A HANDBOOK FOR
BEGINNING TEACHERS

A HANDBOOK FOR BEGINNING TEACHERS
Second Edition

Robert E. MacDonald
California State University, Chico

Seán D. Healy
Kean University

 LONGMAN

An imprint of Addison Wesley Longman, Inc.

New York • Reading, Massachusetts • Menlo Park, California • Harlow, England
Don Mills, Ontario • Sydney • Mexico City • Madrid • Amsterdam

Acquisitions Editor: Virginia L. Blanford
Associate Editor: Arianne J. Weber
Marketing Manager: Renee Ortbals
Project Coordination and Text Design: Ruttle, Shaw & Wetherill, Inc.
Cover Design Manager: Nancy Danahy
Cover Designer: Joseph DePinho
Cover Photos: PhotoDisc
Full Service Production Manager: Joseph Vella
Electronic Page Makeup: Ruttle, Shaw & Wetherill, Inc.
Printer and Binder: The Maple-Vail Book Manufacturing Group
Cover Printer: The Lehigh Press, Inc.

The previous edition of *A Handbook for Beginning Teachers* was published under the title *A Handbook of Basic Skills and Strategies for Beginning Teachers* (Longman, 1991).

Library of Congress Cataloging-in-Publication Data
MacDonald, Robert E.
    A handbook for beginning teachers / Robert E. MacDonald, Seán D. Healy. — 2nd ed.
      p.   cm.
    Rev. ed. of: A handbook of basic skills and strategies for beginning teachers. c1991
    Includes bibliographical references and index
    ISBN 0–8013–1574–3
    1. Teaching—United States—Handbooks, manuals, etc. 2. Classroom management—
United States—Handbooks, manuals, etc. 3. First year teachers—United States—
Handbooks, manuals, etc. 4. Student teaching—United States—Handbooks, manuals, etc.
5. Teachers—In-service training—United States—Handbooks, manuals, etc.
I. Healy, Seán D. II. MacDonald, Robert E. Handbook of basic skills and strategies for
beginning teachers. III. Title.
LB1025.3.M33 1999
371.102'0973—DC21

                                                           98-2663
                                                             CIP

Please visit our website at http://longman.awl.com

ISBN 0–8013–1574–3

45678910—MA—02

To my wife, Sharon, and to my daughter, Shelley
—*R.E.M.*

To my wife and constant inspiration, Pat
—*S.D.H.*

CONTENTS

PREFACE

This handbook is designed to be a practical field-experience guide and methods text for preservice and beginning teachers, K–12. It is a concise, reader-friendly volume that addresses the developmental needs of new teachers as they encounter the complex realities of a contemporary classroom. It describes and explains basic skills and strategies that will enable entering teachers to deal creatively and responsibly with the substantial new challenges that they face.

It is carefully tailored to meet the needs of four groups in particular:

- Those doing their initial field-based course, as a continual source of reference in making sense of what they encounter
- Those preparing to become teachers, for their introductory methods courses
- Those doing their student-teaching, as preparation for their classes, and for use in their student-teaching seminars
- Those at the very beginning, or in the early stages, of their teaching career, as a guide, a reference, and an up-to-date refresher

It can thus serve students throughout their education program and provide a coherent frame of reference for viewing and guiding their experiences from their first entering the program to their eventual work in the first days and weeks of their professional career.

Main Features

The handbook's directness, down-to-earth practicality, and wealth of detailed classroom and personal applications have made it popular with students, a "must-keep" as one student characterized it. Its specific features include:

1. *A strong emphasis on learning to work productively with young people in today's school settings.* Besides separate chapters devoted to classroom management, interactive teaching, and becoming established with new classes, this handbook pays particular attention in the opening chapter to one of the most pervasive and potentially wearing, but least recognized and understood experiences of being a teacher—*being with* students for extended periods of time.

2. *An accent on proactive attitudes and behavior that will help teachers function as creative professionals in a school environment,* including a comprehensive set of strategies for making a healthy and productive accommodation to a modern school organization. The book emphasizes a teacher's need to derive satisfaction from what he or she does and to rise above the mindless routine and boredom that have become increasingly prevalent in today's classrooms. It provides highly practical and detailed ways in which teachers can minimize the inevitable stress of teaching and avoid occupational burnout.

3. *Concentrated attention on the dynamics of lively teaching,* including succinct descriptions of basic interactive maneuvers that allow teachers both to conduct learner-paced instruction and to manage student groups effectively. Together with chapters offering guidelines for classroom motivation and teacher explanations, these sections provide beginners with a manageable, intuitively appropriate framework for building a repertoire of teaching behaviors.

4. *An implicit constructivist psychology of adult learning and continuing teacher development.* Teachers are addressed as self-motivating persons whose behavior is a function of their purposes and needs as people. As such, this handbook attempts to address the needs of developing teachers as they encounter the new challenges of teaching. The two opening chapters are intended to assist beginners in accurately sizing up the nature of the work and the milieu in which they will be working, and in beginning to build attitudes and strategies for maintaining their stamina and sense of purpose in an organizational setting. The book also incorporates a psychology of classroom management that sees class control as a means to educational ends to which the teacher is fully committed, and includes a final chapter that strongly emphasizes the need for beginning teachers to pay close and continuing attention to their own professional development.

5. *A rich store of practical strategies for achieving the proficiencies it features.* The book contains an abundance of professional guidance to help beginners become skilled teachers. Chapter titles and many of the section headings are action-based, appealing to the performance needs of new

teachers in a language designed to get their attention. The title of Chapter 6, "Drawing Students into Encounters with Learning," is at the heart of the handbook's view of what it is to teach.

Throughout the book the reader will encounter short verbatim commentaries of teachers at various levels of professional development. These statements, primarily from student teachers and first-year teachers, were obtained by the lead author from personal journals and personal interviews with contributors to the book.

Organization

There are three parts to this handbook. Part One contains four chapters devoted to *Preparing for Teaching*, the first two chapters being primarily conceptual and orientational. Chapter 1 identifies basic but intangible features of modern teaching that will have an important bearing on a teacher's professional growth and job satisfaction. Chapter 2 focuses on the teacher's relationship to the system itself. It shows teacher development to be integrally related to the kinds of adaptations teachers are able to make to dominant organizational realities. Both chapters offer the new teacher suggestions for making positive accommodations to these prevailing conditions. Chapter 3 provides basic guidelines for preparing instructional objectives, and Chapter 4 consists of fundamental ideas and strategies to help beginners organize for instruction.

Part Two, *Conducting Classroom Activity*, includes five chapters, each of which centers on a major dimension of skilled classroom performance. Chapter 5 focuses on the dynamics of teacher–group relations and offers entering teachers rules for developing sound working relationships with their classes. Chapter 6 explores ideas and tactics for engaging students actively and genuinely in school learning. It emphasizes motivational techniques that appeal to students' intrinsic motivation to learn. Chapter 7 focuses on the teacher as explainer. It features teacher explanations as basic ingredients of good teaching and treats this fundamental skill in considerable depth. Chapter 8 details the specific interactive tactics good teachers use to establish effective two-way communication as a medium for in-depth classroom learning. Chapter 9 describes an approach to classroom management that makes the control function an integral part of a teacher's instructional pattern. It presents a series of low-profile maneuvers for achieving and maintaining order in the classroom.

Part Three, *Following up Instruction*, is devoted to two crucial pre- and postinstructional responsibilities with which all teachers must come to terms. Chapter 10 provides a conceptual framework for approaching the evaluation of classroom learning, together with practical methods for testing and grading. Chapter 11 introduces basic communication strategies for productive parent conferences and effective one-to-one interaction with students. The final chapter offers ideas for managing one's own professional development as a new teacher. It recommends techniques for self-evaluation and self-development in several important areas.

The New Edition

The new edition retains and accentuates all the features of the original hand-book, in particular its directness, down-to-earth practicality, and wealth of classroom applications, qualities that have made it widely popular with students of all ages and degrees of sophistication. In addition, material on the major developments in practice and theory that have proved their worth since the original handbook was published has been seamlessly integrated with the original text. In numerous instances this has been done by recasting a para-graph, or adding one or two new ones, as for instance in the treatment of school context and of discipline. Other developments called for more extended treatment and this will be found in the appropriate place in the text. The major additions are:

- Diversity
- Inclusion
- Cooperative learning
- Collaborative and team teaching
- Multiple intelligences
- Alternative assessment
- Technology for the student and for the teacher
- Thematic curriculum organization

Acknowledgments

We appreciate the persistent efforts of Arianne Weber, associate editor, and Ginny Blanford, acquisitions editor, in making this second edition possible. Their commitment to this book, and their determination to see it through—updated and appropriately expanded—is much appreciated. Thanks also go to Naomi Silverman, its original editor and to many manuscript reviewers for their insightful comments and suggestions: J. Wordy Buckner, Southwest Missouri State University; Robert W. Burke, Ball State University; Karen Foster, Alabama A & M University; Susan B. Harris, California State University, Fresno; Judy K. Lamb, Washington University of St. Louis; James E. McGlinn, University of North Carolina, Asheville; D. John McIntyre, Southern Illinois University at Carbondale; Chogollah Maroufi, California State University, Los Angeles; Andrea Maxie, California State University, Los Angeles; Betty Jo Simmons, Longwood College; Norma J. Strickland, Rust College; and Kim Truesdell, SUNY at Buffalo.

A Message to Teachers in Training

You are entering teaching at a crucial time in the history of American education. As a classroom teacher you will likely be called on to design learning experiences for increasingly diverse, nonacademically oriented populations of young learners. From all indications, you will need to prepare yourself to teach greater numbers of nontraditional and educationally disadvantaged students than encountered by previous teachers. Consider the following demographic patterns:

1. As the general population ages, the proportion of young who are members of minority groups—particularly African-Americans and Hispanics—will expand dramatically. Some states can expect to have a "minority majority" in their schools by the beginning of the twenty-first century. California is already at that stage in its elementary schools.

2. The gap between rich and poor in the United States continues to increase. As this gap grows wider, a larger and larger percentage of children will fall below the poverty line. Forty percent of the poor in the United States are children, and this situation is likely to worsen because the median income of families headed by a person under the age of 25 has declined steadily over the last 20 years.

3. Fewer than 5 percent of U.S. households now conform to the standard model family of past decades: a working father, mother at home, and two or more school-age children. Indications are that 60 percent of the children born in 1983 will live in one-parent homes before they are 18 years old. As shifts in the traditional patterns of marriage and child rearing continue, fewer children will have the emotional and educational advantages of a two-parent family, parents who are themselves educated, and close supervision after school.

These social trends will undoubtedly have dramatic implications for American teachers of the future. For one thing, classroom teachers will need to possess a working knowledge of alternative learning patterns, together with schemes for engaging nonacademically inclined youngsters in new learning. As we move toward the twenty-first century, teaching will require more personalized, learner-centered techniques for teaching the highly diverse mix of students who will enter U.S. classrooms.

Future teachers will need to be able to summon the personal stamina and resourcefulness to face an ever more complex and formidable set of teaching responsibilities. As a means of coping with the complexity of teaching and the heavy demands on your energy it will make, you will need strategies for working within the present-day school organization that will help you to avoid being devitalized by the system, and patterns of professional involvement that will allow you to make best use of your creative capacities.

This handbook is designed to help you size up the challenge facing you as a new teacher in today's schools. It will assist you in preparing yourself to work effectively and productively with the young people you will be expected to teach. It is also intended to help you cope with the demands of the school system and at the same time to maintain high levels of professional competence and creativity in your work.

CHAPTER 1

Having a Realistic View of Teaching

It may be possible to learn in two or three years the kind of practice which then leads on to another 20 or 40 years of learning.

David Perkins

Looking Beyond the Surface Features

One of the first requirements for success in any occupation is to have a good understanding of what that activity will require of you. Many people enter teaching with well-entrenched impressions and expectations of the work, but are dismayed to find the job significantly different from what they had anticipated. Having spent a good portion of their early lives in school classrooms, beginning teachers generally approach teaching with a feeling that they are reentering familiar territory. However, as Lieberman and Miller describe it:

> After years of formal academic preparation, most teachers enter teaching and experience a common jolt. Equipped with theoretical understandings, they lack the practical knowledge that they need for survival.[1]

Some beginning teachers never fully recover from this initial jolt. As a result, about three out of ten new teachers leave public school teaching in this country during the first several years of service.[2] A significant number of those who end up making careers of teaching do so with diminished enthusiasm for the work, often expressing regret that they had not gone into some other occupation. The seriousness of this burnout problem among teaching professionals has become increasingly apparent.[3]

What is it about classroom teaching that makes it difficult for beginners to realistically anticipate and prepare for its impact? In the first place, there is the relative abruptness with which beginning teachers find themselves on their own in the classroom. Teaching is unique among professions in expecting new members to immediately carry out the same responsibilities as people with 10 or 20 years of service. In comparison with other occupations where novices initially spend longer periods of time in on-the-job training, and their job responsibilities increase with experience, teaching has turned out to be more of a "sink or swim" type occupation.

Furthermore, it is difficult to simulate live classroom dynamics or to prepare emotionally for the teacher's role before one has responsibility for a real classroom and a full schedule of teaching activities. Earlier experiences such as observing and talking about teaching can help to prepare you intellectually but not emotionally for the real thing. There is a significant experiential gap between learning about and actually performing the work of a teacher. The flesh-and-blood realities of teaching must ordinarily be experienced in their full magnitude, in all-or-nothing fashion, for a would-be teacher to know their effects. Newcomers to the teaching profession often comment on the discontinuity between preparing to teach and being in charge of and fully responsible for their own classrooms:

> Though I think I learned a lot from my preteaching seminars, nothing that was said or done in education classes could have prepared me for the gut-level aspects of day-to-day teaching. You can talk about it and do everything in your power to psych yourself up for the real thing, but the feeling of having complete control of a classroom full of students has to be a unique experience for someone just starting out. Managing your own classroom is totally different from helping in another teacher's class. I couldn't avoid feeling like a guest during my aiding and student teaching semesters. Now I'm feeling the full force of the responsibility for my own classroom. It isn't that my knowledge of teaching has increased that much, it's just that overnight I'm having to behave like a real teacher. Up to this point I've been a student.*

Finally, the common perception of what it means to be a teacher tends to accentuate the most apparent and well-known aspects of the teacher's role, to the exclusion of other very important, but less tangible characteristics and requirements. For example, people cite the knowledge background required to teach students; but they fail to mention the personal qualities necessary to co-exist with students in a school setting. Other times, teaching is depicted as a job where you work with young people to help them "become something." These characterizations may be useful, but give little insight into the kind of becoming teachers themselves must undergo in order to excel at this type of work.

The following are underlying but pervasive realities of public school teaching that you should be aware of if you are to be psychologically as well as technically prepared for this kind of work:

1. You will be spending your working hours in a confined setting with groups of young people for extended periods of time.

*As mentioned in the preface, the firsthand commentaries to be found at various points throughout the handbook were obtained by the author from personal journals of and personal interviews with the contributors.

2. You must learn to manage multiple, fast-paced activities, and to continually perform control and maintenance functions.

3. You ordinarily work alone as a classroom teacher—making critical decisions, applying your professional skills, and experiencing the satisfactions and frustrations of the job in isolation from people who are doing essentially the same work.

4. You will need to take abstract, nonsituational knowledge and make it meaningful for young learners who will normally lack the motivation and life experience to appreciate its import.

5. You will be joining a *character-intensive* occupation—a kind of work that often draws more heavily on your emotional and interpersonal resources than it does on your formal knowledge.

6. You will be teaching in classrooms that are becoming increasingly multicultural and inclusive. That is to say, you will be responsible for helping students who are diverse in terms of their home language and culture, and some of whom are disabled in a wide variety of ways—physically, intellectually, or emotionally.

This chapter attempts to shed important light on these fundamental though less generally recognized aspects of classroom teaching. Beyond that, the chapter offers insights and strategies for making reasonable and satisfactory adaptations to these realities of teaching in today's classrooms.

Being-With Groups of Young People

One of the first and most important realities faced by beginning teachers is the need to be with groups of young people for relatively long and unbroken periods of time, usually in a confined space and with limited resources. Jackson notes that

> there is a social intimacy in schools that is unmatched elsewhere in our society. . . . Even factory workers are not clustered as close together as students in a standard classroom. . . . Imagine what would happen if a factory the size of a typical elementary school contained three or four hundred adult workers. In all likelihood the unions would not allow it. Only in schools do thirty or more people spend several hours each day literally side by side.[4]

Whether or not teachers and students treat one another with respect, whether or not they have productive times together, whether or not they come to care for one another as people—the certainty remains that they will be together again tomorrow, and the next day, and the day after that, same time, same place. The togetherness condition is such a widespread and fundamental feature of a teacher's work that it is often overlooked when considering job requirements. Yet, of the various job demands placed on public school teachers, there are good reasons for considering being-with-students to be even more fundamental to a teacher's work than the instructional or bringing-them-to-know requirement.

Also, what you manage to teach students will to a large extent depend on the way you coexist with them in the classroom. If you are consistently enthusiastic, inquisitive, and encouraging, you have a much greater chance of fostering meaningful learning than if you are listless, dogmatic, and disparaging.[5]

The ability to consistently be-with young people cheerfully and respectfully calls for a special kind of resolve on the part of a classroom teacher. When people spend this much time together in prestructured relationships, it is easy for them to become tired of one another and the agendas that bring them together. Classroom groups are like families in that relationships among the members can easily reach the point where they become dull and matter-of-fact. The potential for teachers and students in today's schools to drift into apathy and ritualism is always present. When this happens routines and roles come to dictate behavior, and the individuality of both students and teacher gets lost.

Maintaining a Positive Climate

For teachers who care, an important part of being-with young people is the ability to keep the classroom environment energized and upbeat. Often the best teachers are effective spiritual leaders before they are competent teachers of subject matter. These teachers realize that the group atmosphere out of which meaningful learning and positive human relations emerge is one that recognizes and respects individual and group needs. What students learn from lectures, discussions, hands-on activities, working in groups, tapes and films, and assignments, is invariably related to how they feel about themselves, one another, and the world around them. A productive classroom environment reflects the notion that the quality of the student's personal being and being-with-others is the primary consideration. The formal knowledge these young people may come to possess is a derivative of this more fundamental condition. That is to say, if the first condition is not right, the second loses its significance.

To keep group relations from degenerating into stale routine is perhaps the toughest part of a teacher's job. The best teachers have developed the capacity to maintain a relationship that brings the best out of the young people in their classes. They recognize when the group is losing its dynamic edge and are able to provide that needed spark, that injection of new energy, that key suggestion that keeps students interested and productive.

There is a definite art to being-with-students on an extended basis and continuing to foster a group atmosphere that is stimulating and constructive for both students and teacher. As a beginning teacher, it is important for you to learn to be-with-students in ways that are invigorating and that enable and encourage students to become involved in worthwhile learning.

To establish whether you are ready to meet the "togetherness" requirement of classroom teaching, you should take time to consider the following questions:

1. Although I may enjoy being in the company of young people, can I tolerate them when they are at their worst as well as when they are at their best? Do I presently have the patience and resilience to flow with the kinds of behavior I can expect when students are feeling irritable, nonresponsive, or needful of attention? Because the presence of peers tends to foster a wide variety of student behaviors, what can I do to prepare for the occasions when students may show off, use obscene language, or say they don't like my teaching, or defy me? Will I be able to keep a sense of humor when I am confronted by behavior that indicates kids are simply being kids?

2. Will I be able to anticipate inevitable changes in group attitudes and intergroup relationships during the course of a school year? What do I know about group dynamics and group cycles? How will I know when my classes are ready to function as a group rather than as separate individuals? What are some main stages in the evolution of classroom groups? How long will the "honeymoon" period last? Will I be able to recognize and adjust to normal stages in group development when students suddenly become critical and less cooperative? How can I avoid feeling depressed or insulted when the entire class suddenly becomes uninterested or preoccupied with things other than my lessons, and what shall I do to recover their attention and interest? Will I be resourceful enough to come up with ideas that keep classes involved at times when they are unable or unwilling to handle higher-thinking operations or more challenging assignments?

3. Am I prepared to face and deal with the problem that arises when people are together for extended periods and begin to tire of one another's voices, mannerisms, and personal agendas? Can I deal with the fact that students as well as teachers have times when they need their privacy? Will I know when I am bearing down too hard or when I need to vary my style? What constructive measures can I take when I sense I might be getting tired of certain classes or particular students? Are there measures I can take to ensure that teacher and students continue to respect one another's privacy and individuality? What are some effective renewal strategies I can use when I feel classroom relationships are beginning to lose their freshness?

4. What can I do to consistently model a positive and constructive approach to classroom business, even on days when I am feeling less than enthusiastic myself? Will I be able to leave distracting personal problems and agendas at home when I come to school in the morning? Can I consistently provide the positive initiative to get students back on track after a school vacation, a bad lesson, or a class interruption? Am I prepared emotionally to be "an adult with the young" in my own classes? What can I do about any inclination I may have to be a peer rather than an adult leader with my students?

5. Am I acquiring theories of human growth and development that will help me better understand the young people with whom I will be working? What social and emotional stages will my students likely be

experiencing if they are seventh graders, seniors in high school, first graders, high school freshmen? At what grade levels are students most likely to exhibit strong emotional attachment to their teachers, be pre-occupied with themselves and how they look, voice cynical attitudes toward adult authority, tend to say things they do not really mean, or exhibit a dominant need for acceptance and recognition by their peers? Do I have a basis for distinguishing between student behavior that is irritating but to be expected, and behavior that is both socially and developmentally out of line? All of these considerations are explored in more detail later in this handbook (see Chapter 5).

The Immediacy of Classroom Events

In addition, you must be prepared to deal with the crowded atmosphere and rapid pace of classroom events that characterize both elementary and secondary schools. The fast tempo of school activity places a premium on a teacher's ability to make instant decisions, to monitor multiple events, and to maintain crowd control. The number of verbal transactions a classroom teacher is involved in during a typical day can be astonishing. In his studies of schools and teachers, Jackson found that elementary teachers may engage in as many as 1000 interpersonal exchanges in a day.[6] In fact, a teacher's job has been likened to that of a ringmaster in a circus. So it is not abnormal for beginning teachers to be apprehensive about their ability to control people and events as they take full responsibility for one or more classrooms. Such early anxiety is reflected in this comment of a first-year seventh-grade teacher:

> To some extent I like having to spring into action when the bell rings. But I can't think of any other job or even a fast sport where you have to be in control of all of your wits like you do in teaching. I find myself worrying that things might get out of hand. I know I'm spending too much time imagining scary situations and wondering how I'd deal with them. I've got to start thinking more positively because so far I've managed to stay on top of the action once it's underway.[7]

The Need for Instant Decisions

With so many things happening, and in such rapid succession, teachers rarely have time to think about what they are going to do next. They find themselves reacting to classroom situations before they are able to give deliberate thought to each of the many decisions they have to make. This is a practical reality of modern teaching that might call into question the widely held image of teaching as a rational process. In this connection, Jackson has discovered that most classroom teachers find it necessary to change their thinking processes radically as they move from planning to actual teaching:

> When grading exams, planning a lesson, or deciding what to do about a particularly difficult student, teaching looks like a rational process . . . When stu-

dents are in front of him [or her], the teacher's behavior is more or less spontaneous . . . the teacher tends to do what he feels is right rather than what he reasons is right. . . . Amid all this hustle and bustle, the teacher often has little time to think.[7]

This gives us an insight into one of the main sources of stress for people just becoming acquainted with the world of classroom teaching. Their preparatory experience has promoted a logical, rational approach to teaching and provided them with some sense that they will have control over the teaching situations they will encounter. Now, as they enter the bustling world of the classroom, this sense of rationality and control is weakened. They find themselves having to rely to a considerable extent on their instincts and intuitions if they are to stay on top of fast-moving events.

The Need for Multiple Concentration

Because of the complexity and rapidly changing character of classroom activity, you must be able to perform various tasks in quick succession and to manage a number of overlapping responsibilities. For example, while presiding over a class discussion, you need to be deciding

- When and how to intervene
- When and how to elicit and orchestrate student participation, and to attend and respond to student contributions
- How, tactfully, to prevent any one or two students dominating the proceedings
- How to encourage nonparticipating members to join in
- How to integrate all these teaching functions into one smooth-flowing performance, all the while keeping an eye on the time

Jackson attempts to classify the ongoing managerial responsibilities that compete for a teacher's time and attention in a typical elementary classroom. These tasks include: (1) deciding who shall and who shall not speak; (2) acting as a dispenser of supplies; (3) delegating duties and privileges; (4) serving as official timekeeper; and (5) directing movement within the classroom.[8] To manage these diverse responsibilities effectively under busy classroom conditions involves a mental juggling act. It requires what one teaching authority has called *multiple concentration:*

> Multiple concentration is the ability to use many centers of the brain to process information, and based on that information, to reflexively act or speak with successful results. . . . It's the act of combining simple skills in a sequence or using several skills at the same time.[9]

The ability to perform complex teaching acts under busy classroom conditions seldom comes naturally for new teachers. Like most other compound skills, it is something that normally takes considerable practice before you can expect to be proficient (see Chapter 12). However, there are several things you can do to help prepare for the rapid pace of classroom interaction:

1. Recognize that skillful interactive teaching is to a large extent a matter of effective mind control. There are some good readings available on this topic that are appropriate for teachers. One is Robert Nideffer's *Attention Control Training,* another is Timothy Gallwey's *The Inner Game of Tennis* (do not be misled by the title), and a third is Robert W. Travers' and Jacqueline Dillon's *The Making of a Teacher* (see Chapter 4: Acquiring Affect, Poise, and Self-Control).[10]

2. Become involved in physical activities that require you to make instant decisions and to react spontaneously under pressure. Excellent examples are the martial arts, racquetball, tennis, basketball, and other recreational activities that cause you to alternate between broad and narrow focuses of concentration while you are performing.

3. Continue to improve your powers of language and abstract thought through challenging reading, stimulating discussion, and other conceptual activities. The better you are with language, the more likely it is that your classroom input will be spontaneous and free-flowing. Moreover, the more capable you are of abstract thinking, the better grasp you will have of classroom processes and the more adept you will be at multiple concentration.[11]

4. Make a deliberate effort to exercise your skills of multiple concentration in social and formal group situations. Practice your abilities to structure conversation, to draw others into discussion, to respond to others' ideas, to attend to nonverbal behaviors, and to alternate between talking and listening all at one time. Your ability to do this in your everyday life should pay dividends as you are called on to exercise multiple concentration in the classroom.

5. Find opportunities to observe the behavior of such performers as talk-show hosts, whose job it is to orchestrate spirited group interaction under pressure; make note of the kinds of mental acts they are able to perform in a relatively short space of time, of the techniques they appear to be using to help them remain poised and under control in pressure situations (e.g., breathing, moving, joking, stalling for time); assess their abilities to think and make decisions on their feet, their powers of multiple concentration, their skills as speakers and their levels of self-confidence and personal assertiveness.

The Emphasis on Control

Another central fact of life in busy, crowded schools is the emphasis placed on management and control. This has a direct bearing on a teacher's work, particularly in a modern high school. At the high school level the press of numbers and the necessity for crowd control has led to ways of organizing and managing students that is virtually *processing.* Lieberman and Miller describe this system as follows:

Life in schools is life in crowds, for both teachers and students. Because of the large number of students in any given high school, "batch processing" is the order of the day. So that students can be processed in batches, schools divide their days into discrete units of time for the purpose of distinct subject matter instruction. Students and teachers move through the building in mass, and they move every 50 minutes or so on the average of six times a day. Most teachers teach 125 to 150 students in a day.[12]

This organizational feature accounts for the constant movement and the repetitiveness that characterize life in most high schools. It means teachers have to conduct at least five separate classes a day, making it difficult to maintain the kind of freshness necessary to perform at one's best.[13]

The school's preoccupation with control and maintenance often detracts from a teacher's ability to give full attention to actual teaching. The management system of the school requires teachers to take on a variety of noninstructional duties, tasks that contribute to the maintenance of the system. They include monitoring and recording student attendance and promptness, as well as supervisory responsibilities in school corridors, lunchrooms, study halls, and parking lots. As Lieberman and Miller point out, the need to spend so much time attending to the control function can create nagging priority conflicts:

> This recognition of the need for control places teachers in a contradictory position. On the one hand, they want to spend their time doing what they are trained to do, and that is to teach. On the other hand, in order for instruction to take place, order must be maintained. Teachers view this role as a necessary evil; it "comes with the territory."[14]

The system of processing students, designed to maximize order and control, can also have serious effects on what and how a teacher teaches. Teaching patterns become shaped by the tension between the contradictory goals of educating students and those of controlling them and moving them through the system.[15] In the case of secondary teachers, breaking the school day into 50-minute class periods limits a teacher's ability to promote in-depth learning. It can also result in disjointed lessons and cause teachers to feel rushed. It assumes that students and teachers can effectively turn frames of reference on and off as they move from one class to another and from one subject to another. Lieberman and Miller observe that

> as soon as students walk into the room, they are supposed to switch frames of reference. For teachers, a similar switch is necessary. Teachers are expected to put aside the concerns of the previous class and to concentrate on the one sitting in front of them at the present moment. . . . Every teacher makes a separate peace with this concern. . . . For some, the solution is to keep things routine.[16]

Every teacher, then, must come to grips with the problems and contradictions created when schools emphasize controlling and processing functions at the expense of teaching. There are some important things you can do to help ensure that the control function does not come to dominate your teaching. Consider the following measures:

1. Develop a well-defined set of overriding objectives that allow you to keep your teaching priorities in proper focus (see Chapter 3). Continue to fight to make teaching your number one priority and do your best to treat the organizational and managerial responsibilities as support activities.

2. Use motivational techniques that are learning-based rather than control-based. Make it a practice to stimulate learning activity by appealing to students' interests, curiosities, and problem-solving inclinations rather than to their fears, anxieties, and competitive instincts. Techniques for achieving this are discussed in Chapter 6.

3. Find workable strategies for dealing with system-imposed interruptions, transitions, and time limitations. Attempt to provide the best possible learning environment in your own classroom, and be protective of your teaching space. Develop efficient techniques for getting students focused on the subject matter of your class immediately after they come in from the halls, and after breaks and interruptions (see Chapter 4). Find ways of making appropriate use of teaching sessions, whatever their length. (Chapter 2 is devoted to ideas and strategies for making a creative adaptation to the organizational structure of the school.)

4. Develop a system for achieving classroom control that supports rather than interferes with teaching. Adopt effective low-profile class management techniques that flow with your teaching, techniques that make the control function subordinate to teaching and learning. An in-depth treatment of ideas and strategies for accomplishing this is presented in Chapter 9.

5. Create an effective system for handling the organizational and managerial tasks of teaching so they do not become preoccupations. Learn to approach required paperwork, supervisory responsibilities, and other bureaucratic chores in good spirit, but with the kind of efficiency and dispatch that allows you to devote your best energies to teaching. Chapter 2 provides more detailed strategies for achieving this goal.

6. Use the inevitable conflicts and distractions as a motivating factor for you in your teaching. Prepare yourself to face the organizational contradictions that are inherent in public schooling in this country (see Chapter 2). Realize that in *character-intensive* occupations like teaching, successful practitioners are those who find the energy and commitment to rise above the built-in conflicts and resistance of the system. (The concept of *character-intensive* occupations is developed further on in the section, Teaching as Character-Intensive Work.)

Alone in a Busy World

Although teachers spend a great deal of time interacting with young people in the school, they often do not have the time or opportunity to develop close professional relationships with their peers. Gene Maeroff describes the situation in these succinct terms:

> More than many other occupations, teaching is practiced in isolation—an isolation that is crushing at times. Collegiality is nonexistent for many teachers, unless hurried lunches over plastic trays in lunchrooms are viewed as exercises in colleagueship.[17]

This is another fact of life in U.S. schools that should be taken into consideration by anyone planning to make a career of teaching.

For purposes of instructional planning, solving classroom problems, and cultivating new skills, the tendency is for teachers to function in isolation from one another and from outside sources of new information. John Goodlad has attempted to document the extent and seriousness of the isolation problem among U.S. teachers:

> The classroom cells in which teachers spend much of their time appear to me to be symbolic and predictive of their relative isolation from one another and from sources of ideas beyond their own background of experience. . . . We compiled a substantial amount of data pertaining to teachers' links to sources of influence in their teaching and to one another. The teachers we studied had some association with others . . . but rather brief and casual associations. . . . There was little to suggest active, ongoing exchanges of ideas and practices. . . . A large majority said they never observed instruction in other classrooms.[18]

Teachers generally work alone in separate classrooms, and are responsible for their own lessons, evaluation devices, and managerial policies. Even when teachers are together between classes or during lunch, the culture of the school tends to militate against the serious sharing of ideas relating to what they do in the classroom. Whereas they may find it easy to talk about external matters like politics or recreational interests, teachers are generally more reticent to discuss interests, problems, and strategies having to do with their own teaching, much less teaching in general. Lieberman and Miller comment on this reality of school:

> While relations with students tend to be immediate, direct, and engaging, relations with peers may be characterized as remote, oblique, and defensively protective. The rule of privacy governs peer interactions in a school. It is all right to talk about the news, the weather, sports, and sex. It is all right to complain in general about the school and the students. However, it is not acceptable to discuss instruction and what happens in class rooms as colleagues.[19]

One of the reasons teachers are disinclined to share professional concerns with one another is the need to have a break from classroom business when they are away from students. Full-time teaching requires a great deal of time and energy, in and out of school, so most teachers look for relief from this highly involving activity when they leave the classroom. There is often an unspoken agreement not to "talk shop" when teachers meet between classes or on social occasions.

Another reason is the inevitable differences in motivation and skill level among teachers, which leads to subtle competitions and professional jealousies within a school faculty. Teachers who are struggling with teaching and control problems are normally reluctant to discuss or solicit help for their problems, particularly in the teachers' room, for fear of being perceived as incompetents. In the words of one early career teacher of secondary English:

> I'd like to know how other teachers in the school deal with some of these smart alecky seniors. I can't be the only one these kids wise-off to. But everyone seems to act so self assured about their teaching when we're together in the teachers' room. I'm caught between wanting to share my problem and fearing the possible consequences of my honesty. I don't want to be seen as the weak sister in the group.

Similarly, highly competent teachers are often inclined to keep their success stories and teaching ideas to themselves, sensing that colleagues might view it as bragging.

One of the problematic effects of teacher isolation is its tendency to inhibit teacher growth and to discourage the joint efforts of teachers to work together for needed improvements in their schools. Goodlad's studies have shown this to be a nagging problem:

> The teachers we studied appeared, in general, to function quite autonomously. But their autonomy seemed to be exercised in a context more of isolation than of rich professional dialogue with a plethora of challenging educational alternatives. . . . Teachers rarely worked together on schoolwide problems. . . . Teacher-to-teacher links for mutual assistance or collaborative school improvement were weak or nonexistent. . . . Although outside resource people were available, they drew upon them only a little and said that they were of limited value."[20]

The relative isolation of classroom teaching can produce chronic feelings of loneliness for teachers who are not prepared to face this basic reality of the job. The need to continually plan and work alone in a human-service occupation like teaching is an emphatic test of a teacher's self-confidence and personal resourcefulness. New teachers, in particular, may experience periods of insecurity and self-doubt on realizing that the long-term responsibilities for teaching objectives, lesson content, student discipline, and other important decisions rest exclusively on their shoulders.

The following are steps you can take to overcome the professional isolation of classroom teaching, and to increase your own teaching skills:

1. Find opportunities to team-teach periodically with other teachers in your school. This can ordinarily be arranged for one or more periods if two people have the will to make it work. Planning and sharing teaching responsibilities with a compatible colleague can be an enlightening and enjoyable experience. It provides you with an opportunity to share practical strategies for teaching, to observe a different teaching style, and to solicit constructive feedback on your own teaching patterns.

2. Ask a trusted colleague to visit one of your classes on occasion. This can be an opportunity to get constructive feedback and suggestions from someone other than an administrator. Offer to exchange visits if that is feasible. Besides being a chance to receive ideas that may add to your teaching, a visit from a fellow teacher can be an opportunity to show things that you do particularly well, to unveil a classroom "act" that to this point has gone unappreciated by the other adults in the school.

3. Make arrangements to visit other teachers and other schools from time to time. Once having completed their preservice teaching requirements, many full-time teachers become mired in their own classrooms for extended periods of time without ever getting a glimpse of fellow teachers in action. Their professional frames of reference become limited to what they see and do in their own classrooms. By making arrangements to observe other teachers and other school settings periodically, you are able to achieve a broader, more up-to-date perspective on your own teaching.

4. Read several professional journals. Professional reading will allow you to keep abreast of major topics and issues in U.S. education as well as new ideas and developments in areas that you teach. Use professional reading as a means of keeping yourself in touch with other active and inquiring minds within the profession. (For specific recommendations, see Chapter 12.)

5. Volunteer for curriculum development projects and other constructive professional activities. Take opportunities to attend educational conferences and meetings where you can share professional concerns with other educators. Attendance at the annual statewide meetings of the National Education Association (NEA) and of the American Federation of Teachers (AFT) are excellent opportunities to meet with a wide range of teachers, to attend numerous workshops given by teachers and, frequently, nationally known and respected experts, and to survey the most recent books, material, and equipment. This is equally true of the local or national meetings of subject-matter organizations such as the National Council for Teachers of Math (NCTM), the National Council for the Teaching of English (NCTE), the International Reading Association (IRA), the National Council for the Social Studies

(NCSS), and the National Science Teachers Association (NSTA), and of the Association for Supervision and Curriculum (ASCD), which publishes *Educational Leadership*[21] (for the Internet addresses of these organizations see note 21). Many school districts make it possible for their teachers to go to these meetings, and some are willing to hire substitutes for teachers who wish to pursue professional growth activities on school time. Whether they do or not, you should make it a point to be involved in activities that will help you renew your enthusiasm for, and keep a continually fresh perspective on, your teaching.

6. Regard district-sponsored inservice (sometimes poorly regarded by teachers) as opportunities to learn *something* of value, maybe a lot. Generally speaking, you get out of an activity as much as you put in.

A word of caution, however: do not try to do too much in your first year or two!

The Abstract Nature of Formal Teaching

Another reality that makes a teacher's job uniquely challenging is the abstract nature of teaching and learning in a school setting. School learning tends to be quite artificial in comparison with the learning young people experience outside of school. As Gardner reminds us,

> Authorities generally agree that, outside of schooled settings, children acquire skills through observation and participation in the contexts in which these skills are customarily invoked. In contrast, in the standard classroom, teachers talk, often presenting material in abstract symbolic form and relying on inanimate media such as books and diagrams in order to convey information. Schooling generally treats subject matter that one cannot readily see or touch, even as those sensory modes of taking in information seem singularly inappropriate for most school tasks.[22]

Most people, young or old, learn best when they are actively involved in real-life situations that call for new competencies or new understandings. They learn more effectively when their own perceived needs and purposes are at stake and when they can learn at their own pace. Formal education, however, is based on the premise that responsible participation in a complex society requires certain understandings and abilities that people cannot be expected to acquire through life experience. The only way young people can learn some things about the world is from a distance, or nonsituationally. They need to learn certain life skills apart from and prior to the occasions when they will have use for them.

This creates a difficult dilemma for the school. It has a responsibility to prepare young people for life outside the school, yet in attempting to accomplish this it finds itself working against the grain of human nature. By definition, *nonsituational learning* is abstract learning because it is removed from the context in which it has application. In order for it to be meaningful, the learner must possess a sufficient stock of knowledge, and existing ideas and experiences to make a personal connection with the new ideas. As Frank Smith maintains:

> Making sense of what is going on is something all school children must do if there is to be any chance that they will learn, and they must do this by relating the situations they find themselves in to prior knowledge. . . . So a primary concern of teachers must be with what children already know, if only to avoid making impossible demands on them by confronting them *with nonsense*.[23] (authors' emphasis)

Nonsituational learning also places a premium on the learner's imagination because learners must be able to construct mental images of objects, events, people, and situations that lie beyond the school environment, and be able to do this on cue. When teachers ask students to conceptualize happenings of the Civil War era or to appreciate a poem satirizing life in metropolitan New York, the students must instantaneously formulate mental representations of distant objects and events if they are to meaningfully process this kind of school learning.[24]

The more mature the learner, the more likely that person is to possess the necessary motivation, perception, imagination, and mental organization to profit from nonsituational learning. To the consternation of many adults, most young people entering college are not highly proficient abstract learners, and many have not yet even reached what the Swiss psychologist Piaget called the stage of formal operations. This is of course even truer of high school students, and overwhelmingly so of students in the lower grades.[25] They find it difficult, or impossible, to remove themselves mentally from their immediate environments and to work with realities that have no concrete referents for them at this stage in their intellectual and emotional development.[26] These students are bound to have problems coping with instruction that is exclusively verbal. When they are forced to learn material that has no real meaning to them, they can do little but end up simply going through the motions, repeating or regurgitating material without comprehension. Their *apparent* learning, is in fact illusory, and the learner often becomes bored, frustrated, and a behavior problem for the teacher. A recent study involving 20,000 students at nine very varied high schools found that "an extremely large proportion of students—somewhere around 40 percent—are just going through the motions."[27]

In order to make formal learning more than a mechanical and impersonal game, you must be prepared to translate what is to be learnt into much more concrete terms, while gradually increasing the abstract elements in order to lead students on to full formal reasoning. A large part of your instructional task will involve providing what one writer has called "scaffolding," devices that can enable a learner gradually to reach a higher level of mental functioning.[28] Techniques for accomplishing this are the basis of effective teaching methods.

Chapters 6, 7, and 8 contain practical suggestions for making classroom learning less abstract and more meaningful for young learners at all levels.

In the meantime, the following are some central guidelines that you should keep in mind as you attempt to compensate for the abstract nature of formal teaching and learning:

1. Make an effort to provide as much context as possible when introducing new learning. Grounded understanding depends on the formation of new relationships. People learn best when new learning makes a connection with existing perceptions, abilities, and understandings. You can help put students in a frame of mind or "mental set" to see those relationships when you begin lessons by providing relevant background information, by posing problems, or by challenging students' existing knowledge structures.

2. Give students practice in imagining and projecting themselves into life situations beyond the confines of the school. Students often need vivid imaginations to profit from abstract learning. You can assist them in cultivating such imagination by taking opportunities to apply visualization techniques and other devices that will help students identify with learning situations that lie outside the boundaries of the school.

3. Become proficient in the use of visual aids and other concrete props to help make your teaching less abstract. Use a wide variety of teaching supplements, including physical objects, newspapers, films, videotapes, role playing, simulations, and so on, to provide concrete references and high-quality vicarious experiences for your students. Make every effort to bring the outside world into your classroom.

4. Personalize your teaching by consistently addressing students' existing perceptions, needs, experiences, and understandings as they relate to new learning. Develop a learner-centered teaching style that attempts as often as possible to proceed from questions and inquiries rather than from information and conclusions. Make it a practice to appeal to students' interests, ideas, and values in the second person, for example, "How will you know when . . . ," "What would you do if . . . ," "How does this look to you?," "How else might it have turned out?"

5. Take steps to make school learning an active rather than a passive process. Outside of school we generally learn by doing, through constant transactions with our environments. Design your learning activities so students will have to use initiative, thinking ability, and problem-solving strategies; always attempt to structure lessons so students will have to invest something of themselves in the new learning.

6. Provide continuous opportunities for students to practice new learning and to receive appropriate feedback on their progress. In out-of-school situations people normally learn things that have current relevance to their lives. This means they get ongoing practice and immediate feedback to determine whether or not the new learning works. To maximize school learning, teachers should attempt to simulate this out-of-

school learning process, as closely as possible. (See Chapter 10 on methods of evaluating this kind of student work by way of Authentic and Performance Assessments.)

Teaching as Character-Intensive Work

People frequently come to teaching expecting a more technically exacting type of work, the sort of activity where a skilled performance will ordinarily produce certain positive and measurable results. They assume that the knowledge base they acquired in college will be the main prerequisite to success in teaching. With formal education being an integral part of the "knowledge business," successful classroom teaching is widely thought to depend on the academic learning and technical training teachers bring to it. The best teachers, so it is very generally supposed, are highly knowledgeable people who are able to transmit their ideas and know-how directly to the uninitiated.

There is a problem, however, in considering teaching to be essentially technical, knowledge-based and knowledge-intensive work in the same sense that engineering, television repairing, and accounting are knowledge-intensive pursuits. In these latter occupations, persons with the appropriate technical knowledge and ability to apply it can ordinarily be successful in their respective jobs. Job requirements normally entail a relatively direct application of that knowledge to materially manipulatible and controllable tasks according to certain fairly well established rules and procedures. These are occupations in which other human qualities may also be necessary, but in which special knowledge and/or skill is the critical determinant of success.

Teaching is a fundamentally different kind of activity. It is work in which, to a large extent, success often depends on the capacity to deal with multiple, complex *human* variables that are difficult to control or even to affect through specialized knowledge, in particular, the beliefs, attitudes, habits, and actions of other people. As in varying degrees with nursing, police work, social work, and certain other human-service occupations, modern-day teaching asks you to apply your knowledge in settings in which the odds may often be stacked against you. The situations you are attempting to control or influence are human situations where you must frequently contend with the genetic endowment, the earlier experience, resistance, skill deficiencies, and differing outlook and plans of the people you are serving, as well as those of your hierarchical superiors.

Whereas a great many jobs are primarily physically or intellectually challenging, teaching is an occupation that also draws heavily on your inner resources. It will require the application of your total personality rather than simply the specialized knowledge or technical skill you have acquired. Lightfoot makes the point this way:

> It is difficult to disentangle teacher character from teacher competence. . . . The teacher is deeply engaged in his work as a whole person because an effect is required on the student as a whole person. . . . Teachers make use of

powerful affective resources to motivate learning by developing empathetic relationships with students.[29]

Public school teaching tests the emotional maturity and stamina of an individual to a much greater extent than most knowledge-intensive jobs. It is the kind of activity that often involves interacting with other people, most of them young, immature, and inexperienced, under stressful conditions. So in addition to the more obvious knowledge requirements, it calls for substantial investments in patience, empathy, and human concern.

Good teaching requires an abiding strength of commitment to one's occupational mission, a kind of single-mindedness that allows a person to cut through distractions and bureaucratic tangles, refusing to be distracted by the conflicts, frustrations, and adversities that seem to go with the job. Arthur Combs defines accomplished teachers as those who are able to use themselves effectively to carry out their own and society's purposes in the education of others:

> Research has shown that effective teaching is the product of certain kinds of purposes. . . . The good teacher sees his appropriate role as one of commitment to the helping process. . . . He has trust in his own organism. He sees himself as essentially dependable, as having the potentiality for coping with events. . . . He is not exclusively concerned with details but can perceive beyond the immediate to the future.[30]

As a teacher, you can expect to see some of your best efforts go unrecognized and unappreciated. You must be prepared to give more than you can hope to get back in the way of social or material reward. This is in contrast to many knowledge- and skill-based occupations where outstanding performances are more visible and more highly remunerated, and where practitioners generally have a greater degree of personal control over the outcomes of their work.

With these considerations in mind, it becomes appropriate to regard teaching in its most fundamental sense as character-intensive work, a type of occupation in which what you are as a person counts for at least as much as what you know. Failure to recognize its character-dependent nature leads to an unfortunate misidentification of what it takes to achieve success and fulfillment as a teacher in today's schools.

In appreciating the character-intensive nature of teaching, there are a number of important things you can do as a beginning teacher to get ready for a productive career. Many relevant ideas and suggestions are presented in Chapter 2 under the subheadings Maintaining Supra-System Perspectives, Staying Vital, Dealing with Conflicting Agendas, The Self-actualizing Teacher, and Coming to Terms with the System. In the meantime, here are some general recommendations for adapting to the character-dependent nature of classroom teaching:

1. Recognize that in a character-intensive occupation like teaching your major satisfactions will need to be internally rather than externally de-

rived. Money, prestige, and material achievements are less available in teaching than in most other professions, so you should be cognizant of the more intangible or hidden benefits teaching has to offer. The final section of this chapter examines some of these more subjective rewards and suggests steps you can take to avail yourself of teaching's special opportunities.

2. Accept the day-to-day challenges of classroom teaching and realize the positive byproducts to be derived from character-intensive work. Some of the important side effects of teaching can be increased self-confidence, a better command of language, and substantial increases in interpersonal skill, and perhaps above all, a growing sense that you are involved in a truly worthwhile, *human* enterprise. Teaching tends to be excellent basic training for a wide variety of other opportunities and challenges likely to be experienced in life.

3. Continue to cultivate your people-skills as basic keys to success and fulfillment in teaching. Your skills at human interaction are fundamental to this kind of work. The ability to be a sensitive and articulate conversationalist pays high dividends in teaching. This includes the patience and empathy to be a caring listener, and the aptitudes for entering into genuine dialogue with others (see Chapters 8 and 12).

Diversity in the Classroom

As we mentioned in the Preface, classrooms are becoming increasingly diverse. Students have of course always differed in ability, even if tracked into supposedly homogeneous classes; there have always been poor and rich, and the United States has from the beginning had a wider range of peoples than almost any other nation. Now, however, the differences are becoming more marked and more general. Children from cultural and ethnic minorities, Hispanic and African-American in particular, but with increasing numbers of students from southeast Asia and the Orient, will form an ever growing proportion of young people in the next few decades.[31] At the same time, it seems safe to predict that more and more children will come from poverty, and more and more will come from homes in which both parents work, or in which there is only one parent, often too much out of the home or too preoccupied with maintaining the home to give the children the attention and nurturing they need.

In addition to these sources of increasing diversity, there is the move to what is termed "inclusion," or "inclusive education." This is an outgrowth of the 1976 federal legislation, usually referred to as PL 94–142. This enactment gave *all* students, for the first time, the right to a free and appropriate education in "the least restrictive environment." The updated version of that law, *Individuals with Disabilities Act* of 1990, requires even more specifically that "to the maximum extent appropriate" students with disabilities be educated in the same classrooms as students without. All children, or older students, who have a disability but who are nonetheless able to gain from being in the same classroom as those without disabilities, must be educated alongside them, unless they are so disruptive that neither they nor the rest of the class can learn. What has always been one of the more difficult aspects of teaching, keeping *everyone* in a class engaged with work of appropriate interest and difficulty, is thus becoming more challenging every year.

You will therefore have to seriously consider whether you are prepared, or are currently preparing to meet this challenging aspect of contemporary and future classroom life. Many schools try to ensure that teachers with and without special education preparation and experience work in the same classroom, so that students get the special or extra help they need. Many, however, still do not, or employ paraprofessionals or teacher aides for what is highly skilled and professionally demanding work. Particularly when you share a classroom with someone trained in special education, you enjoy a valuable support and their presence has the added advantage of making it possible for you as a beginning teacher to work alongside a more experienced professional, hitherto rare as previously mentioned. The best approach is for any new teacher to arrange to meet with a future colleague even before the first time they both meet the new class, and to keep doing so frequently thereafter, so that they can work out together how to deal with the class as a whole, and how to deal with students who need more individual help.

Here are a few other suggestions to help you deal with this aspect of beginning to teach:

1. Whether or not your college coursework includes extensive material on diversity, do all you can to observe and if possible to work with individual students with disabilities, students referred to as limited English proficient (LEP), and students different in backgrounds and in culture from your own. This will give you valuable practical insight into the attitudes and techniques you need to acquire to help varied students learn. It will also give you firsthand experience of how students with particular difficulties, and students who are in some respect "other," need intense, concentrated, and emotionally demanding teaching. Above all, it will serve to remind you of the humanity of such students before you get into a situation in which numerous pressures will make it difficult for you sometimes to keep this in mind.

2. If your required coursework in this area is limited as it still is in many states, get to know as much as you can about the various types of disability and of the teaching approaches that each makes necessary. This is equally true if your future classroom, in common with so many, is likely to have a number—perhaps even a majority—of students for whom English is their second language, sometimes very much the second one.

3. Diverse classes can be taught only to a limited extent as if they were homogeneous—taught, that is to say, by the teacher talking to everyone from the front of the class and requiring the same attention and

work from all. Since the number and type of diversities is so much greater, even though it can be quite wide even in "tracked" classes, it is essential that you become thoroughly familiar with methods of teaching that involve students working with students, in pairs or in small groups (see Chapters 6 and 8). Always bear in mind the fact that, as one recent writer put it, "cognitive development and socialization are paired"; in other words, that students' learning develops to a considerable extent out of their relationships with others.

4. If there is a strong likelihood that you will be teaching in schools where a majority of the students will be from one minority or another (or possibly from two, or possibly many), make every effort to learn all you can about the customs and perspectives of the people, and at least some of the everyday phrases in the language.

5. Equip yourself with a far wider variety of teaching approaches and materials than you probably experienced yourself as a student, and recognize the absolute centrality of interest and a sense of purpose in *any* student's decision to learn, or in their absence, *not* to learn. The student always has the final word.

The Intangible Rewards

It may be said that teaching is an occupation with challenges that are largely invisible to those who have not worked in classrooms, but it also brings with it a number of intangible benefits for those who are able to appreciate them. Just as it is essential for you as a beginning teacher to be realistic about the challenges, it is also important for you to be aware of the nonmaterial rewards that accompany this sort of work.

One of those benefits is the personal growth opportunities provided by classroom teaching. In comparison to a great many other occupations, including most jobs requiring primarily technical skill, teaching is a totally involving kind of work that continually draws on your emotional and interpersonal resources as well as your technical knowledge. Having made the classroom plunge, one is pressed to develop these resources at an accelerated rate to meet the demands of the job. Early-career teachers have been known to make dramatic leaps in self-confidence, language and public speaking ability, and capacity to deal with other people, after concentrated exposure to classroom teaching. With few exceptions, those who experience the exigencies of classroom teaching find themselves much better prepared for child-raising, community service activities, alternative career opportunities, and other personal and interpersonal challenges.

Another occupational benefit that tends to be unique to teaching is the opportunity for a teacher to recharge during summers and other school vacations. This is often perceived as a mere job "perquisite," and is usually described simply as "having your summers and vacations to yourself," a characterization that quite fails to convey the essence of what this time away from the classroom can do for you. Teaching is the kind of work that requires a constant supply of emotional and creative energy, and one must thus be able to step back periodically and find ways to replenish these crucial resources. Also, in an activity like teaching where people are especially prone to becoming stale because the structure of each class period, each day, each week, and each semester readily produces a routinization of thinking and acting, it is absolutely necessary to re-think one's whole approach to what can very easily become just "the job." Time away from school can allow you the opportunity to do this periodical reviewing and renewing.[32]

A third attractive feature is the opportunity to work with developing young people. You will have occasion to spend your working hours with people who are full of potential and energy. Although these hours spent with the young can be personally demanding, they can also be gratifying and rejuvenating. Contrary to what their overt behavior may sometimes suggest, most students are still experimenting, caring, trusting, and searching for where they fit into the world around them. If you teach in an elementary school, you will ordinarily get students before they have become cynical and jaded, before they develop the ego barriers that make them unapproachable. Even though many students in high school may also seem to have reached this stage, for most it is still a pose, and given purposeful teaching, they can work with energy, enthusiasm, and concentration. In short, there is something refreshing and inspiriting about a job that entails working with young learners, however frustrating and exhausting it may be at times. Being in their company keeps you on the cutting edge of what is new and vibrant in a society in which many jobs tend to be lifeless and uninspiring—but it can be exhausting!

Finally, an aspect of teaching that has been regarded as a liability, namely, the fact that you often, especially in high school, work apart from other adults, can in some respects be a positive feature of the job. For creative teachers, working alone turns out to be a blessing in disguise. Once you are in the classroom on your own, you have a private work space you can use to develop your own style. This enclave separate from the rest of the school may be thought of as a studio where you can develop your own unique talents and interests as they apply to teaching and learning. It is a place where you can do special things with your own students. Teaching, then, is an occupation that gives you considerable privacy to create an environment that is uniquely yours, and within that special environment, to perform the act of teaching largely to your own specifications.

If, on the other hand, you enjoy working with adults, many elementary and middle schools now offer opportunities for collaboration, in the form of team teaching, an arrangement in which three or four teachers share the responsibility for teaching a common group of students. Sharing ideas with colleagues about what and how to teach can be a stimulating and rewarding experience especially if one is a beginning teacher. It provides a chance to learn from those with more, or different experience, and to specialize to some degree in one or two subject areas, while one's fellow team members concentrate on other parts of the curriculum.

As a new teacher, consider the following things you can begin to do to take advantage of teaching's latent rewards:

1. Recognize what it takes to continue to grow in this profession. Beginning teachers often make dramatic personal and professional gains during the first several years, then settle into nongrowth patterns for the remainder of their careers. Chapter 2 offers ideas and strategies for overcoming serious occupational hurdles and achieving a "creative orientation" as a teacher, and Chapter 12 contains many suggestions for, as its title promises, "Managing Your Own Development as a Teacher." Develop a lifestyle that supports your need for continual renewal as a teacher. Use your summers and shorter vacations to accomplish recreation in the generic sense of the word, that is, *re*-creation. Teachers frequently fall into do-nothing patterns during their time away from school. The kind of recreation style they adopt is often counterproductive in terms of their need for personal renewal. It can cause a teacher to come back to school feeling more lethargic and out-of-sync than before. An especially good source of ideas on the type of recreation we are talking about here is Bruno Hans Geba's *Being at Leisure: Playing at Life.*[33]

2. Allow yourself to experience the unique satisfactions that can come from working with young learners. Learn to savor those special moments in teaching when you are glad you have chosen to work with youngsters rather than adults. Accept the fact that you are forfeiting opportunities to be around people who are more knowledgeable, stable, and predictable, for the chance to work with those who are naive, restless, and unfinished. Make this one of your main reasons for being there.

3. Take advantage of the special things you can do *because* you have a classroom to yourself. Make the most of opportunities to rearrange the furniture to suit your teaching purposes, to bring in exciting materials, and to use unorthodox approaches, without having to get permission. Short of exhibiting bad taste or becoming an impossible eccentric, allow yourself to do things in the classroom that represent your own special interests and talents.

◆◆◆   SUGGESTED ACTIVITIES AND QUESTIONS   ◆◆◆

1. What are some of the things that appeal to you about teaching as an occupation? Do you think of teaching as a glamorous kind of work? How accurate do you think that notion is? What are some common misconceptions about the work of a teacher? How do these ideas become established?

2. What are some of the lingering images you have of teachers from your own days in school? Try writing a description of several teachers that continue to stand out in your mind from your school experiences. Do you have favorable or unfavorable recollections of these people? What kinds of roles do you suppose these teachers were attempting to play (e.g., stern taskmaster, everybody's friend, subject-matter specialist)?

3. How do you see your own role as you enter the field of teaching? Do you have particular objectives you want to accomplish in teaching? What kinds of role conflicts do you anticipate as a classroom teacher?

4. Find occasions to talk with six to eight classroom teachers about what they perceive their main roles to be. Which among these various role perceptions do you consider to be most realistic? Most idealistic? Why?

5. How do you feel about a job where one of the main requirements is being able to manage and organize groups of people? As you imagine yourself in a teaching situation, how would you attempt to resolve the potential conflict between your role as someone responsible for creating and maintaining order and your responsibilities as a promoter of learning? Have you been in other responsible positions in your life in which you felt there were conflicting expectations placed on you (e.g., military service)?

6. What do you anticipate will be some of the main problems you encounter as a teacher? Attempt to identify things you can begin to do to help make these expected problems less severe.

7. What are your present thoughts and feelings about working in a school environment all day with groups of young people? What special qualities do you possess that would allow you to adapt well to the "togetherness condition" of teaching? Are there some specific things you might do to make it easier for you and your students to "live together" over the long stretch?

8. In terms of its pressures, teaching has been compared to the job of an air-traffic controller. How does this comparison strike you? Are there other similarities? Dissimilarities?

9. Try to remember times when you have found yourself in environments that were highly unfamiliar or when you have felt overwhelmed by busyness, noise, movement, and so forth. Attempt to describe the sort of shock you felt. What were some of the things you did to attempt to deal with the problem? How long did it take you to adjust to these situations? What did you learn on these occasions that can help you as a teacher?

10. Describe some of the ways people deal with the "stimulus overload" they experience in situations like teaching. What sorts of defense mechanisms do people typically rely on in these instances? Describe what you would consider positive adaptations to the shock we sometimes experience under these conditions. What would you regard as less constructive types of responses?

NOTES

1. Ann Lieberman and Lynne Miller, *Teachers, Their World and Their Work.* Alexandria, Va.: Association for Supervision and Curriculum Development, 1984, p. 7.

2. Kevin Ryan observes that "teaching increasingly is becoming a short-term career, with the average teacher leaving the profession in less than ten years. Teachers who have unsuccessful and unpleasant early experiences do not

make strong commitments and often begin to look for ways to escape from teaching." (In Kevin Ryan, *The Induction of New Teachers*. Bloomington, Ind.: Phi Delta Kappa Educational Foundation, 1986, p. 8). Darling-Hammond, executive director of the National Council on Teaching and America's Future, reports that "as many as 30 percent leave in the first few years, while others learn merely to cope rather than to teach well." Linda Darling-Hammond, "What Matters Most: A Competent Teacher for Every Child." *Phi Delta Kappan 54*, (November 1996): 195.

3. See Sara Freedman, Jane Jackson, and Katherine Boles, "Teaching: An Imperiled Profession." In Lee S. Shulman and Gary Sykes (Eds.), *Handbook of Teaching and Policy*. New York: Longman, 1983, pp. 261–299.

4. Philip W. Jackson, *Life in Classrooms*, 2nd ed. New York: Holt, Rinehart and Winston, 1993, p. 229.

5. Richard C. Sprinthall and Norman A. Sprinthall, *Educational Psychology: A Developmental Approach*, 3rd ed. Reading, Mass.: Addison-Wesley, 1981, p. 393.

6. Jackson, *Life in Classrooms*, p. 11.

7. Philip W. Jackson, "Talking About Teaching." In Kevin Ryan and James Cooper (Eds.), *Kaleidoscope, Readings in Education*, 3rd ed. Boston: Houghton Mifflin, 1980, p. 229.

8. Jackson, *Life in Classrooms*, p. 12.

9. Joseph Hasenstab and Connie Wilson, *Training the Teacher as a Champion*. Nevada City, Calif.: Performance Learning Systems, 1989, p. 75.

10. See Robert M. Nideffer and Roger C. Sharpe, *A.C.T. Attention Control Training*. New York: Wyden Books, 1978; W. Timothy Gallwey, *The Inner Game of Tennis*. New York: Bantam Books, 1974; and Robert W. Travers and Jacqueline Dillon, *The Making of a Teacher: A Plan for Professional Self-Development*. New York: Macmillan, 1975. In his book, Nideffer offers some premises that are basic to the attention control techniques he would advocate for teachers: "When you're anxious your ability to deal with a large amount of information is reduced. . . . Knowing *what you* should pay attention to is critical. When people feel uncertain in a situation, they tend to try to pay attention to everything. At that very time attention is narrow and you're least able to succeed. By taking time for some advance planning, you can stop the tendency to overload yourself" (p. 59).

11. Norman A. Sprinthall and Lois Thies-Sprinthall, "Educating for Teacher Growth: A Cognitive Developmental Perspective." *Theory Into Practice 19*, No. 4 (1980): 278–285.

12. Lieberman and Miller, *Teachers*, p. 40.

13. See Stuart B. Palonsky, *900 Shows a Year: A Look at Teaching from a Teacher's Side of the Desk*. New York: Random House, 1986; Theodore R. Sizer, *Horace's Compromise: The Dilemma of the American High School*. Boston: Houghton Mifflin, 1984; and Vito Perrone, *A Letter to Teachers: Reflections on Schooling and the Art of Teaching*. San Francisco: Jossey-Bass, 1991.

14. Lieberman and Miller, *Teachers*, p. 41.

15. See Linda M. McNeil, *Contradictions of Control: School Structure and School Knowledge*. New York: Routledge and Kegan Paul, 1986, especially Chap. 7, "Defensive Teaching and Classroom Control."

16. Lieberman and Miller, *Teachers*, p. 42.

17. Gene I. Maeroff, "A Blueprint for Empowering Teachers." *Phi Delta Kappan 47*, (March 1988):474.

18. John I. Goodlad, *A Place Called School*. New York: McGraw-Hill, 1984, pp. 186–187. Citing the 1989 OERI report, "What Works: Research about

Teaching and Learning, "Brophy and Good write that, "as many as 45 percent of the teachers reported *no* contact with one another during a school day, and another 32 percent reported infrequent contact with colleagues. Thomas L. Good, Jere E. Brophy, *Looking in Classrooms.* 7th ed. New York: Longman, 1997, p. 463.

19. Lieberman and Miller, *Teachers,* p. 11.
20. Goodlad, *A Place Called School,* pp. 186–187.
21. http://www.NCTM.org; http://www.NCTE.org; http://www.NCSS.org; http://www.NSTA.org; http://www.IRA.org.
22. Howard Gardner, *Frames of Mind: The Theory of Multiple Intelligences.* New York: Basic Books, 1983, p. 357.
23. Frank Smith, *Comprehension and Learning: A Conceptual Framework for Teachers.* New York: Holt, Rinehart and Winston, 1975, p. 10.
24. Rosemary A. Rosser and Glen I. Nicholson, *Educational Psychology: Principles in Practice.* Boston: Little, Brown, 1984, pp. 487–489.
25. For recent confirmation of this fact, see Leon F. Gardiner, *Redesigning Higher Education: Dramatic Gains in Student Learning.* ASHE-ERIC Higher Education Report, Washington, DC: The George Washington University, 1994. "A study of first-year physical science students at Rutgers University and Essex Community College (NJ) found that 2/3 had not yet become formal thinkers" (p.10).
26. N. L. Gage and David C. Berliner, *Educational Psychology,* 4th ed. Boston: Houghton Mifflin, 1988, p. 128.
27. Laurence Steinberg, *Beyond the Classroom: Why Education Reform Failed and What Parents Need to Do About It.* New York: Simon and Schuster, 1996.
28. Barak Rosenshine and Carla Meister, "The Use of Scaffolds for Teaching Higher-Level Cognitive Strategies." *Educational Leadership 50,* (April 1992): 26–33. "Scaffolds" include "concrete prompts," devices used, for example, by teachers "to help students learn the strategy of generating questions" by having ready "question words—*who, what, when, where, why, and how.*"

    Michael F. Graves, Bonnie B. Graves, and Sheldon Braaten, "Scaffolded Reading Experiences for Inclusive Classes." *Educational Leadership 54,* (February 1996):14–16.

    The authors cite David Pearson's statement that "scaffolding allows us . . . to provide the cueing, questioning, coaching, corroboration, and plain old information needed to allow students to complete a task before they are able to complete it independently."
29. Sara Lawrence Lightfoot, "The Lives of Teachers." In Lee S. Shulman and Gary Sykes (Eds.), *Handbook of Teaching and Policy.* New York: Longman, 1983, p. 250.
30. Arthur W. Combs, *The Professional Education of Teachers: A Perceptual View of Teacher Preparation.* Boston: Allyn and Bacon, 1965, pp. 71, 85.
31. Eugene García, *Understanding and Meeting the Challenge of Student Cultural Diversity.* Boston: Houghton Mifflin, 1994, p. 260.
32. It becomes important, though, for you to learn how to achieve personal and professional renewal during vacations from work. Just being away from the job does not guarantee it. For this reason, you should regard vacation time as a potential benefit to you in your professional life. It becomes an actual benefit when you are able to use it to further your professional growth.
33. See Bruno Hans Geba, *Being at Leisure, Playing at Life.* La Mesa, Calif.: Leisure Science Systems International, 1985.

CHAPTER 2

Learning to Work Creatively Within the System

The Nature of the Challenge

Probably the most formidable challenge facing you as a beginning teacher is that of adapting to the demands and pressures of the school organization without sacrificing your initiative and creativity as a teaching specialist.[1] The sort of personal accommodation you make to the system itself can have an important bearing on whether you achieve a degree of professional autonomy in classroom teaching or settle for the role of functionary within the school bureaucracy. It helps to have a good initial understanding of how the system works and how it can affect your teaching patterns.

Most first-year teachers have to work their way through an initial *survival period* (what one might refer to as the period of "*sheer survival*") in which their overwhelming concern is demonstrating to themselves and others that they are capable of being a teacher.[2] During this adjustment period their main energies are usually devoted to coping with class schedules, time pressures, class management problems, and other such urgencies. This survival stage is typically a short one, however. Novice teachers will ordinarily move rather quickly through this time of doubt and instability, arriving at a set of routines that allows them to reduce the pressures and make the job more manageable. Having become familiar with organizational patterns, they are inclined to be less security-minded and primarily concerned with adapting their workaday situation to align more closely with their own personal needs and preferences.

This second level of accommodation, or *pragmatic orientation* (which will also be referred to as the period of "*mere survival*") not uncommonly turns out to be an occupational plateau from which teachers never advance, or to which they return even after reaching the third level, because, as Sarason made clear

> Constant giving in the context of constant vigilance required by the presence of so many children is a demanding, draining, taxing affair that cannot easily be sustained. . . . To sustain the giving at a high level requires that the teacher experiences getting. The sources of getting are surprisingly infrequent and indirect.[3]

By continuing to devote their best resources to the organizational and managerial aspects of teaching, teachers may learn to play the role sufficiently well to keep a job, but never develop the autonomy, sensitivity, and classroom maneuverability that characterize a *creative orientation* to this work (the stage that we will refer to as *"beyond survival"*). The resulting occupational rut can lead to serious job dissatisfaction and professional burnout, not to mention ineffective or even counterproductive teaching.[4] The task, then, is to arrive at a relationship to the system that allows one to continue to grow as a teacher.

This chapter offers insight into the requirements for creative teacher performance in a school organization. It discusses the factors that contribute to lifeless, routine-bound teaching and offers perspectives and strategies for achieving a suprasystem orientation, for managing conflicting roles and agendas, and for maintaining one's vitality and integrity in the institutional setting.

Patterns of Accommodation

By recognizing the variety and sequence of accommodations teachers normally make to school systems, and by anticipating the institutional forces that can serve to inhibit teacher growth, you are in a better position to confront the organizational hurdles that must be surmounted to achieve your potential as a public school teacher. This section describes in more detail the three levels of system accommodation already mentioned, namely, that of *sheer survival*, that of *mere survival*, and that which finally goes *beyond survival*.[5] Being aware of these as stages of teacher development will give you a framework for conceptualizing the kind of professional growth you can realistically aspire to within a modern school bureaucracy, and how.

Sheer Survival As beginning professionals, teachers at this survival level find themselves preoccupied with personal adequacy and job security. They are concerned with getting and holding a job, controlling their classes, and satisfying students and supervisors. These concerns are apparent in the following statements of three first-year teachers:

> I'm enjoying my classes so far, but right now I'm a little nervous about the evaluation I've got coming up. I'll be cruising along just fine until someone comes in and sits down in the back of my classroom. I couldn't stand to get a bad evaluation at this stage.

It's especially important to me that I get off to a good start with my classes. I want my students to like me. If they like you, they'll be more cooperative and you'll have a better chance of getting through your first year without serious discipline problems. So having good rapport with my students is one of my most important goals right now.

At the moment I'm mainly interested in finding a job. I've been told that social science positions are quite scarce. But I've been in school too long to spend another year without work.

Survival-oriented teachers often feel overwhelmed by the scope and scale of their new responsibilities. They are not helped by the fact that

formative learning is still obtained on the job, without much systematic and substantive help from colleagues and supervisors. Teachers remain largely autonomous in the classroom and often are left to "wing it." . . . they plan the best they can, improvise when necessary, make good and bad decisions, and "survive with dignity."[6]

Their first encounters with the complexities of classroom teaching tend to be disorienting, causing them to limit their fields of vision as they react frantically, sometimes mechanically, to the fast-moving, multiple agendas of a typical teaching day.[7]

Being above all concerned with their own performances, survival-oriented teachers often fail to attend to other critical aspects of the teaching situation. They may have difficulty keeping their fingers on the pulse of the class, or reading and responding to cues that strategy adjustments are in order. As a result, teachers at this level can expect to have some initial difficulty with classroom control.

Mere Survival Teachers at this stage have become socialized to the ways of the school and are no longer primarily preoccupied with personal competence and job security. They have succeeded in reducing the complexity of teaching to manageable proportions through routines that enable them to satisfy major role requirements, while providing important measures of stability and predictability. These teachers have usually achieved orderly classrooms, systems for handling required paperwork, adaptations to the prescribed curriculum, and workable relationships with administrators and parents.

By reducing teaching to a set of dependable routines, the pragmatically oriented teacher is able to systemize the teaching process, simplify the teaching day, and avoid having to function continuously, or at all, in a creative mode. As Lieberman and Miller concluded from their studies of classroom teachers,

Given many children, and much subject matter, routine becomes easier than risk. And dropping a subject or two is better than the insecurity of teaching something you know little about.

And they cite the pioneer study of Willard Waller back in 1932 to the effect that

> the established teacher has been playing safe so long that she has lost the necessary element of recklessness without which life becomes painful.[8]

This preoccupation with efficiency and manageability generally results in mechanical approaches to teaching and learning. The teacher becomes essentially a presenter of content, often a very proficient one, concerned above all to "cover the material," to get through the text. He or she is disposed to view teaching as rule-governed behavior and frequently functions best with "teacher proof" materials, that is, materials that come with instructions, such as a teachers' manual. Such teachers will tend to rely primarily on extrinsic forms of motivation.

Despite the fact that survival is no longer a central concern for teachers at the stage of sheer survival, they still devote a major share of their attentions to the nuts and bolts of their work. The ability to cope effectively, as they see it, with the system still tends to dominate their consciousness. They are occupied with time pressures, numbers of students, availability of materials, noninstructional duties, and the politics and economics of teaching. Here are typical statements representing the dominant concerns of two third-year secondary teachers:

> I'm going to have to find another system. I won't continue to take home this much paperwork.

> There has to be a way to get more of this work done during the school day. I'll just try to squeeze some of it in during lunch. If they want me to teach this many students, I'm going to expect fewer preparations. Also, I believe I've been here long enough to deserve a room of my own. I'm tired of moving.

At this level, the teachers' absorption with the apparent "realities" of working in a public school often makes it difficult for them to see beyond the system. As a result, they tend to confuse organizational agendas (means) for educational goals (ends). Their notion of teaching competence is more likely to derive from prevailing role definitions—what other people define the job of the teacher as—than from consciously applied principles of teaching and learning. For example, they will be inclined to look to such external indicators as test results, rather than to individual learning patterns, for evidence that teaching goals have been achieved.

Beyond Survival Fully functioning teachers develop patterns of working within the school organization that allow them to concentrate on objectives that reach beyond the system itself. They are able to bring suprasystem perspectives to their teaching. These teachers are able to be productive and creative in looking for and finding ways of serving the educational needs of young human beings in spite of workloads and school climates that could serve to distract them from their primary mission. They are often actually stimulated by the challenge of performing under hectic conditions so that they develop a capacity similar to that of the subject of a two-year-long study. This new teacher, in her second year

> developed an intimate . . . knowledge of how the school worked, and with this knowledge she became increasingly sophisticated at manipulating the institution to help ease the problem of negotiating a satisfying place within it. . . . She became more reflective in practice.[9]

Such teachers have learned to cope satisfactorily with the exigencies of school life and they seem to enjoy the complicated juggling act that characterizes superior teaching. They have developed a style in response to major dilemmas which, in the case of elementary school teachers, Lieberman and Miller enumerate as[10]:

- More subjects to teach than time to teach them
- Coverage versus mastery
- Large-group versus small-group instruction
- When to stay with a subject or a routine and when to shift
- How to discipline students without destroying the class
- How to deal with isolation from other adults

And in the case of secondary teachers as[10]:

- Personal versus organization constraints
- Dealing with the classroom and with the whole school
- Packaging and pacing instruction to fit into allocated time periods
- Proportioning subject matter expertise and affective needs in some way
- Figuring out how to deal with mixed loyalties to the faculty and to the student culture

The major concern of creatively oriented teachers is the effect they are having on their students. They tend to employ methods and objectives that derive from a belief that human learning and development need to be aided and fostered rather than continually driven and directed. These teachers ordinarily possess well-developed powers of communication and self-expression and will strive to promote forms of self-expression in their students as an overriding objective. They place a high premium on intrinsic motivation and on the inner-self development of young learners. This is revealed in the following exchange between two veteran sixth-grade teachers:

> **TEACHER A:** I'm going to do less with formal grammar this time around and put more emphasis on impromptu writing.
>
> **TEACHER B:** Yes, I'm with you on that. I believe these kids definitely need opportunities to form ideas before they get bogged down in rules.

TEACHER A: This, of course, will mean more papers to read, but I'm willing to do that if I can begin to make a dent in some of the
negative attitudes toward writing they bring into my class.

TEACHER B: That's what we're here for. I don't mind the extra work either
if I can see some improvement in their writing.

Teachers who perform at this level tend to approach teaching as an art
form. One of their most important identifying characteristics is their ability to
function in an indirect teaching mode (see Chapter 4). They recognize that
meaningful learning cannot be forced. As such, they will attempt to provide a
solid foundation for new learning and to adapt their teaching to the learning
styles and rhythms of their students. These individuals are inclined to put a
great deal of themselves into their teaching.

Anticipating the Hurdles

A great many people with the potential to become better than average teachers have difficulty realizing that potential within the structure of a U.S. public
school.[11] In response to the system forces they encounter, most teachers
adopt a pragmatic accommodation early in their careers and remain at that
level until they leave teaching. These teachers do a satisfactory job of meeting
major role expectations, but they fail to develop a creative orientation toward
their work. Their best efforts are devoted to meeting system requirements
that are frequently at cross-purposes with their development as skilled classroom practitioners.[12]

The most likely candidates for occupational burnout are pragmatically
oriented teachers whose routines have become stale, causing them to experience serious job frustration and dissatisfaction. According to Seymour Sarason, burnout among professional people "involves a change in attitude and
behavior in response to a demanding, frustrating, unrewarding work experience." One of the negative changes is "a loss of concern for the client, and a
tendency to treat clients in a detached, mechanical fashion."[13] Other characteristics include "increasing discouragement, pessimism, and fatalism about
one's work; apathy; negativism; frequent irritability and anger with clients and
colleagues; preoccupation with one's own comfort and welfare on the job; a
tendency to rationalize failure by blaming the clients or "the system"; and resistance to change, growing rigidity, and loss of creativity."[14]

In a sense, we might say burnout occurs when teachers feel buried within
the school organization.

Developing a Creative Pattern

It is imperative, then, that you give serious consideration to the quality of the
relationship to the system itself if you are to achieve maximum effectiveness
and satisfaction in your work.

By examining the patterns and dispositions of creative teachers, you can gain insight into the kinds of personal investments that will allow you to make the most of your opportunities in teaching.

Maintaining Supra-System Perspectives

In order to make a healthy adaptation to a modern school bureaucracy, you must be capable of standing above the organization conceptually and psychologically. You must be able to see the system for what it is and have the personal strength to resist being overpowered by it. Systems (also known as "organizations," or "institutions") come into being, or are deliberately set up, to enable a group of people to reach some goal. They provide ways of integrating the efforts of many different kinds of individuals, and different operations, over long periods of time, so that the goal can more easily be reached.

Systems of some sort are always necessary, but sooner or later they seem to take on a life of their own. Ways of doing things become routinized, relations between people become bureaucratized, which is to say fixed, rigid, and power-centered. Those in them come to regard maintaining the system, its ways of doing things, as more important than the purposes for which the system was originally designed and created in the first place, or is now needed to fulfill. "Maintenance becomes more important than mission," as one writer aptly put it. Systems, no matter how successful in the past, must change with the changing times to meet new social and personal needs, or they become obstacles, but they almost always resist change, or are slow and reluctant to move. Ironically, very often the greater their record of success, the more they resist change, and schools are no exception.

Teachers with a creative orientation to their work are able to recognize the limitations as well as the merits of institutionalized schooling in meeting the needs of individuals. They expect neither more nor less of these organizations than they are capable of delivering. Such teachers construe school systems as vehicles for achieving purposes that go beyond the school itself. They are not as likely to confuse the requirements of institutional maintenance with the imperatives of human growth and development. In this they will differ from the many teachers whom two researchers in a very recent study found to be doing " 'teacher work' . . . organizing the stuff (a curriculum for a particular grade or subject, learning techniques and methods that 'work for me,' controlling and managing students, and sorting students (assigning grades)." They

> were not anxious for substantive change. Collaborative work and shared decision were neither practiced nor much admired by the leaders of this veteran staff. That is, these teachers were doing exactly what the "teacher craft" and their school's culture expected of them and had prepared them to do; they were doing "teacher work."[15]

It is crucial that you make the distinction between maintaining the system and promoting human development because major institutions such as schools, and especially those who pay for and run the schools—taxpayers, parents, administrators, and often teachers themselves—tend to suppose that what has been, and is, must, for that very reason, continue to be. Much school learning (and *ways* of learning it), remain in the curriculum because they have always been part of the schooling tradition, that is, "it's something any well-educated person ought to know (and teachers telling students is how they ought to learn it)." A good deal of what students learn in school is deemed important simply because it prepares them for what they will learn in school next year or the following year. The reality of the U.S. school system is that it is largely self-contained. It has its own goals and values, its own rules for how the game is to be played, and its own language for defining organizational agendas."[16] It is one thing for a representative of the system to accommodate to that reality as a means of pursuing broader educational goals, or as a strategy for negotiating their first few weeks or even months of teaching. It is something altogether different, however, to allow yourself to be encapsulated and perceptually disabled by it.

Creative teachers are precisely those who are determined and able to keep one foot in and one foot out of the system. They manage, difficult as they may find it, to keep themselves grounded in principles that reach beyond the organization and its programs, as reflected in this comment by a veteran teacher of eleventh-grade U.S. history:

> I'm not satisfied just to have my students pass tests. I can't see requiring them to memorize names and dates if there's no carryover. They've got to practice historical thinking when they leave the school, otherwise I really haven't taught. This class should help them to see history in the making as they read newspapers and watch the news. It's vital that these young people develop a realistic sense of where we've been and where we seem to be going as a country.

The following are some important things you can do to help maintain supra-system perspectives as a teacher:

1. Take time periodically to reflect on your most important purposes as a teacher. Allow your frame of reference to reach beyond the boundaries of the school. Apart from the specific content objectives that appear in your daily lesson plans, what sorts of principles and purposes are important to you in your teaching? (See Chapter 3). Do they include human development and social development goals? In the ideal, what kinds of people do you see yourself as helping to emerge through your teaching? In what specific ways can the school contribute to making a better community and a better society?

2. Make a consistent effort to keep the ends and means of the school in proper focus. Recognize the fallacy of using organizational concepts to evaluate the performance of the system itself. This practice tends to be self-justifying. Test scores, grade-point averages, daily attendance figures, and percentages of high school graduates may indicate that the

system is functioning well in itself, but they do little to demonstrate the effectiveness of the schooling process in enhancing life beyond school. You would do well to keep in mind the contention of two observers that

most urban schools and many suburban schools are "teachers' schools" . . . i.e., teachers believe they own them . . . In a teachers' school, the message is a simple one. "Do what I tell you, the way I tell you, and everything will be all right. That is what you will have to do in the real world, so learn to obey those in charge now."[17]

3. Avoid relying on system requirements as prods to get students involved in school learning. A teacher introducing a learning activity with the reminder that "this will be on the test," indicates that he or she is preoccupied with the school's concern to measure and grade student's performances rather than with the benefit the student has derived from the process. It shows a complete lack of sensitivity to the learning and developmental needs of young people. Chapter 6 sets out an approach to classroom motivation designed to involve students actively in learning without having to use the system and its requirements as the primary form of incentive.
4. Develop a critical attitude toward the specialized language of the school labyrinth in this country. For example, if you can recognize the value assumptions that underlie concepts like "performance objectives," "academic subjects," "scholastic aptitude tests," and "remedial classes," you will be in a better position to assess just how valid they are as *educational* means as distinct from *system* requirements.

Staying Vital

Resourceful teachers refuse to allow the demands, the resistances, or the impersonality of the system to rob them of their creative edge. To function productively as a teacher in a modern school system, you must consistently bring fresh energy to the job. As a model for the kind of spirit and enthusiasm you would like students to exhibit, you should feel a strong need to keep yourself energetic and alive.

Considering the long hours, the repetitiveness of the work, and the feeling of fighting an uphill battle, it takes a special effort to consistently display a constructive and optimistic outlook with groups of young people, and to come up with material and approaches that get students involved. Exemplary teachers, however, find effective means for meeting this challenge. Like superior athletes and entertainers, they learn to pace themselves during the day, so that, for example, they limit the amount of direct, whole-group instruction they do to what they can manage at their full energy level, and deliberately structure in periods during which the students are fully engaged in working individually or in smaller configurations. They also develop a knack for using their personal resources constructively, being careful not to waste their emotional reserves in brooding, complaining, nagging, or chastising. Other contributing factors are the abilities of exceptional teachers to leaven what they and the students do with laughter and their dispositions to avoid taking themselves or the institution too seriously.

Regularly to bring positive and creative energy to this type of work, you will need to develop reliable ways of recharging your batteries when you sense you are beginning to run out of ideas and enthusiasm, and to go stale. The following are some strategies for renewing your teaching energies and perspectives from time to time:

1. Take opportunities to detach yourself from the day-to-day pressures of your work for a period of time. Time away from the job gives a person an opportunity to achieve a fresh vantage point. Cultivate at least one hobby or recreational activity that calls for different mental and physical skills than those you are accustomed to using in school.

2. Make a concerted effort to keep yourself as physically fit as possible. Insist on the kind and amount of sleep, and physical exercise that will allow you to feel fully refreshed in the morning and that will maintain your energy level throughout the school day. Do not ignore the close relationship between your physical well-being and your ability to function mentally and emotionally as a teacher.

3. Pay serious attention to what you eat. Demanding work such as teaching requires major energy. Sugary, fatty, instant foods sap that energy. You certainly don't need to go *on a diet*, but like athletes, you need to think "nutrition."

4. Allow yourself time for serious reflection on the nature of your work. To maintain their creative edge, most good teachers make it a practice to periodically review and perhaps reconstruct their fundamental views of education and teaching, taking into consideration their most recent experiences with these processes. In-depth professional and philosophical reading can often be the stimulus for new motivation (see Chapter 12). One indication that teachers are growing with the job is the realization that their basic outlooks and motivations are undergoing a metamorphosis as their experience widens and deepens.

Dealing with Conflicting Agendas (Role Conflict)

The role of a public school teacher is especially complex. It requires that teachers be able to manage multiple conflicting responsibilities. This can be frustrating and disconcerting for those who have not prepared themselves for the reality that dealing with contradictions and dilemmas is part of the teacher's job.

One potential conflict derives from the fact that the school is, on the one hand, a primary agent of *socialization* and as such has an obligation to help young people make a smooth adjustment to society as it presently exists. On the other hand, it is also responsible in our society to be an agent of *education* as human enlightenment, and in this perspective has stated commitments to promote the kinds of thinking skills, social ideals, and change, all of which dispose people to become critical of the status quo. This dilemma is unique to the schools of open societies such as our own. Schools in dictatorships or autocracies are, by definition, primarily and often exclusively instruments of socialization and subordination.

The processes of education and socialization are not easily combined. The former tends to be a broadening or liberating influence, while the main thrust of the latter is to promote conformity.[18] Pragmatically oriented teachers tend to eliminate, or at least alleviate, the stress produced by these conflicting agendas by concentrating on one of these school functions and ignoring or simply giving lip service to the other. Those who settle for the pragmatic accommodation have, whether they realize it or not, opted for socialization at the expense of the school's educational role.

Mechanical and superficial approaches to teaching and learning, doing "teacher work," are not only easier; they also facilitate the testing, grading, and sorting of students for job placement or further schooling. They do little, however, to promote meaningful learning or higher (or indeed any) thinking processes in students. So, although it is possible to justify all of these as necessary for implementing its social maintenance function, this kind of teaching is difficult to justify from an educational standpoint.

Another source of role conflict is the fact that teachers find themselves in the position of being both executives and counselors in their relationships with students. The executive role is essentially supervisory, directive, and critical. The other, that of counselor, is essentially supportive, advisory, and facilitative of the student's pursuit of knowledge.[19]

Teachers with a firm and well-understood creative orientation are able to sustain appropriate tension between the requirements of the contradictory roles they are asked to play. They strive to keep alive the *educational* mission of the school when it struggles to compete with the social adjustment emphasis. Such teachers also manage to maintain supportive and facilitative relationships with students in spite of forces that would cause them to be preoccupied with their executive responsibilities.

Here are some suggestions for dealing constructively with the conflicting agendas that are often part of the teacher's role:

1. Do not repress these conflicts when you find them to exist within the system. Make an effort to meet them head-on. Value conflicts and contradictions are part of the American way of life and can be expected to appear in our education systems. The problems they create for you and your students should not be thought to reflect personal weaknesses or inadequacies on your part. The tension you feel when you allow yourself to face up to such conflicts can turn out to be energizing rather than debilitating for you.

2. Accept the reality of classroom teaching as character-intensive work in which those who make the most positive impact and achieve the most personal satisfaction are people who are able to avoid the path of least resistance. Realize that truly creative performance in most any endeavor involves a willingness to buck the odds and resist entrenched patterns, but remember to keep a low profile, to avoid confrontation unless it is thrust on you. Nonetheless, be prepared to take carefully calculated risks when you are satisfied that the interests of your students call for them to be made.

3. Make it a point to periodically review your own priorities. By having clearly defined purposes and schemes for achieving them you are in a better position to see the logic of system patterns and to assess their compatibility with your own teaching needs. This allows you to maintain a sense of purpose and direction in the midst of institutionalized conflict or confusion.

Teaching Professional or School Employee?

Another potential conflict stems from your double role as both teaching professional and employee of a particular school system. As paid employees, workers generally have no decision-making authority beyond that granted them by their employers. On the other hand, trained professionals in public service occupations are typically allowed considerable autonomy when it comes to decisions that bear on their abilities to carry out their social service commitments. Whereas employees are obliged to perform in a manner that meets the expectations of a particular employer, professionals have an ethical commitment to the profession, or in effect to the larger society, to perform a social function that overrides the perceived needs of individual employers.[20]

For conscientious and reflective teachers this raises important questions about the basis of their authority. It causes them to ask: For whom am I really working? Is my first obligation to the teaching profession (i.e., to the society at large), or am I ultimately responsible to the particular school district that pays my salary? Who are my clients? Are they the students in my classes, or their parents, or all of the people in the school district who contribute to my salary? If the students are my clients, what is my professional obligation to them? Do I have a professional responsibility to prescribe learning experiences that I deem appropriate for these particular clients? What is my responsibility in cases in which my professional judgment is different from or in conflict with the prescriptions of the school system? If I allow the school system to dictate not only teaching objectives but also the means for achieving them, can I still claim professional status? Teachers have to go on asking themselves these questions because, as Fenstermacher pointed out

teaching is . . . unique among human service professions. It is unique in what it demands from its practitioners and the purposes its practitioners serve in the larger society. . . . It is—must be—a profession different from any of which we are immediately aware. To think of teaching in this way is to think of it as a *fundamentally moral undertaking.*[21]

Teachers with a pragmatic orientation will generally refuse to struggle with the dilemmas posed by these questions. The authority question is not a live issue for them. They are satisfied to consider it a legal rather than a philosophical or moral question. These teachers see themselves as employees who have been hired by the local community to perform a task in which the boundaries are clearly defined. Their views of teacher authority tend to be system-bound.

By approaching the issue of teacher authority from a purely technical point of view, pragmatically oriented teachers allow themselves to concentrate on the means and mechanics of teaching and to avoid the difficult questions having to do with purpose. One effect is to leave the schools more vulnerable to narrow parochialism, to the special interests and prejudices of laypersons who are apt to favor the socialization function over the educational function.

Creatively oriented teachers have an acute sensitivity to the conflicting roles they are asked to play. As we have maintained, a distinguishing characteristic of teachers who are able to perform at this level is their commitment to purposes that lie beyond the school organization itself. These people are able to achieve a satisfactory balance in this difficult authority issue, and since teaching means so much to them they do everything they can to live with the requirements imposed by the school system while at the same time doing justice to professional standards.

The following are suggested strategies for approaching the authority question and the conflicting expectations surrounding it:

1. Take a personal interest in examining the authority base from which you work. The question of whether your decision-making authority derives from your commitment and knowledge as a teaching professional or from your contractual responsibilities to the school district carries important implications for your work and satisfaction as a public school teacher.
2. Realize that as a conscientious, critical-minded teacher there will be times when the expectations placed on you as a school employee may put you in conflict with your perceived responsibilities as a professional educator. Be prepared to face the dilemma that these conflicting notions of authority pose for you and be armed with grounded arguments supporting what you are doing. Have the courage of your convictions, and be ready to stand up to the system when you are convinced it is requiring you to compromise your professional and moral obligations.
3. Take the optimistic view that the system—especially at the present time—is susceptible to positive influence by competent and assertive people with genuine commitments to educational excellence.

The Self-Actualizing Teacher

In the final analysis, it takes a good deal of psychological strength to work creatively and humanely in a modern school organization and not be dominated by the system. It helps to have achieved the personal adequacy and autonomy to be able to stand apart from the system and not depend on it for one's primary need-satisfaction. Abraham Maslow's model of the *self-actualizing* person has much to offer as a basis for the creative orientation in teachers.

In describing the quality of detachment in self-actualizing people, Maslow makes the following observation:

> It is often possible for them to remain above the battle, to remain unruffled, undisturbed by that which produces turmoil in others. . . . It becomes possible for them to take personal misfortunes without reacting violently as the ordinary person does. They seem to be able to retain their dignity even in undignified surroundings and situations. Perhaps this comes in part from their tendency to stick by their own interpretation of a situation rather than to rely upon what others feel or think about the matter.[22]

Maslow describes a related characteristic, the attribute of autonomy, in these terms:

> One of the characteristics of self-actualizing people is their relative independence of the physical and social environment. . . . They are not dependent for their main satisfactions on the real world, or other people, or culture, or means to ends, or in general on extrinsic satisfactions. Rather, they are dependent for their development and continued growth on their own potentialities and latent resources. . . . This independence of environment means a relative stability in the face of hard knocks, blows, deprivations, frustrations, and the like. These people can maintain a relative serenity and happiness in the midst of circumstances that would drive other people to suicide.[23]

In effect, the self-actualizing person has an uncommon ability to function within two reality structures at once and not allow one reality to be obscured by the other. Exceptional teachers are able to ensure that organizational needs and agendas do not cause them to lose sight of the ordering principles from which they work.

The following are steps you can take to become more self-actualized as an individual and a professional educator:

1. Find time in your busy schedule to be alone, a time for personal reflection and renewal.
2. Be able to locate your "personal center." Learn to trust the inner core of your personality for a sense of stability and direction. Continue to develop other aspects of your self by making time for art, music, outdoor activities, and travel, any and all of which draw on and nurture your intuitions, your imagination, and your emotions as well as your logical and analytical processes. Strive to be more than a specialist in

your work as a teacher, concerned with human growth and development no less than with subject matter.

3. Make an ongoing effort to understand your own internal needs and motivations. This includes knowing your own purposes and dreams and how they affect your work as a teacher. It is important to remain aware of your personal strengths as well as of changes in abilities and outlook that will make you a better teacher.

Coming to Terms with the System—General Strategies

As a summary of this chapter, the following is a set of general guidelines for making a healthy and creative accommodation to teaching in a modern school organization:

1. *Know where you are bound and where you are free.* Do not allow yourself to continually dwell on situations in which you feel hassled or constrained. Identify the areas where you have latitude to exert your personal influence and devote your best resources to making a difference in these areas. Teachers are of course tightly bound to time schedules, assigned classes, record keeping chores, and other organizational requirements. They often feel somewhat looser constraints when it comes to such things as prescribed curriculums, schoolwide discipline procedures, or parent-conferencing policies. You can usually expect a good deal of freedom to develop a teaching style and to express your own personality in the classroom once the door is closed. Teachers have considerable leeway in most schools and in most teaching areas to take unconventional approaches to teaching the subject matter of their assigned classes. In one of the areas where you can have considerable impact, namely, in your relationships with students, you will normally have a great deal of freedom to determine the nature of those relationships.

2. *Keep yourself focused on positive, constructive goals that have personal meaning for you.* Design ongoing projects, inquiries, or activities that you can pursue relative to your teaching, projects that represent your own special interests and aptitudes. For example, in experimenting with a significantly different method of working with nonachieving students, or in pursuing ways for extending student learning into some kind of community involvement, you can derive a sense of autonomy and significance that may be harder to achieve if your efforts and purposes are entirely system-determined.

    The fact that teachers are busy people working in a fast-paced environment is not in itself the thing that causes burnout and job dissatisfaction. Often it is the hectic pace in pursuit of agendas one has not chosen, the fact of constantly being in a position of having to adapt oneself to someone else's ideas. Creative teachers are inclined to be initiators and meaning-makers, proactive rather than reactive people.

Their response to apparent constraint or adversity is to take initiative, to move to control situations rather than waiting for these situations to control them.

3. *Be ready, willing, and able to stand up to the system when necessary.* Expect some dissonance between your own educational agendas and those of school systems. Develop the courage to oppose courses of action that you find to be in fundamental disregard for your beliefs and the needs of your students—but be careful to do it as quietly and tactfully as possible, with due respect for the knowledge and experience of your colleagues! Become organized and articulate in representing your own educational purposes and commitments if you are called upon to do so. Be equipped to support what you do with sound and convincing rationales.

The frequent impersonality, inflexibility, and machine-like qualities of a modern school bureaucracy is best countered by the initiative, courage, and fresh perspective of vital, people-oriented educators with strong purposes. You may find strength and courage in John Stuart Mill's contention that "one person with a belief is equal to a force of ninety-nine who have only interests." Of course, the more support you can generate from like-minded colleagues, the better chance you have of influencing the system in a desired direction.

4. *Know the hidden agendas of the system and use them to your advantage.* Make yourself familiar with the inner workings of the organization and the most important people within it (who are not necessarily those at the official top of the hierarchy). Learn ways you can use the system (in contrast to working against the grain of the system) to accomplish your purposes. For example, present-day school administrators tend to be preoccupied with the political and public relations aspects of running a school, frequently finding less time to be interested in the substance of educational activity within the school. Realizing this, you can often gain needed support for personal projects or activities, which might otherwise fall on deaf ears, by featuring their timeliness, their potential visibility, or their political or economic value to the system. At the same time, do not be surprised to find less than genuine interest in the content of your personal agendas. Determine which administrators have a special interest in teaching and learning and which are preoccupied with the smooth functioning of the school organization.

It will behoove you to understand the personalities of those key people within the organization who can make your job more, or less, pleasant for you, including support personnel, counselors, fellow teachers, and administrators. Insightful teachers know when and how to approach administrators with problems, requests, or a desire to share accomplishments. They know which people in the school can be counted on to support innovative efforts, those who can provide helpful political clout, and those to approach or avoid when you want to share a problem or interest (teachers' lounges are usually poor places to find constructive conversation about education and teaching). System-wise teachers have learned how to gain the support of school secretaries and custodians when they need a favor. They are able to use the "informal power structure" of the school (often consisting of an especially influential group of teachers, or perhaps a veteran secretary) to accomplish purposes that may not be achievable through more direct channels.

5. *Organize and pace your teaching activities to make the most of your personal resources.* There are a number of things you can do to pace your activity during a long teaching day to ensure you are using your mental and physical energies to best advantage:

   a. Plan your teaching so you will not have to talk for most of the day. Break up your lessons with activities that allow you a degree of relaxation from a constant teacher-centered format.

   b. Adopt an interactive style that allows you to work effectively with students in a less judgmental, less confrontational manner than most teachers are accustomed to (refer to Chapter 8). A smoother, less ego-charged interactional pattern can be a tremendous energy saver for you, and can be far more effective as a teaching style.

   c. Make an effort to arrange your teaching schedule to accommodate your own mental cycles. If you are a morning person, lobby to have your most strenuous classes before lunch. Take measures to build in relaxation times for yourself during the day, short periods when you can calm your mind and body. If possible, find a quiet spot in the school where you can engage in simple relaxation techniques.

   d. Identify the best time to plan for your teaching, and recognize that planning requires considerable time and concentration. If it is morning, get in the habit of doing your planning before school. Do not leave it to the last thing in the day when your creative energy is at its lowest ebb. Adopt a planning routine that allows you to stay on top of a busy teaching schedule with a minimum of stress.

   e. Be conscious of your own creative style. Are you one who formulates ideas and projects deliberately or do you depend on flashes of insight while relaxing, eating a meal, or driving in your car? If the latter is your style, you may need to adopt a relatively open-ended and flexible approach to planning your lessons (not to be confused with an off-the-top-of-the-head approach to teaching). You will, for example, want to learn to take advantage of ideas for teaching approaches that suddenly occur to you, by keeping a pen and notepad with you in your car, on your bedstand, at the dinner table, and so forth. A microcassette recorder, small enough to carry around in your pocket or bag can be a convenient way of storing thoughts until you can write them down. Try to complete as much of your work as possible before you leave school. By using "prep" periods to advantage and by using techniques such as peer editing to provide feedback on writing assignments, student exchanges of papers for correcting short objective tests, or teacher aides to help with paperwork, you can cut down on the amount of homework left after a day at work.

f. Work out an effective system for handling paperwork. Schools, in common with other modern organizations, depend heavily on paper flow as their main form of communication. Get into the habit of sorting your mail, returning information to the school office, preparing evaluational materials, and so forth, promptly and efficiently so these organizational chores do not pile up and become nagging worries. A computer, and the specialized software that now exists to assist teachers in keeping up with paperwork, storing records, working out grades, and so on, is becoming more and more of a must. Succeeding chapters will detail numerous other reasons for you to become comfortable with the electronic world.

6. *Maintain a suprasystem perspective on your work.* Do not expect more of the system than it is capable of providing. Get to the place where you are not continually disappointed and dismayed by the failure of the institution to live up to your expectations. A healthy sense of humor, one that does not reflect resignation or cynicism, can do wonders. Recognize the limitations of school organizations when it comes to meeting the inner needs of individuals. Learn to get satisfaction from some of the unplanned, intangible successes you experience during a typical week of teaching, for example, a note from a shy student expressing appreciation for your special efforts, a productive lunchtime sharing session with a like-minded colleague, the excitement of an in-depth class discussion that refuses to end with the bell. Maintain ideals that extend beyond the system itself, with the realization that in a character-intensive occupation like teaching the meaning and satisfaction you derive from your work will depend far more on the personal effort and vision you bring to it than on what is provided by the organization. Any worthwhile and lasting improvement in schools is dependent on the quality of individual teachers, such as you, in classrooms such as yours. Remember that institutions *can* change, and that many schools have already done so. By hanging onto your creative orientation, you will be ready for change, which is inevitable, and prepared to take your part in the process.[24]

◆◆◆ **SUGGESTED ACTIVITIES AND QUESTIONS** ◆◆◆

1. Arrange to do interviews with seven or eight teachers in schools where you are involved. Use these discussions to gain insight into such things as (1) the main concerns that occupy them as teachers; (2) the theories of learning they work from; (3) their approaches to the conflicting roles they face; (4) their attitudes toward the external demands and distractions they encounter in their work; and (5) the kinds of energy, enthusiasm, and creativity they apply to teaching. Based on your interviews, how would you characterize the present accommodations of

these teachers to the school system? Do you find any veteran teachers who still exhibit a survival orientation? Did you get any idea of why? Would some of the teachers qualify to be considered creative teachers? What evidence are you using to support these judgments?

2. Take the opportunity to talk to as many school students as possible (at various levels) regarding their perceptions of "good teachers." What are the qualities most frequently associated with high-quality teaching in the minds of these young people? Do they square with the concept of creative teaching developed in this chapter?

3. Identify any creative projects you have undertaken in your recent life, apart from school assignments, that have turned out to be growth enhancers for you, that is, that have caused desired changes in specific habits, levels of awareness, personal sensitivities, appreciations, and so forth. Describe as precisely as you can the sort of positive growth you believe to have resulted in yourself. How effective do you feel you are in monitoring your own personal growth as an individual and as a teacher? How close are you to being a self-actualizing person?

4. Pinpoint one or more aspects of your personality or interpersonal style in which positive change could improve your chances of becoming a creative teacher, for example, listening skills, self-expression, stress tolerance, critical thinking, multiple concentration. Design specific courses of action for making these strength areas rather than liabilities. For example, on deciding you are generally a better talker than you are a listener, take deliberate steps to remedy this imbalance by adopting strategies for improving your listening skills in everyday situations. As other examples, skills of critical thinking and self-expression can generally be improved by making time for more substantive reading and thoughtful discussion.

5. How would you characterize your present level of concern as a developing teacher? Are you interested mainly in completing teacher training and locating a job? Are you concentrating on finding a particular type of job that will allow you freedom to teach a certain way and accomplish specific purposes? Or are you mainly concerned for an opportunity to work with young people, while attaching less importance to the particular school situation?

6. What are some of the ideals you have set for yourself as a teacher? Do any of the ideals you have identified amount to your main reason for choosing teaching as a career? Do you anticipate that these ideals will change as your immediate needs and circumstances change, for example, as you achieve a full-time job, tenure in a school, a stable income?

7. Can you identify with the particular attitudes and patterns of the level two, or pragmatically oriented, teacher? Have you had many teachers with this approach to teaching during your years as a student? Can you imagine yourself performing at one or another of the teaching levels described in this chapter?

8. What kind of an "organization person" do you see yourself as being? Apart from your experiences as a student, have you had the opportunity to work or function for any period of time in a highly structured organizational setting, for example, the military, a government job, a youth camp? How do you handle situations in which a good share of your time and behavior is structured by impersonal rules and regulations? Do you consider yourself a person who accepts authority easily? What ideas can you offer for maintaining individuality and creativity in a bureaucratic environment? To what extent do you subscribe to the idea that highly competent classroom teachers must be self-actualizing people? Give reasons to support your opinion.

NOTES

1. See Stuart B. Palonsky, *900 Shows a Year: A Look at Teaching from a Teacher's Side of the Desk.* New York: Random House, 1986; see Chapters 3 and 7; Theodore R. Sizer, *Horace's Compromise: The Dilemma of the American High School.* Boston: Houghton Mifflin, 1984; see Part IV; and John I. Goodlad, *A Place Called School.* New York: McGraw-Hill, 1984; see Chap. 6.
2. Francis F. Fuller, "Concerns of Teachers: A Developmental Conceptualization." *American Educational Research Journal* 6 (1969): 207–226, 211–212.
3. Seymour Sarason, cited in Richard H. Dollase, *Voices of Beginning Teachers: Visions and Realities.* New York: Teachers College Press, 1992, p. 83
4. See Herbert I. Freudenberger, *Burn Out: The High Cost of Achievement.* Garden City, N.Y.: Doubleday, 1980.
5. The three levels of system accommodation developed here reflect the lead author's unpublished studies of teacher growth patterns in combination with notable work that has been done on teacher developmental stages and the changing concerns of teachers as they become stabilized in teaching careers. See Sharon Feiman and Robert Floden, *What's All This Talk About Teacher Development?*, Research Series No. 70. East Lansing: Institute for Research on Teaching, Michigan State University, February 1980, pp. 94–107; Paul R. Burden, *Developmental Supervision: Reducing Teacher Stress at Different Career Stages.* Paper presented at the Annual Conference of the Association for Teacher Educators, Phoenix, Arizona, February 1982; and Gene E. Hall and Susan Loucks, "Teacher Concerns as a Basis for Facilitating and Personalizing Staff Development." *Teachers College Record*, 80 (September 1978): 36–53.
6. Dollase, *Voices of Beginning Teachers*, p. 129.
7. See Thomas L. Good and Jere E. Brophy, *Looking in Classrooms*, 3rd ed. New York: Harper and Row, 1984, Chap. 2.
8. Ann Lieberman and Lynne Miller, *Teachers: Their World and Their Work.* Alexandria, Va.: ASCD, 1984, p. 21.
9. Geoffrey Bullough, *First-Year Teacher.* New York: Teachers College Press, 1989, p, 134.
10. Lieberman and Miller, *Teachers*, p. 82.
11. See Jack Frymier, "Bureaucracy and the Neutering of Teachers," *Phi Delta Kappan* (September 1987): 9–14; and Patrick Welsh, *Tales out of School.* New York: Penguin Books, 1986; see Chaps. 8 and 10.

12. See Goodlad, *Place Called School*, Chap. 6.
13. Seymour B. Sarason, *The Culture of the School and the Problem of Change*. Boston: Allyn and Bacon, 1982, p. 203.
14. *Culture of the School*, p. 204.
15. Ralph Parish and Frank Aquila, "Cultural Ways of Working and Believing in School: Preserving Things the Way They Are." *Phi Delta Kappan* (December 1996): 300–301.
16. See Barbara Benham Tye, "The Deep Structure of Schooling." *Phi Delta Kappan* (December 1987): 281–283.
17. Parish and Aquila, "Cultural Ways," pp. 302–303.
18. See Neil Postman, *Teaching as a Conserving Activity*. New York: Delacorte Press, 1979; see Chap. 1; and Ira Shor, *Critical Teaching and Everyday Life*. Boston: South End Press, 1980; see Chap. 2.
19. See Linda M. McNeil, *Contradictions of Control: School Structure and Classroom Knowledge*. New York: Routledge, Kegan, Paul, 1986, especially Chap. 1.
20. See Myron Lieberman, *The Future of Public Education*. Chicago: University of Chicago Press, 1960, especially Chap. 8.
21. Gary Fenstermacher, "Some Moral Considerations on Teaching as a Profession," In John I. Goodlad, Roger Soder, and Kenneth A. Sirotnik, *The Moral Dimensions of Teaching*. San Francisco: Jossey-Bass, 1990, pp. 146–148. (Italics added.)
22. Abraham Maslow, *Motivation and Personality*. New York: Harper and Row, 1954, p. 212.
23. *Motivation*, pp. 213–214.
24. For information on the numerous school improvement and school restructuring projects that are developing across the country, refer to the materials mentioned in Chapter 12 under "Professional Reading."

CHAPTER 3
Designing Appropriate Learning Objectives

Owning Your Teaching Goals

As a teacher it is important that you be able to give a general structure to what takes place in your own classroom. You will want to feel classroom events are under control. However, in your efforts to cope with the hectic pace of modern teaching, it is easy to fall into a pattern of simply reacting to classroom situations rather than moving activities in some clearly established direction. At times you may find yourself confusing ends and means, and engaging in activity for the sake of activity. The best way to ensure that this does not become a regular occurrence is to have a firm grasp of your teaching goals. In order to be a proactive teacher, an initiator rather than a reactor, you need to be aware of your main purposes and priorities as an educator. At any point in your teaching, it is important to be aware of what you are attempting to accomplish with your students, and why.

You can usually obtain some initial guidance in formulating instructional objectives from course and program descriptions, curriculum frameworks, and other teachers. The structure you obtain from such external sources is often helpful and necessary, but you cannot rely on it to give you the basic sense of direction you need to become a self-sustaining professional. To attain this sense of direction you need to start by giving serious attention to the long- and short-range aims that will guide your teaching. You must focus on what you want your students to achieve in your classes, and, again, why. In short, you will need to "own" the learning objectives you work from in order to proceed confidently and autonomously in your planning and in your relations with students, parents, and school administrators.

Implicit and Explicit Goals

One of your reasons for coming into teaching is undoubtedly a concern to have a positive impact on students. That is, you have certain aims you want to achieve in your teaching. In all probability, at this point, the goals you have set for yourself and your students are implicit, that is, taken for granted, rather than explicit, or worked out in detail. In other words, you believe in the value of education, you want to help young people develop their potentials as human beings, and you want them to acquire certain skills and understandings in the areas you will be teaching. However, if you are like most beginning teachers, you have not had occasion to analyze these broad goals and to transform them into realizable learning objectives for your students.

When you begin to examine your teaching goals, along with goal statements from curriculum guides and programmed materials, you realize that although goals taken from these sources may serve as worthwhile points of departure, they are too general to be functional in structuring specific learning activities. For purposes of planning classroom learning, they need to be converted to precise and often measurable terms. For example, a teaching goal that aims "to promote students' powers of self-expression" must eventually be reduced to pointed descriptions of what students will actually do to demonstrate increases in self-expression before the goal can be used as a basis for designing lessons or determining student achievement.

Also, when you are able to get these various statements of purpose on paper, some prescriptions will clearly appear incompatible with others. A goal such as "students will develop skill at democratic processes" would pretty obviously be in conflict with one that prescribes unquestioning acceptance of existing institutional patterns; for example, "students will learn to accept authority in preparation for future roles in the world of work."

To eliminate this sort of contradiction, you may have to go back to first principles, to consider what American schools exist for, and then to decide what your major goals *should* be. Chief among those principles will no doubt be the fact that the classrooms in which you will be teaching exist in a free, participatory democracy, and that everything you do ought in some way, however small, to aim at contributing to the continuation of that democracy or at least should be consistent with its continuing existence and extension. In this perspective, teaching that encouraged or actually required passive acceptance and mindless subordination would be subversive of the very purpose of the schools in which you teach. It is important for you to bear it constantly in mind that success in multiple-choice tests, high SAT scores, and other commonly accepted indicators of "education" may be no more than signs that a student has been well *schooled*, that is, has been able and willing to play the school game in order to please others or to get ahead, no matter how or at whose expense. If you fail to help students do well in relation to these indicators, you will of course be judged by others to have failed as an *instructor* (and will be acting irresponsibly insofar as students need this kind of school success to move ahead), but if you do no more, you may judge yourself to have failed as a *teacher*.

It will be necessary, then, for you to make certain decisions regarding the educational goals you adopt for your teaching.[1] You will need to decide in the first place, what they are, and then how they are to become manifest in your day-to-day teaching activities, how compatible your various teaching objectives are with one another, and how they align with the school's goal statements for the classes you teach.

This chapter is designed to help you with this decision-making process. It also provides practical strategies for preparing learning objectives, and calls your attention to some of the major considerations that should enter into the development of teaching goals. More specifically, the content of the chapter serves to assist you in (1) distinguishing between principles, goals, and objectives; (2) establishing teaching objectives that represent your most important purposes and priorities as a teacher; (3) making necessary distinctions between different types and levels of learning objectives; (4) writing highly specific objectives for use in teaching situations in which they are appropriate; and (5) classifying instructional objectives into three major domains of learning as a basis for specifying a variety of learning outcomes.

Educational Purposes, Goals, and Objectives

As suggested earlier, you should know that statements about what students are going to be able to do, can vary widely from highly general statements of educational goals to very detailed descriptions of what students are expected to be able to do following direct or indirect teaching (see Chapter 4) or other forms of learning experience. Educational purposes, the general educational goals of the school, describe the broad intent of formal education in this country. The following are some examples of these:

> Education should develop the whole child
> Education aims to promote character development
> Education should prepare students for the world of work
> Education should equip students for life in the twenty-first century
> Education seeks to develop an appreciation for art and beauty

Such large-scale descriptions of educational purposes are often formulated by national committees or commissions that usually include educational leaders as well as interested laypersons. They are deliberately general, serving more as statements of educational philosophy than as precise teaching objectives.

Broad educational statements have an important function in that they give educators a place to start and provide reference points from which to develop school curriculums. They can be used as general statements of purpose and as screens for determining the appropriateness of specific elements within school programs. For example, if one main purpose of a teacher or a school is to promote independent thinking, this gives us a basis for questioning the value of activities in which students are being spoon-fed ideas with no opportunity to reflect on their implications. Educational purposes, then, are important to you at stage one in your organization for teaching because they serve to provide a broad justification and framework for teaching and learning.

At the other end of the spectrum are the highly specific learning objectives that describe intended learning outcomes in precise and measurable terms. These explicit statements of what students should be able to do following direct or indirect teaching (see Chapter 4) as evidence of learning are variously referred to as *"behavioral objectives," "performance objectives,"* or *"terminal objectives."* Here they will be referred to simply as "objectives." Some examples of these could be:

> The learner will be able to list the 50 states in the United States
> The learner will be able to identify the 12 cranial nerves
> The learner will be able to tell how a first-class lever works
> The learner will be able to recite to the nine times table correctly
>   from memory
> The learner will be able to compose three different salutations for a
>   personal letter

Much more will be said about objectives a little further on, after an examination of the basis on which they are constructed, that is, goals or aims.

Identifying Broad Learning Goals

Subject-Specific Goals

The first and most obvious goals you will be working with are those that are particular to the subject or subjects you will be teaching. These serve as reference points for your large-scale planning; they provide valuable structure for your subject-level and unit-level organization. The following are examples of subject-specific goals:

> Students will develop an appreciation for modern art forms
> Students will be able to identify significant periods in U.S. history
> Students will understand the essence of scientific method
> Students will understand the requirements of physical fitness
> Students will become familiar with high-quality literature

Goal statements for various subject areas can usually be found in state and district curriculum guidelines as well as in textbooks and programmed materials for your teaching areas. You can normally expect to have considerable leeway when it comes to interpreting and adding to these subject-specific goals.

You will have some fundamental choices to make here. Your subject goals should reflect what you think is most important for students to achieve in a general sense in the classes you are teaching. Whether these educational goals are entirely your own or largely provided for you, it is important for you to have a good idea of what is appropriate in the way of broad goals for particular teaching areas. This will help you avoid getting bogged down in subject-matter fragments and losing sight of the larger purposes for learning.

As a history teacher, for example, what are some ultimate goals for students of history? Should they be learning to think like historians? Should they become disposed to recognize historical antecedents for significant national and international events as they occur in their lives? Should they be developing a general interest in the past? In the case of science, as another example, what broad learning outcomes should it produce? Should students learn the facts of science merely, or the application of scientific method? Should they have a working knowledge of basic differences between empirical and intuitive modes of thought in their everyday lives? If you are to own your teaching goals, these are the sorts of fundamental considerations you will need to entertain and make decisions about to guide you in the selection of material and methods that you will initially employ in your teaching, even if, as is very likely, you later adapt them in the light of experience.

Human Development Goals

A second type of educational goals is especially important as you attempt to establish your own purposes and priorities in the classroom. These are human development goals, which underlie the group process and development objectives you set for your classroom and the young people in it, those that reach beyond subject-matter learning. In the first instance, these goals specify the kinds of intergroup behavior and relationships that allow you and your students to function together in ways that are necessary for education to take place. You might think of these as your *enabling goals* because they enable teaching and learning to proceed in a reasonable, cooperative, and humanly justifiable manner. Some examples would be:

Class members will treat each other decently
Class members will address one another respectfully
Class members will learn to value those who differ from them *in any way*
Class members will acknowledge one another's rights to an opinion
Class members will honor group time commitments
Class members will respect one another's rights to attend to class proceedings

When your enabling goals are not being met, they should become your most immediate priorities. For example, in a classroom in which name calling or class interruptions have become prevalent, your development goals should take precedence over your academic ones. In the circumstances, it will be less important to teach subject matter than to concentrate on more fundamental social and interpersonal skills which are, in any case, among the multiple intelligences identified by Howard Gardner (see later in this chapter).

Your development goals should also reflect the most important concepts and ideals you hold for human growth and maturation, the ultimate goals you are striving to achieve with the developing young people in your classes. Here are some examples:

Students will show sensitivity to the various forms of life around them

Students will learn to accept people with disabilities as equal in every other respect

Students will come to accept responsibility for their own behavior

Students will become inclined to share in decision-making processes that affect their own lives

Students will develop dispositions to approach personal problems confidently and rationally

In short, your developmental goals are those that allow you to achieve purpose and direction in your teaching, and make it all worthwhile. They are the goals you look to when you are confused or when you sense a conflict in your teaching pattern. As one pair of teacher educators have described them, your developmental goals could be called your *superobjectives*. They are the goals that permeate your teaching performance and hold it all together.

The superobjectives give coherence and meaning to a teacher's performance. . . . A teacher who does not have superobjectives can manifest only a patch-work of unrelated skills and disjointed activities. . . . The acquisition of superobjectives is just as important an aspect of teaching as is the acquisition of specific skills. A teacher who acquires only the specific skills is like an actor who has learned his lines but who does not understand the part.[2]

Transitory and Dispositional Learning

In contrast to the more immediate learning objectives you will be focusing on in your day-to-day teaching, you should think of your broad goals as long-range prescriptions representing the basic understandings and dispositions that you want to become a part of the learner. To fully appreciate their significance, it might be helpful to consider for a moment the ideal progression of school learning from the memorization of simple facts, through the understanding of complex subject matter, to the development of important life habits. Too often what we teach in school ends with the transfer of information, with simply telling students things (e.g., good writing requires careful proofreading, advertisers often use illogical means to sell products). With the exception of skill-based classes like writing, physical education, and shop, school curriculums frequently feature the transmission of facts rather than the development of skills. For our purposes we can think of this as *transitory learning*, because it tends to fade rather quickly if it is not put to some functional use. It infrequently takes students to the next level, which would entail the ability to use this information (e.g., to become proficient at proofreading or at discerning logical fallacies in television and newspaper ads).

Furthermore, even when schools do promote skill acquisition, unless students are influenced to practice these skills in many contexts they are rarely advanced to the level of everyday habits. They seldom become manifest in life patterns, or what we might call *dispositional learning.* For example, students who are told that proofreading is important, and may even have learned how to proofread in school, often are not inclined to give a second reading to things they write on their own time. They have acquired a good deal of information, and perhaps some school-related skills, but they lack the readiness— or the desire—to actualize this new learning. Although they may have "learned a lot," it has been mostly learning in the weak rather than in the strong sense, because what they have learned tends to have remained at school. It does not become an integral part of their behavioral patterns.

Dispositional learning, on the other hand, goes beyond simply knowing about or being able to do and affects what the student actually does do.[3] Learning in this stronger sense penetrates to the *being* of the learner. When learning reaches the *being-level,* students have not only learned about certain things and how to do certain things, but they have learned to *be* certain things: They have learned to be inquiring, to be thorough, to be caring, to be patient, and so on. When you attempt to incorporate dispositional or being-level goals into your teaching, your focus is on the kinds of life habits you want to foster in developing young people, on the behaviors and attitudes you would encourage to the point at which they have a chance to become second nature for your students. Here are some examples of being-level goals:

Students will learn to disagree without being disagreeable
Students will come to respect their own life-space and that of others
Students will be disposed to take pride in the work they produce
Students will show evidence of carryover of school learning to their
    everyday lives, for example, being inclined to see "history in the
    making" in newspapers and other media, being disposed to take
    physical education home with them in the form of personal exer-
    cise programs, being inclined to apply rational and scientific prin-
    ciples to solve personal problems.

Dispositional learning requires that the learner adopt certain attitudes and values in addition to understanding certain things. When teachers systematically attempt to promote the learning of attitudes and values, they find themselves prescribing learning goals in what has come to be called the *affective domain* (discussed in a later section of this chapter).

In aiming at goals that would foster specific life habits and values in students, it is important for you to be aware of the controversy surrounding the teaching of values in U.S. schools. There are those who maintain that values and attitudes are best developed in the home and the church. Some people believe teachers are violating a student's fundamental right to freedom of choice when they attempt to promote certain value preferences.[4] However, as you cannot avoid fostering certain human values to the exclusion of others whenever you set out to manage and instruct a classroom full of students, it is not a matter of whether you should or should not attempt to teach human values in your classes. Instead, it is a question of which particular values and attitudes you should be fostering in your students, and how you justify your choices.[5] You are encouraged to further examine both sides of this controversy, and to make your own reasoned decision regarding the role of values in the school curriculum.[6]

◆◆◆ **A P P L I C A T I O N   E X E R C I S E S** ◆◆◆

1. Test your ability to recognize three types of teaching aims by labeling the following goal statements as broad educational purposes (BEP), subject-specific goals (SSG) or human development goals (HDG).
   a. Students will understand how values are formed.
   b. Class members will demonstrate respect and support for one another during times of individual vulnerability (e.g., solo class performances).
   c. To develop the whole child.
   d. To understand the importance of the Civil War in U.S. history.
   e. To prepare young people for the world of work.
   f. To have students learn to work cooperatively and productively in small groups to accomplish assigned group tasks.
   g. To acquaint the student with good dramatic literature.
   h. Students will take pride in a job well done and consistently give their best efforts to projects calling for creativity and self-expression.
   i. To instill an appreciation of the requirements of democratic citizenship.
   j. Students will adapt constructively to minor frustrations and disappointments they encounter in an organizational setting.
   k. Students will develop the abilities to solve mathematical problems encountered in day-to-day life.
2. Specify one or two subject-specific goals for the grade level and curricular area (or areas) you presently teach or hope to teach. Provide a rationale for your goal selection. Why are these goals important to the individual or to society?
3. Attempt to specify at least three human development goals that you will seek to achieve in your teaching. These may include *group-process* or *enabling* objectives as well as *dispositional* or *being-level* goals that are particularly important to you. In deciding on being-level objectives, a good place to start is by taking inventory of some of the positive human qualities and interpersonal dispositions that you *yourself* possess and would like to model for your students (e.g., basic trust, empathy toward the underdog).

Moving from Broad Purposes and Goals to Specific Objectives

As indicated, broad educational purposes are not intended as objectives for daily lesson planning. They are not specific enough, and they are subject to too many different interpretations to be useful as statements of just what learning the school or teacher considers important to have occur, and so in your teaching you need to be able to move from these more global statements of purpose to much more specific learning objectives.

Intermediate Goals

As will be discussed in Chapter 4, the progression from general educational purposes to precise learning objectives is made easier if you establish *intermediate* or *narrowing* goals to assist you in translating your aims into practical applications. Intermediate goals are considerably more explicit than broad goal statements, but less explicit than objectives. These intermediate-level goals are useful for unit planning and long-range organization. They can help teachers focus on main understandings, attitudes, or learning processes they want to promote, without having to specify the precise learning activities that it will be necessary to stipulate in daily lesson planning. The following are examples of intermediate-level teaching goals:

> Students will understand the main causes of big-city air pollution
> Students will appreciate the need for safety in woodshop
> Students will learn how to write short essays on a topic of their
> choice
> Students will learn self-restraint

Thus, if one of your subject-specific goals should be for students "to understand how their federal government works," a more explicit intermediate goal might be that students "know how a bill becomes a law," whereas an objective would be for students to "be able to list, in correct order, the steps a bill follows through Congress, specifying the requirements for passage in each step." As another example, if you should be working from a statement of a broad educational goal, or purpose, that says "students will become proficient in written English," a possible intermediate goal would specify that students "be able to write grammatically," leading to an objective that stipulates, "students will compose two- to three-page autobiographical sketches, demonstrating proper subject-verb agreement and correct spelling in each sentence."

Writing Performance Objectives

Once you have established a framework of broad and intermediate goals for your teaching, you are in a position to begin developing specific instructional objectives for the classes you will teach. We have seen that educational goals are more or less broad statements of intended outcomes for student learning. In contrast, objectives are detailed statements of what you intend learners to be able to do during or after instruction, or other kinds of learning activities, that they could not do before. Although there are a number of ways to write objectives, there are some general rules to observe in meeting the requirements of highly specific, measurable objectives:

Rule 1. Describe what you expect the student to be able to do.

Rule 2. Specify this by way of an *action verb* that states what the student will do (e.g., list, identify, arrange, weigh, describe).

Rule 3. Describe the criterion or criteria for evaluating an acceptable performance (e.g., name at least four colors of the rainbow, hammer three nails 1 inch deep, run a mile in six minutes).

Rule 4. Specify important conditions under which the student will perform the behavior (e.g., run a mile before breakfast, kick three field goals in a championship game, solve a quadratic equation during a classroom session).[7]

The following are some examples of objectives that meet these criteria:

Learners are to spell with 95 percent accuracy the dictated words in each spelling lesson

Given a reference manual, the student will write a job application letter in correct form with no grammatical errors

Given the name of a note and the scale, a member of the chorus will be able to sing the note accurately nine out of ten times

On a level surface, the student will be able to do 30 push-ups in three minutes

Using no references, the student will be able to write five ways that socialist and capitalist countries are alike and five ways they differ

When presented with pairs of paintings, the student will be able to select which painting is the work of an Impressionist painter seven out of ten times

As you examine these objectives, you will notice that each contains an action verb that leaves little doubt about what the student is to do to satisfy the learning requirement. With correctly worded objectives it is easy to see how the teacher can tell if the objective has been reached. When writing objectives, verbs that are vague, ambiguous, and that do not lend themselves to measurement should be avoided. Words such as "know," "understand," "analyze," "appreciate," "comprehend," and "realize" are not action verbs. Although they do refer to human learning and behavior, they do not denote observable actions or, in themselves, produce measurable outcomes, and they cannot, therefore, be used when writing objectives. They, however, are appropriate for describing goals.

In addition, each of the objectives just mentioned makes clear the performance conditions and the degree of accuracy expected.[8] One quick way to test a learning prescription to determine if it is specific enough to qualify as an objective is to ask yourself whether several independent learning evaluators would see or hear the same thing.

◆◆◆ APPLICATION EXERCISES ◆◆◆

1. Classify the following as a subject-specific goal (SSG), intermediate goal (IG), or objective (O):
   a. Students will evaluate the effectiveness of their experiments.
   b. When dissecting a frog, students will identify organs of the digestive system.
   c. Given a worksheet containing 20 addition problems requiring regrouping, students will correctly solve 17 problems during class.
   d. Students will gain knowledge of the electoral system.
   e. Students will understand the process for electing a president.
   f. Students will become familiar with several varieties of modern art.
   g. Given a work of propaganda, the pupil will be able to spot the propaganda devices and faulty logic in the piece.
2. From the following items, identify those that state or call for an observable or audible action.
   a. The student will appreciate the music of Bach.
   b. From memory, the student will name the Allied countries of World War II.
   c. The learner will describe the function of baking powder in the making of bread.
   d. The learner will know the Constitution and its amendments.
   e. The student will learn to write properly.
   f. The student will learn the names of six common tools in metal shop.
   g. The student will understand how paper is made.
   h. The student will write a short essay demonstrating proper use of the eight major punctuation marks.
   i. To show the effects of smoking on the individual.
   j. The student will draw a diagram of the combustion engine.
3. Examine each of the following statements and determine whether it meets the conditions necessary for an objective. Rewrite any improperly written objectives in the proper form.
   a. At the end of the course the student will understand the fundamental concepts of long division.
   b. The student will learn about the structure and organization of Congress.
   c. Students will be able to say what the correct time is for any clock settings.

    d. Students will develop a clear understanding of the biological princi-
ple of photosynthesis.

    e. The student will be able to identify the major parts of speech in sev-
eral unfamiliar sentences.

Main Categories of Educational Objectives

Cognitive Learning

Up to this point in our discussion of learning objectives we have focused on school learning tasks associated primarily with traditional subject-matter learning. For example, memorizing multiplication tables, learning to spell, comparing national economies, and writing job applications all involve essentially mental or intellectual processes. These learning activities and others of a similar nature that call for memorizing, remembering, analyzing, formulating, reasoning, judging, and so forth are called *cognitive learning* tasks. The educational psychologist Benjamin Bloom and his associates describe objectives in the cognitive domain as

> Objectives which emphasize remembering or reproducing something which has presumably been learned, as well as objectives which involve the solving of some intellectual task for which the individual has to determine the essential problem and then reorder given material or combine it with ideas, methods, or procedures previously learned. Cognitive objectives vary from simple recall of material learned to highly original and creative ways of combining and synthesizing new ideas and materials.[9]

Classifying Cognitive Objectives Bloom's group developed a useful taxonomy (or classification system) of cognitive objectives that allows teachers to better understand the kinds of cognitive tasks they are prescribing for their students. It contains six cognitive levels, ranging from simple and concrete to more complex and abstract mental operations.[10] Consider the following summary of these six cognitive levels:

1. *Knowledge.* Knowledge is defined in the *Taxonomy*, which long predates more recent developments in cognitive science, as the bringing to mind, whether as a result of their being remembered, committed to memory, or learned by rote, of bare facts, such as dates, events, persons, and places. It includes basic principles and generalizations, if merely retrieved from memory. This represents the lowest level of learning outcomes in the cognitive domain, and would now be generally thought of as "memory" or "recall."

2. *Comprehension.* The second level of cognition encompasses a minimal kind of knowledge, a mental operation requiring some degree of understanding. It entails the ability to grasp facts or ideas and make use of them without relating them to each other (e.g., paraphrasing or even

interpreting something gained from reading or listening). At this lowest level of understanding, students in a foreign language class should be able to translate a paragraph from Spanish to English, while students in a social studies class might explain in their own words the causes of the Civil War. Also at the comprehension level, the learner may be able to extend thinking beyond the data by making simple inferences. As an example, students in science would be able to draw conclusions from a simple demonstration or experiment.

3. *Application.* At this level, the learners can use knowledge in new and concrete situations. The knowledge may be in the form of general ideas, concepts, principles, or theories that must be remembered or applied. The science student, for example, who draws conclusions from a particular experiment at the comprehension level is now able to apply the basic principles to related experiments or scientific happenings. The social studies student can relate concepts or principles concerning the separation of powers to current problems.

4. *Analysis.* This level of cognition involves the taking apart of information and the making of relationships in order to discover hidden meanings and the basic structure of an idea or fact. The student is able to "read between the lines," to distinguish between fact and opinion, and to assess degrees of consistency or inconsistency. Thus, the science student is able to distinguish between relevant and extraneous materials or events, or the social science student is able to work out why a particular historical character acted as he did (interpersonal intelligence).

5. *Synthesis.* The learner is able to put together existing knowledge in new ways. Thinking at this level involves the analysis and recombination of information to develop a structure or pattern the student did not have before learning (an act of creation). The learner draws on elements from many sources in addition to those of the particular problem under consideration. For example, the science student may propose a unique plan for testing a hypothesis. The mathematics student may make a discovery or generalization not evident from the given communication. The art student discovers how to use color theory to create a mysterious painting (visual-spatial intelligence).

6. *Evaluation.* This is the cognitive ability to judge the value of material (e.g., a statement, poem, research report) for a given purpose. The judgments are based on distinct criteria for such decisions. As examples, students in an English class would be able to judge the merits of a story or a play, or students in social studies would be able to appraise how well our country's democracy works.

Psychomotor Learning

Although cognitive learning has received most of the emphasis in formal education, it is obvious that school learning often involves more than just mental or intellectual operations. In fact, there are areas within our school curriculums that heavily depend on the learning of coordinated physical movements as the main basis for student achievement, for example, physical education, auto shop art, and woodworking. Here we are concerned with *psychomotor learning*, or learning tasks that involve physical skills and often complex mind-body interactions—for example, handwriting, shooting a basket, or playing a musical instrument. In contrast with cognitive learning tasks, which involve exclusively mental processing of information, learning objectives in the psychomotor domain are, as Bloom and his associates describe them, "objectives which emphasize some muscular or motor skill, some manipulation of objects and materials, or some act which requires a neuromuscular coordination."[11]

There is, of course, a cognitive component to most psychomotor objectives, but their basic purpose is to describe physical behavior.[12] We tend, somewhat misleadingly since they never occur by themselves, to separate cognitive and psychomotor objectives because they usually require somewhat different practice conditions. The outcomes of cognitive learning are ordinarily inferred from verbal behavior, whereas in psychomotor learning changes in the speed, accuracy, integration, and coordination of body movements are more directly observable.

Goals and objectives in the psychomotor domain are especially important to elementary school teachers. In the lower grades, merely teaching a youngster to hold a pencil or crayon may constitute an initial objective and using the pencil or crayon properly can become a more advanced one.

To try your hand at distinguishing between cognitive and psychomotor learning tasks, examine the following behavioral objectives and attempt to determine which are psychomotor objectives:

1. Given six equations with one unknown, students will be able to solve at least five.
2. Students will be able to march around the room three times in step to a military march.
3. Students will give examples, in their own words, of recent legal decisions regarding equal rights.
4. Students will be able to keyboard an average of 60 words per minute for 5 minutes with fewer than four errors.
5. Given a situation in which a faulty conclusion is presented, students will analyze the data and identify the errors in logic.
6. Students will be able to print the letters of the alphabet, duplicating the model in the writing manual.

You will generally find that such forms of physical behavior, with or without apparatus, are easy to describe in behavioral terms because the required competence is always tied directly to a clearly defined overt action. For example, skill in throwing a baseball is directly observable. It does not require some indirect evidence, such as writing an essay to demonstrate mastery.

Classifying Psychomotor Objectives As with objectives in the cognitive domain, psychomotor objectives can be classified according to level, from simple to complex. One classification system developed by Kenneth Hoover provides an easily grasped model for designing learning objectives in the psychomotor domain.[13] It consists of a four-stage sequence of skill development tasks that will be useful to you at points in your teaching where your focus is on a performative skill:

1. *Observing.* At this level, the learner observes a more experienced person performing the activity. The learner is usually asked to observe sequences and relationships and to pay particular attention to the finished product. Sometimes reading directions substitutes for observation, although often reading supplements direct observation. For example, the beginning tennis student may read a manual and then watch the instructor demonstrate certain techniques.

2. *Imitating.* By the time learners have advanced to this level, they have acquired the rudiments of the skill. Individuals follow directions and sequences under close supervision, making a deliberate effort to imitate the model. The total act is not important at this stage; neither is timing nor coordination. The tennis player, for example, may practice a prescribed stance or stroke.

3. *Practicing.* The entire sequence of steps is performed repeatedly at this level. Conscious effort is no longer necessary once the performance becomes more or less habitual in nature. At this level, we might reasonably say that the person has acquired the skill.

4. *Adapting.* This fourth stage of skill development is often referred to as "perfection of the skill." Although some individuals develop much greater skill than others in certain areas, there is always room for improvement. The process involves adapting minor details that, in turn, influence total performance. These modifications may be initiated by the learner or the teacher. This is the process engaged in, for example, when a good basketball player becomes a better one.

Affective Learning

Human learning can entail not only mental achievement and the development of physical skills, but it almost always involves feelings and attitudes. *Affective learning* is the term used to identify the feeling, valuing, and attitudinal components of learning processes. When students indicate that they have enjoyed reading a particular book, what they are really saying is that they have learned not merely to be *able* to read but to gain satisfaction from the process. The act of reading itself is essentially a cognitive skill. Coming to enjoy reading or valuing a particular book lies in the affective domain.

Affective learning also encompasses personality development. One of a teacher's goals might be to lead an overly shy student who never raises a hand in class to join actively in classwork. This is a good example of an affective goal. Consider some other instances of affective learning:

Willingly obeys playground regulations
Enjoys listening to chamber music

Becomes interested in community problems
Recognizes form and beauty in art, dress, and architecture
Is sensitive to human need and pressing social problems
Enjoys reading
Likes solving problems

Each of these statements reflects a behavioral disposition that goes beyond knowing about something and indicates an attitude toward or an inclination to be involved with some situation. Notice also that each statement points to learning that is not observable per se. Just as thoughts or thought processes cannot be directly observed, such is also the case with emotions, feelings, values, and attitudes. Terms like "appreciates," "enjoys," or "shows interest," are acceptable for communicating broad or intermediate goals in the affective domain, but are inappropriate when the need is to describe affective behavior in precise terms.

What a student feels can only be inferred from observing what the student does. Because the affective domain encompasses such intangibles as emotions and attitudes, however, affective objectives are even less easy to specify than cognitive ones. The indicators we use to decide whether or not students know certain elements of school subject matter (particularly at lower levels) are better established than those we have for determining whether students do in fact appreciate or value aspects of school learning.

When analyzing an affective goal such as "the learner will enjoy history," teachers of history would use essentially the same procedure in reducing the goal to behavioral terms as they would with cognitive objectives. They would attempt to identify in precise terms the sorts of actions that would allow them to infer students were enjoying history. Students might, for example, do some or all of the following: (1) opt for a front row seat and be especially attentive during history class; (2) talk impromptu with other students about history; (3) carry around a history notebook; (4) spend their own money on historical paperbacks; (5) come to school early to ask questions about the history they are reading; or (6) regularly browse in the school library, the Internet, or The History Channel for historical material.

A list such as this does illustrate that some affective goals *can* be expressed in behavioral terms. It takes a good deal of observation, however—whether direct or indirect—to permit a decision on whether an affective goal has really been attained, especially since some, if not all, of the signs can easily be counterfeited. Students can, for instance, put on a show of attention, or make a show of carrying around (while not actually opening) a history notebook. Direct observation, of course, is what the teacher personally sees. Indirect observation is what other people—the student's classmates, the librarian, the guidance counselor—tell the teacher.

Classifying Affective Objectives Krathwohl, Bloom, and Masia produced a taxonomy for categorizing affective goals that is similar to the one Bloom and his associates devised for classifying cognitive goals.[14] This classification describes a continuum of emotional involvement in terms of the degree to which a student is affected by it, and one may never know that, or know it for sure. Early in this process, one can be simply peripherally involved with a particular idea or object, aware of its existence, but not investing strong emotion in it. Farther along in the *Taxonomy*, we see how one becomes more deeply involved, as in responding to the object or idea, developing positive feelings for it, or even making it a whole way of life. The following is a summary of these five levels of affective development:

1. *Receiving (attending).* The learner becomes aware of an idea, thing, or process and is willing to listen to a given communication. From a teaching standpoint, the concern is with getting, holding, and directing the student's attention. The student may advance from merely passive receiving to actively directing attention to the communication, despite competing or distracting stimuli. For example, the student listens for rhythm in poetry or prose as it is read aloud.

2. *Responding.* The student shows an interest in the subject. At this low level of commitment, the student displays an interest in the learning object, but has not yet learned to value it. From obedient participation, the student may advance to making a voluntary response and finally to having a pleasurable feeling about, or sense of satisfaction with, the subject matter. This could be expressed by the goal, "Reads poetry for personal pleasure."

3. *Valuing.* As the term suggests, the student has come to regard a person, an idea, or an activity as important. Individuals are now motivated by commitment. At the lower end of the valuing continuum, learners might hold a belief somewhat tentatively; at the other end, their value becomes one of conviction. In fact, one who holds the value strongly may attempt to persuade others to adopt this way of thinking. Instructional goals and objectives related to attitudes and appreciations are appropriate at this level.

4. *Organization.* After having become committed to the value, the learner organizes personal values into a value system. Finding that more than one value may apply to a situation and that sometimes values conflict, the person finds it necessary to gain a better understanding of the values and then to organize them into a system of dominant and subordinate values. At this level learners will be able to defend their value choices according to an established rationale. Objectives relating to the development of a philosophy of life would fall into this category.

5. *Internalization.* At this level, individuals have a value system that has regulated their behavior for a sufficiently long time for it to be possible to say that they have developed a characteristic lifestyle based on a philosophy. Values have become integrated into some kind of consistent system. Instructional goals and objectives concerned with the student's general patterns of adjustment (personal, social, emotional) would be appropriate here.

The Benefits of Classifying Objectives into Domains

It is, of course, not to be imagined that these three learning domains are mutually exclusive. Most of the time you are teaching you will be operating in two, or all, domains at once. Although some learning behaviors may be more easily classifiable into one or another of the three domains, others entail a complex interplay among the three types of learning. A student reciting Lincoln's Gettysburg Address is simultaneously demonstrating memory (cognitive/knowledge), concern to get it right and, one hopes, a feeling for Lincoln's language and ideals (affective/valuing), and perhaps gesturing (psychomotor/practice). Emotion is an essential aspect of intellectual processes, and motor and mental skills have an affective dimension. Yet, some behaviors are more intellectual than emotional, whereas others are more emotional than intellectual. Still other action requires more mental and physical dexterity than anything else. As a teacher, you should remember which domain is more important to you at the moment and set your objectives accordingly.

An ability to analyze learning in these three areas helps to clarify our thinking about what we are attempting to teach. Some believe the most important effect of this classification system has been to increase the emphasis given to higher-level cognitive activities (sometimes referred to as HOTS, higher-order thinking skills, as distinct from lower level ones, LOTS).[15] There is a tendency for teachers to concentrate on lower-level skills within the cognitive domain to the exclusion of the higher-level ones.[16] In other words, we may be more inclined to ask students to *remember* a specific date from the Civil War period than to *analyze* causes for the Civil War. It is important to get beyond these lower-level skills in teaching, and the classification of objectives in the *Taxonomy* allows a check to see that we have objectives at the various levels of complexity.

More recently, Howard Gardner's work has given good reason for supposing that each individual student possesses intellectual strengths in a variety of fields, which he has called "intelligences." He has in general departed from the notion that people have one big, fixed intelligence expressible in a number, one's "IQ," which applies to whatever one is learning or doing. Rather, he plausibly argues, we all have underlying *intellectual* potential, can be "smart," in seven (possibly more) separate ways: linguistic (word-smart), logical/mathematical (number-smart), bodily-kinesthetic (movement-smart), spatial (art-smart), interpersonal (people-smart), intrapersonal (self-smart). As he wrote:

> [F]ar from being divorced from cognition, our capacities to interact with other individuals, to enjoy works of art, or to participate in athletics or dance, each involve highly developed forms of cognition. [Multiple Intelligences] theory seeks to establish the pervasiveness of intellectual activities in areas where it has hitherto often been excluded.[17]

This means that your objectives should cater to as many different ways of thinking about the subject matter as you reasonably can. So that, for instance, if the class were studying the Great Depression era, in addition to the politics of the era, its music, dance, and popular literature, the means of getting about (Model-T Fords, streetcars, prop-driven planes, etc.), the sports of the time, would all figure in what students could research and exhibit in the interest of having them form a realistic picture of that historical period. "A skilled teacher," as Gardner has elsewhere maintained.

> is a person who can open a number of different windows on the same concept. . . . [He or she] functions as a "student-curriculum broker," ever vigilant for . . . texts, films, software that can help convey the relevant contents in as engaging and effective a way as possible, to students who exhibit a characteristic learning mode.[18]

Bloom's *Taxonomy* and Gardner's *Multiple Intelligences* both serve to remind us of the complexity of productive learning, allowing us to see it in several important dimensions while pointing up the error of emphasizing one type of learning process or one kind of intelligence to the neglect of others that are equally important. Thus, although we may regard the learning of history or mathematics as essentially cognitive processes, a fuller perspective on learning should move us to ask whether it is realistic to neglect the affective domain or other mental capacities in teaching areas in which motivation is a perennial problem. How many students can't, don't, or won't learn mathematics either because they see no value in it for them, or have been put off, possibly forever, by an unduly abstract approach to the subject that leaves them baffled, able to plug numbers into formulas but not to use mathematical knowledge to solve problems and to understand the world around them more fully? In a similar vein, for any of us inclined to view physical education classes in terms of isolated skill development, an ability to view learning in broader terms would help us to recognize the need for the addition of some important cognitive and affective objectives (such as finding physical activity mentally stimulating, or liking some form of exercise) in an area where psychomotor objectives have generally been allowed to predominate.

As John Dewey pointed out over 50 years ago, "collateral learning . . . formation of enduring attitudes, of likes and dislikes . . . may be and often is much more important than the spelling lesson or lesson in geography or history that is learned." "What avail is it" he asked,

> to win prescribed amounts of information, to win ability to read and write, if in the process the individual loses his own soul: loses his appreciation of things worth while, of the values to which these things are relative, if he loses desire to apply what he has learned and, above all, loses the ability to extract meaning from his future experiences as they occur?[19]

Moreover, classifying objectives in this way highlights important relationships between these different types of learning. It becomes evident that goals in one domain are often reached through another domain. For example, good teachers frequently attempt to develop interest (an affective goal) in a particular area so the student will learn it (a cognitive goal). On other occasions, new cognitive learning can change student attitudes. Outstanding teachers have the ability to reach cognitive goals through the affective domain. It turns out that the most liked and respected teachers are often described by students as those who take a deep interest in them, who challenge them, who understand their anxieties, who respect their opinions and do not embarrass them, who maintain high interest, and who instill a love of the subject. These attributes are affective in nature.

Finally, recognizing basic differences between cognitive and affective objectives allows teachers to skillfully use each type to best advantage. Cognitive objectives can be used as teaching tools for purposes of informing and guiding the learner. We might think of the main function of these objectives as facilitating communication between teacher and student. On the other hand, the function of an affective objective is quite different. It is intended to be used by the teacher to observe whether the learner values what is being taught. When there is good evidence that students do not value certain learning experiences, this should serve as a signal for the teacher to reexamine his or her teaching approach as well as her relationships with students. Whereas a cognitive objective indicates the extent to which students understand a subject, an affective objective indicates whether students value the subject sufficiently to make contact with the subject, particularly outside of class.

♦♦♦ APPLICATION EXERCISES ♦♦♦

1. Classify the following objectives as representative of the cognitive, affective, or psychomotor domains:
   a. The student will voluntarily read outside material related to current events.
   b. Learners are to develop skill in swimming so that they can, using any stroke they choose, swim 50 meters within two minutes.
   c. The student will identify the differences between facts and opinions.
   d. Given a model of a hypothetical cell, the student will identify the cellular structures.
   e. The student will correctly operate the photocopier.
   f. Students will express an interest in visiting a local art museum.
   g. The learner will show an appreciation of outdoor sports.
   h. Students will be able to list some of the characteristics of social insects.
   i. The student will correctly focus the microscope.
   j. When given ten Spanish sentences, students will be able to translate at least seven into English without error.
   k. The student will volunteer to remain after class to help clean up the classroom.
2. Consider the following examples of student behavior and decide which level of cognitive learning each represents (i.e., knowledge, comprehension, application, analysis, synthesis, or evaluation).

The student:
  a. Describes in his or her own words the three major causes of the War of 1812.
  b. Composes a short musical score.
  c. Employs principles of nutrition and a list of foods to prepare three menus for well-balanced meals.
  d. Names the 50 States of the Union.
  e. Judges a presidential decision.
  f. Compares the actions of the characters in a short story.
  g. Provides an example to support an idea.
  h. Proposes a solution to a problem from accumulated data.
  i. Enumerates the parts of a lathe.
  j. Chooses from several alternatives.
  k. Translates a paragraph from Spanish to English.
3. Examine the following affective objectives and decide which level of affective development each represents (i.e., receiving, responding, valuing, value organization, or value internalization:
  a. Science students will develop a commitment to the need for clean air and water and will become active in encouraging others to do so.
  b. Students will listen patiently and good-naturedly to the opinions of peers who may have different points of view.
  c. Students will entertain an interest in poetry, and during a free reading period will select a book of poetry as one of their choices.
  d. Students will learn to value honesty and will show this by not cheating on tests and assignments, and by discouraging others from doing so.
  e. High school students will accept responsibility for establishing career choices by seeking and organizing relevant job information at a career fair.

Making Your Objectives Relevant

One of the main reasons for using objectives is to enhance communication between the teacher and the learner. Clear and unambiguous statements of learning intentions go a long way toward helping students know what you expect them to be able to do. However, getting students to agree that learning objectives are relevant and worth pursuing may be another matter. Students become used to reading textbook chapters, doing math problems, writing compositions, bringing in newspaper articles, and so on, simply because that is what school requires. They often approach what they perceive as learning chores with little enthusiasm because they do not see how they connect with their present or future lives.

Some general strategies for helping students see the relevance of formal learning objectives are:

1. Taking time to discuss with your students the objectives that will be the focus for classroom learning. Rather than simply telling students that certain new learning is important, use an inductive approach in these discussions, one that in its ideal allows you and your students to derive learning objectives together.

2. When starting a new unit, beginning with real-life applications of school learning and work backward to what the students are to be able to do. For example, make it a practice to confront students with realistic situations in their present or future lives in which they will have occasions to use percentages or to communicate their ideas in writing. Take time here to develop a problem-solving frame of reference toward new learning before focusing on precise objectives and learning tasks.

3. Whenever possible, allowing students to view new learning in wholes rather than in fragments. For example, students in a writing class are most likely to see the relevance of an objective stating "the learner will demonstrate proper subject-verb agreement" when this particular skill element is presented in context (e.g., after they have had opportunities to write for an audience and to experience a need for better grammar). Basketball players are more apt to see the point of an objective calling for a particular level of competence at free-throw shooting after they have played the game and found themselves lacking in this particular subskill.

4. Providing opportunities for students to immediately begin practicing new learning in their out-of-school lives. Have them bring in examples of applications they encounter in the mass media or in their physical and social environments. Have them keep journals documenting their efforts to practice new language skills, to recognize history in the making, or to make use of mathematics in their daily lives. By making such carryover activities an integral part of new learning, you help develop a perception that classroom learning objectives have relevance to something beyond school.[20]

Deciding What Your Approach Will Be

In attempting to decide how precisely you should specify the learning objectives for your own teaching, there are several things you should take into consideration: (1) what you want to achieve; (2) the subjects you are teaching; (3) the grade level and ability levels of your students; (4) the expectations of the school administration where you are teaching; and (5) your readiness as a beginning teacher to proceed without highly detailed objectives.

Some subject areas, such as mathematics and physical education, lend themselves more readily to the specification of measurable criteria for student achievement. These are skill areas in which results are more readily observable. In other subjects, like English and social studies, indicators of achievement are often less possible, or even impossible, to define in precise terms, although specific objectives may nonetheless be possible for some learning tasks (e.g., spelling lessons, map-reading projects). Precise objectives are more difficult to write (and are often less appropriate) in the higher grades because of the increased complexity of the subject matter and because the teaching goals more frequently involve understanding and appreciation. Teachers in the lower grades are normally teaching more easily definable skills to students functioning at more concrete levels of cognition. It is generally easier for elementary school teachers to adopt a pattern of stipulating objectives, and with less doubt as to their appropriateness. Teachers at the senior high and college levels need to be careful not to trivialize learning that calls for the individual creativity or higher thought processes of students. They will ordinarily have more difficult decisions to make when it comes to applying performance criteria to student learning.

On taking a teaching position, you will need to find out well in advance of the beginning of the school year what the district and school expectations are for teacher lesson planning. Some districts require teachers to submit written objectives and/or lesson plans for the subject(s) they teach every week or every month. They may or may not insist that these objectives be written in behavioral form. Regardless of how extensively you will apply them in your teaching, it is important for you to have knowledge of and be able to write performance objectives.

As a beginning teacher attempting to find your own way with lesson planning and writing of objectives, you would be well advised to make some use of performance objectives, while bearing in mind the fact that rigid adherence to this type of objective can easily lead to mechanical teaching and learning and the waste of chance happenings, such as a snowstorm or an unexpected visitor, which make children unusually ready to learn—what Maria Montessori called "teachable moments." It is above all important that your approach to learning objectives be as reasonable and flexible as possible. Here are some additional pointers:

1. When teaching intellectually mature students (i.e., those who have reached the stage of formal operations), make sure that learning does not remain at the straight information level by distributing cognitive objectives across the six levels of learning and across the different domains. Some knowledge- and comprehension-level objectives are usually necessary, but it is essential that your planning move on to the development of application, analysis, synthesis, and evaluation objectives.
2. Do not be reluctant to specify in detail what you want your students to get out of a lesson for fear of discouraging incidental learning. Remember, you can always add objectives to describe any learning you want students to demonstrate in addition to what you had originally planned. You can also make allowances in your lesson plan for spontaneous exploration of topics that were not included in the objectives.

3. It is not necessary or desirable to develop long lists of objectives for each unit of instruction. The appropriate number of objectives depends on many factors, but perhaps most importantly on the subject content and grade level of the learners. Usually, the more sophisticated the learners, the fewer the objectives required.

4. There may be times when you want to avoid announcing learning outcomes before involving students in a new learning experience. Eisner, one of the critics of performance objectives, recommends the use of what he calls *expressive objectives* for some learning activities. According to Eisner, an expressive objective

> Identifies a situation in which pupils are to work, a problem in which they are to engage; but it does not specify what from that encounter, situation, problem, or task they are to learn. An expressive objective provides both the teacher and the student with an invitation to explore, defer, or focus on issues that are of particular interest or importance to the inquirer.[21]

A teacher who takes a class on a field trip to a local hospital for the purpose of allowing students to experience human activity in that setting realizes that each student will achieve different learning outcomes from the experience. In this case, the teacher may consider it more imporant to work from an expressive rather than a behavioral objective.

A SUMMARY OF GUIDELINES FOR DESIGNING TEACHING OBJECTIVES

1. Make the objectives that govern your teaching and your relationships with students your own. Take time at the beginning of each new teaching module (i.e., year, semester, unit) to make clear to yourself, in writing, the learning objectives *you* wish to achieve. This will pay important dividends in terms of helping you to keep your teaching organized and focused.

2. Keep in mind the distinction between *goals* and *objectives* and recognize that objectives should be based on and derived from goals, and the goals themselves from purposes.

3. Be clear on your immediate objectives for each lesson, but do not lose sight of your human development goals. Regard these as among your most important priorities as an educator.

4. Know what your *enabling objectives* are and what enabling objectives are necessary for the achievement of your immediate objectives.

5. Be capable of writing objectives that are clear about what learners will do, contain an action verb, and include conditions of performance.

6. Be able to write objectives in the three main learning domains (cognitive, affective, and psychomotor), and know how these domains relate. Realize that teaching goals in one domain may be reached through another domain.

7. Be able to write objectives that represent a progression from simpler to more complex levels of learning. In most teaching areas it is appropriate to include objectives that promote higher thought processes (cognitive domain) and those that foster the internalization of new learning (affective domain).

8. When trying to determine behavioral components of affective goals, think of people who exhibit these qualities (what do they *do?*).

9. Recognize the usefulness as well as some of the limitations of objectives. A decision to use or not to use them is one you will have to make for yourself. Base your decision on experience. Try them and see how they work for you.

10. The following are some concluding generalizations to consider:
    a. The effort you devote to developing objectives can reduce the work and uncertainty involved in deciding what and how to teach. Teachers make decisions every day about what is and is not important. Your objectives communicate these decisions.
    b. Sound evaluation of student learning requires the specification of objectives.
    c. Cognitive learning is usually inferred from verbal behavior.
    d. Factual learning that never becomes manifest in skills or habits is learning in the weakest sense. Your human development goals are aimed at promoting habits and dispositions, or learning in the strong sense.
    e. Objectives are means to certain ends, not ends in themselves. Most important, a good objective should describe an important learning outcome. Failing that, a beautifully stated objective may be of little use.
    f. Objectives become more difficult to write in the higher grades because of the increased complexity of subject matter and because teaching goals more frequently involve understandings and appreciations.
    g. Intentional learning is generally superior for students who are supplied with objectives, but on the other hand, the possibilities of incidental (unplanned) learning may be lost.

◆◆◆ **SUGGESTED ACTIVITIES AND QUESTIONS** ◆◆◆

1. Attempt to obtain a districtwide goal statement of a school system with which you are acquainted. Does it mention such things as "democratic values," "individual development," "social adjustment," "cultural traditions," or "vocational preparation?" What do you take to be its major emphasis?

2. Compose a statement of your present philosophy of education that takes into consideration some of the main developmental needs of to-day's young people as well as major requirements of life in a complex technological society.

3. Write a short critical appraisal of how instructional objectives can help or hinder you in your teaching.

4. In your own words describe an *expressive objective*. Mention several possible learning activities in one of your teaching areas that could call for expressive objectives rather than specific performance objectives.

NOTES

1. The process of goal development can be more manageable and rational if you have begun to formulate a workable philosophy of education and teaching for yourself. This should be an ongoing endeavor as you prepare for a teaching career. This part of the handbook is particularly designed to encourage you to reflect on the goals you carry with you into teaching.

2. Robert W. Travers and Jacqueline Dillon, *The Making of a Teacher: A Plan for Professional Self-Development.* New York: Macmillan, 1975, p. 30.

3. Hoover observes that "although evaluation of learning achievement has emphasized the can-do dimension, it is the does-do dimension that every teacher seeks. Thus, an individual who has internalized a specific value voluntarily behaves in a manner indicating that he or she holds that value" (Kenneth H. Hoover, *The Professional Teacher's Handbook*, 3rd ed. Boston: Allyn and Bacon, 1982, p. 16).

4. Searles argues that "ethical right demands that each individual be allowed to make up his [or her] own mind as to values and subsequent modes of conduct. Therefore the instruction system (of the school) has the right, and in a deep sense, the duty, to present the individual with the alternatives of behavior and leave him free to choose his [or her] own pattern" (John E. Searles, *A System for Instruction*. Scranton, Pa.: International Textbook Company, 1968, p. 47). Searles suggests that the dilemma regarding the teaching of values might be resolved if the school would agree to promote only "behavioral and procedural" values, and not "substantive" ones.

5. Childs, in a classic statement on the moral basis of deliberate education, maintains that "education is a value-conditioned activity. The school seeks to cultivate values in the young by means of both the subject-matters and the methods that it employs in its program. . . . The moral element is preeminently involved in all of those selections and rejections that are inescapable in the construction of the purposes and the curriculum of the school. . . . The fact that the outcomes we seek involve the lives of the immature deepens—it does not diminish—our responsibility to know what we are trying to accomplish when we undertake to educate" (John L. Childs, *Education and Morals*. New York: John Wiley, 1967, pp. 16, 17).

6. For a pointed discussion, featuring two opposing views on the role of the schools in value development, see the articles by Lawrence Kohlberg and Edward A. Wynne in James W. Noll (Ed.), *Taking Sides: Clashing Views on Controversial Educational Issues*, 5th ed. Guilford, Conn.: Dushkin Publishing Group, 1989, pp. 44–63.

7. This set of requirements for writing nonambiguous behavioral objectives is adapted from Ronald T. Hyman, *Ways of Teaching*, 2nd ed. Philadelphia: J.B. Lippincott, 1974, p. 43.

8. It may not always be necessary to include these two performance criteria to be satisfied that you have a useful behavioral objective. For example, objectives like "Students will be able to describe the main causes of World War II," or "Students will write business letters utilizing three different types of salutations" may be sufficiently nonambiguous for your purposes. The particular subject matter, students, and context will no doubt have a bearing on the degree of specificity required.

9. David Krathwohl, Benjamin S. Bloom, and Bertram B. Masia, *Taxonomy of Educational Objectives, Handbook II: Affective Domain*. New York: David McKay, 1964, pp. 6–7.

10. Benjamin S. Bloom (Ed.), *Taxonomy of Educational Objectives: Handbook I: Cognitive Domain*. New York: David McKay, 1956. See Part Two, pp. 62–197.

11. Krathwohl, Bloom, and Masia, *Taxonomy II: Affective Domain*, pp. 6–7.

12. P. G. Kapfer and G. F. Ovard, *Preparing and Using Individualized Learning Packages*. Englewood Cliffs, N.J.: Educational Technology Publications, 1971.

13. Hoover, *The Professional Teacher's Handbook*, pp. 11, 14. Krathwohl, Bloom, and Masia, *Taxonomy II: Affective Domain*, pp. 45–62.

14. Krathwohl, Bloom, and Masia, *Taxonomy II: Affective Domain*, pp. 45–62.

15. John A. Glover, Roger H. Bruning, and Robert W. Filbeck, *Educational Psychology: Principles and Applications*. Boston: Little, Brown, 1983, p. 333.

16. The widespread emphasis on less complex forms of cognitive learning has been documented by studies showing that more than 95 percent of the learning demanded by broad samples of teaching materials in an area like world history remains at the memory-recall and comprehension levels. See D. Trachtenburg, "Student Tasks in Text Material: What Cognitive Skills Do They Tap?" *Peabody Journal of Education* 52 (1974): 54–57.

17. Howard Gardner, *Frames of Mind: The Theory of Multiple Intelligences*. New York: Basic, 1983, p. 285.

18. Howard Gardner, *The Unschooled Mind: How Children Think and How Schools Should Teach*. New York: Basic, 1991, p. 246.

19. John Dewey, *Experience and Education*. New York: Macmillan, 1938, pp. 48–49.

20. Fred M. Newmann and Gary G. Wehlage, "Five Criteria of Authentic Instruction." *Educational Leadership* (April, 1993): 9.

21. E. W. Eisner, "Instructional and Expressive Objectives: Their Formulation and Use in Curriculum." In W. J. Popham, E. W. Eisner, H. J. Sullivan, and L. L. Tyler (Eds.), *Instructional Objectives*. (AERA Monograph Series on Curriculum Evaluation, No. 3). Chicago: Rand McNally, 1969, p. 31.

CHAPTER 4

Organizing Subject Matter and Planning Lessons

*Let the main object be: To seek and to find a method
of instructing by which teachers may teach less but
learners may learn more.*

John Amos Comenius, 1628 A.D.

Getting a Handle on the Planning Process

As you assume responsibility for your own classes, you will have a need to do both long- and short-range planning for your teaching. This will be an early test of your organizational skills and your ability to view your instructional role in large perspective. You may find yourself in somewhat of a muddle over where to start, how much planning is necessary, who the planning is for, where to find help, and so on. Instructional planning can in fact be a complex and confusing subject if it is not approached in the right manner. Before you plunge in and begin the task of organizing courses, units, and lessons, it is important to have a clear notion of capable planning.

It is rare for teachers not to feel some initial uncertainty about their readiness to organize courses of study and to prepare to teach groups of students. One elementary student-teacher expressed her early planning anxieties this way:

> I was hopeful I'd be able to use my cooperating teacher's lesson plans for a while, but she wants me to do all of my own planning. This is certainly a new experience for me. It's the first time in my life I've had to make decisions like this. It seems like quite a lot of responsibility. But I knew I was going to have to do my own planning sooner or later. I might as well get my feet wet.

Such apprehension mainly occurs because competent instructional planning assumes a relatively broad view of the teaching-learning process and some in-depth command of the subject matter one is preparing. The task of planning for teaching would be considerably simpler if our only concern was to identify the content to be learned by our students. The fact that we want to have some control over what kind of learning that results from their contact with the subject makes the planning process more involved. It means we have important decisions to make regarding not only the basic content and general goals we will be working from (we can normally expect some of this to be provided by curriculum guides and textbooks), but the specific learning outcomes we will be concerned to have students achieve and the methods we will employ to have them reach these objectives.

When you begin identifying in precise terms the type of learning you wish to promote in your teaching, it becomes apparent that these learning objectives will not result from a random or haphazard process. The subject matter must be organized and sequenced in ways that give rise to thought and both enable and encourage application. Competent planning, then, requires not only a clear idea of goals, but the ability to decide what learning to focus on, the best sequence of learning experiences, and the type of class activities and teaching approaches for the subjects you will be teaching. It draws on a teacher's abilities as a subject-matter specialist, a learning psychologist, a teaching strategist, and a designer and evaluator of what has been learnt. If it were not for the fact that organizing for instruction is something all teachers must give immediate attention to, the subject of planning for teaching might better follow rather than precede those sections of the handbook that deal with the conduct of classroom activity.

As it is, this chapter addresses a central aspect of preparing for teaching, and it also serves as an advance organizer for the skill-development chapters that follow. In addition to providing basic ideas for course, unit, and lesson planning, it discusses main types of lesson focuses and previews some fundamental teaching strategies and styles. The chapter is designed to help you overcome the initial disadvantage of having to organize subject matter and plan lessons before you have had substantial experience with teaching. By attempting to reduce instructional planning to its essentials, it seeks to make the planning phase of teaching more manageable.

Levels of Planning

Organizing for instruction normally takes place at three different levels: course or program planning, unit planning, and lesson planning. Each type of planning has a different purpose, a different level of generality, and covers a different time span.[1]

In its most fundamental sense, instructional planning means being involved in the design of the curriculums or courses you teach. It means developing your own teaching content from the beginning. However, new teachers are seldom in a position to author the courses they teach. Lack of experience in curriculum development is one factor making that unrealistic. Another is the fact that most entering teachers find themselves teaching in established subjects or programs in which a good deal of curricular structure is already present. Also, in the case of elementary school teachers, planning at the elementary school level often has unique constraints. When working in basic-skill areas with firmly implanted curricular guidelines, elementary school teachers are more likely to be involved in intermediate and short-range planning than with program-level organization.[2]

One should not suppose, though, that course development is the only possible kind of course-level planning. Whether or not they have been involved in the original course design, all teachers should be involved in large-scale planning in which they consider subject-matter elements, learning goals, and teaching methods in terms of the whole course or program. They should become accustomed to planning segments of content or learning units in relationship with other learning units and making reasoned decisions about the order in which these units are taught. The order of teaching units should be deliberately planned, not allowed to happen arbitrarily or just because suppliers of teaching materials have provided a particular sequence. Dependence on teachers' manuals or other prepackaged materials deprives teachers of the vitally important process of thinking things out for themselves.

Following overall course layout, unit organization is an intermediate level of planning, normally involving two- to four-week blocks of teaching, and a point at which teachers often make their most important instructional decisions. Daily lesson planning is the third level and most immediate type of planning. It is important for you to be able to plan at each of these levels and to have your daily lessons become extensions of the initial organizing you have done at the course and unit levels.

Course-Level Planning

As a professional teacher, it is important that you be acquainted with the process involved in constructing a year- or semester-long course of study, including the determination of basic learning goals, course content, and instructional procedures. There may be occasions when you will have an opportunity to apply large-scale planning skills in designing a new course or program, one that is of special interest to you, perhaps in an area that is new to your school. Also, understanding the process of course development allows you to better identify with the thinking that has gone into the preestablished courses you teach. It gives you a better context for the things you do in your classroom on a day-to-day basis, and makes it easier for you to feel ownership of the subject matter you teach.

Whether or not you are engaged in designing a course of study from the beginning, course-level planning usually involves the following steps:

1. Identifying (or reviewing) the central goals and purposes of the program or course you will be teaching

2. Selecting course content, then organizing and sequencing it to make it as coherent and teachable as possible
3. Determining the amount of time to be spent on the various topics in the sequence

Identifying Course Goals

The process of course planning begins when you determine what you plan that students are to learn from this particular subject or course of study: What major understandings, skills, and attitudes are to be emphasized during the year? General goals are those that you want to focus on at this early stage in your planning, course aims that you can summarize in one written paragraph. As an example, a *general goal statement* for a course in junior high school science might read as follows:

- The major goals of this course are to help students develop (1) the rational thinking processes that underlie scientific method; (2) the basic terms and concepts that allow us to interpret, predict, and theorize about scientific events; (3) the fundamental skills involved in procuring and organizing scientific information; and (4) those scientific values, appreciations, and attitudes that allow us to investigate and better understand our lives and our environments

In another instance, a possible goal statement for a course in basic mathematics (seventh- to ninth-grade level) could contain this kind of information:

- This class aims to promote useful life skills in basic mathematics for non–college-bound students. It stresses being able to apply fundamental mathematical concepts and procedures in everyday-life situations such as counting one's change, comprehending and figuring simple percentages, and balancing one's checkbook. The class attempts to build students' confidence in their abilities to perform basic mathematical operations as situations require. It seeks to diagnose and help eliminate the main sticking points students encounter in performing mathematical calculations and procedures.

You will notice that each of these brief course descriptions touches on fundamental skills and attitudes as well as basic understandings that are to be promoted. They are both balanced statements of intent that attempt to take into consideration not only the need to teach subject matter, but the learning needs of students, and the need for the subject to have carryover value in the student's life.

A statement of course aims can help you begin to get a clearer idea of what you want to emphasize and what you want to avoid in your teaching. The previous description of course aims for basic math suggests that students in such classes often have a history of negative experiences with the subject. They desperately need to experience a reversal of this pattern. Based on this kind of awareness, a teacher may decide to adopt a set of developmental goals that center on promoting positive self-concepts and feature the need for all students to experience some successes in this class.

Well-conceived course goals should also serve to describe the kind of emphasis that is to be placed on student initiative, imagination, and higher thought processes in a particular class. The following summary of goals for a high school U.S. history course is an example:

- This course is designed to provide a basic understanding and appreciation of major events, ideas, and personalities that have had a central impact on our nation's development. Its subgoals are (1) to have students recognize important periods in the history of this country and the prominent individuals and events that made these eras significant; (2) to make students aware of major crises in the nation's history and the patterns we have developed for meeting national problems; (3) to help students recognize the precarious nature of democratic institutions, and to appreciate the crucial investments of previous Americans in forming the foundations for our present way of life; and (4) to prepare students to realize that they are observing history in the making as they read newspapers, watch newscasts, and take part in events. Students will be encouraged and expected to perceive the history of their country as a dynamic rather than a static process. They will be called on to identify with historical personalities, to evaluate the decisions of former leaders, and to infer cause-and-effect relationships between historical events. An effort will be made to view factual knowledge in a broad context, to identify specific names, dates, places, events, and so forth within a timeline of larger happenings.

It obviously takes a good deal of thought and effort, not to mention knowledge of subject and students, to summarize one's course goals in this concise manner. Course aims contained in curriculum guides and preestablished courses of study can be helpful, but it is very important for you to think carefully about why *you* plan to teach particular subject matter. Of course, regardless of how self-reliant you may become in defining basic goals for your teaching area(s), it is important to remain aware of potentially binding district or state guidelines for the subjects you teach. In school districts or subject areas in which curricular prescriptions are relatively firm, you should make an attempt to understand the thinking that has gone into these decisions. If you cannot identify with the course-level goals that have been provided, it may be difficult for you to become highly involved in what you are teaching. If you find externally prescribed goals in some respects incompatible with your own rationally derived teaching aims, you will need to do all you can to reconcile them with those of the curriculum.

Selecting and Organizing Course Content

The next step in course-level planning is deciding what course content will achieve its goals,[3] and organizing the central ideas in a way that will make them most interesting and understandable. You will want to determine the order in which these main components are to be taught.

Topic Selection Teachers with qualifications to teach a particular subject will have some initial idea of the kinds of major topics or concepts that should be included in a course of study for that area. For further help in content selection, they can usually depend on assistance from textbooks, curriculum guides, and preestablished programs.

An appropriate list of topics for a course in general math, for example, might include[4]:

> The set of whole numbers
> Measurement
> The system of decimal fractions
> The metric system
> Subtraction and division of whole numbers
> Finite decimal operations
> Addition and multiplication of whole numbers
> Set theory
> Whole numbers—bases other than ten
> The number line
> Real numbers

Or, as a group of master-topics for a course in junior high earth science, teachers might want their students to acquire some understanding of:

> Astronomy
> Ecology
> Geology
> Meteorology
> Oceanography
> Paleontology
> Mineralogy
> Physical geography

Having identified the major topics or concepts that are to form the framework of a particular course of study, you should be prepared to devote considerable thought to the internal organization of the course. To maximize course coherence and teachability, subject matter needs to be organized in a way that takes into consideration any necessary relationships among its various components (logical organization) as well as the learning needs of the students you will be teaching (psychological organization).

The Logical Organization of Subject Matter With some subjects, it will be more critically important to give early attention to the logical requirements of course organization than is the case with certain other subjects. For instance, a fifth-grade reading program, featuring basic study skills, needs to be structured so that a unit on Reading for Main Ideas is allowed to serve as a foundation for a unit on Outlining. Or, to provide a more detailed illustration, the list of potential topics for the hypothetical math course in the previous example will need to be structured in a more cohesive and sequential fashion before further course organization can proceed in a meaningful way. These topics should be grouped under appropriate major headings, for example:

Measuring

The metric system
Measurement

Whole numbers

Subtraction and division of whole numbers
The set of whole numbers

Decimals

Finite decimal operations
Real numbers
The system of decimal fractions

Sets

Set theory
The number line
Whole numbers—bases other than ten

The groups should then be sequenced to represent the order in which these major areas of concentration will be featured within the course:

Whole numbers
Sets
Decimals
Measuring

Within the individual groups the sequence of course topics should also be carefully determined. Once this is accomplished the master outline of course topics should be expected to look something like this:

Whole numbers

The set of whole numbers
Addition and multiplication of whole numbers
Subtraction and division of whole numbers

Sets

Set theory
Whole numbers—bases other than ten
The number line

Decimals

The system of decimal fractions
Finite decimal operations
Real numbers

Measuring

Measurement
The metric system

These are examples of how the internal structure of the subject dictates the way in which course content is organized and taught. Generally, the planning for traditional academic courses and basic skill subjects, in which program or course development proceeds from the simple to the complex, requires stricter attention to the logical requirements of course organization than subjects in which the sequencing of basic units of study can afford to be less tightly structured. In areas such as history, physical education, home economics, music, and art, internal relationships among course elements are often less crucial. Planning for these subjects requires relatively less attention to logical organization of subject matter and more regard for the creative aspects of one's organization (not to suggest that sound planning in more highly structured subjects does not call for imaginative application).

Planning a U.S. history course, for example, provides opportunities for considerable variation in standard approaches to content organization. In contrast to skill subjects that build from simple to complex (e.g., math, reading) or theoretical subjects that proceed from concrete to abstract (e.g., government, economics, philosophy), history courses are typically organized to accommodate time sequences. This has led to unduly restricted notions of how history should be taught. The main topics in U.S. history courses are generally organized chronologically in terms of main time periods. This allows teachers to focus on the progression of historical events and to emphasize cause-and-effect relationships within the subject matter. Yet it is possible to structure a U.S. history course quite differently. Instead of approaching the main topics chronologically, by introducing first the "Colonial Period," then the "National Period," followed by a unit on "Western Expansion," and so forth, the course might be organized to feature central concepts or themes (e.g., nationalism or war), rather than, or as occasional departures from, major time periods. Although the more traditional approach may help students understand and appreciate causal factors or the timing of events in history, the alternative form of organization would aim to emphasize underlying issues, overriding themes, and the student's ability to *think* about history, to connect the past with the present, to understand modern problems in light of earlier times, to see the wider picture.[5]

The Psychological Organization of Subject Matter While the logical ordering of course content focuses on necessary relationships within the subject matter itself, it does not take into consideration the learning needs and requirements of those who are expected to learn this material. Although logical organization helps to ensure, at least on paper, that common course threads get tied together and basic understandings and procedures are taught first, it is not concerned to provide the type of course structure that will provoke the interest and involvement of one's students. In other words, it is a subject-centered rather than a learner-centered form of organization, and as such may as effectively hinder as promote learning.

The subject matter for a course of study can also be organized psychologically, that is to say from the learner's standpoint, to take into account the learning styles and abilities of the students for whom the course is intended. This is the other dimension of course organization you will have to attend to as you do large-scale planning for your teaching. Here we are concerned with selecting and structuring course content so that it connects with students' interests, experiences, perceptions, and knowledge backgrounds. There are some things you can do at this early stage in your planning to make a course of study as learner-centered as possible:

1. Select content that is appropriate to the developmental levels of students.
2. Make an effort to have main course topics connect with real-life applications.
3. Design the course in a way that allows students to develop interests, perceptions, and frames of reference before they get to the more abstract and theoretical parts of the course.

Developmentally Appropriate Content   This is clearly the first and most critical consideration in organizing course content that is psychologically appropriate for the students with whom you will be working. There is evidence to indicate that during their school years a young person's educational development proceeds in age-related stages, and that the young learner tends to make sense of the world and experience in significantly different ways at each successive stage.[6] For purposes of educational planning, consider some of the following basic developmental characteristics:

1. In some important ways young children's thinking and learning are very different from those of adults. Children from approximately the beginning to the middle elementary school years (in what Piaget called the *preoperational* stage) make sense of the unknown world outside them in terms of the known world within. Egan tells us that their "major intellectual tools and categories are not rational and logical but emotional and moral. . . . True learning at this stage must involve their being able to absorb the world to the categories of their own vivid mental life and to use the world to expand the intellectual categories they have available."[7] Young children tend to learn best from stories and games that have clearly established meanings and contain basic concepts of good-bad, love-hate, fear-security.[8]
2. Students from approximately the middle elementary to the late high school years are fascinated by the world around them, by the extremes

of what exists and what is known.[9] Part of this fascination stems from the sense of mystery and personal challenge they perceive in the external world. They are interested in exploring the limits of the practical reality with which they are now having to deal.[10] During this lengthy middle period in their schooling, students tend to be predominantly *concrete* thinkers: They are readily able to form concepts of objects or situations for which they have immediate references, but they have trouble with hypotheticals and high-level abstractions.[11] At this stage in their mental development, young people tend to learn concepts and generalizations (a big part of school learning) best when the ideas are approached inductively, that is, from the particular to the general. However, their interest is largely in the particulars. For them to make sense of what is being learned, the story form is still important at this educational level. According to Egan, "History is best understood at this stage as a kind of mosaic of bright elements—anecdotes, facts, dramatic events—which are composed into a small story, which in turn is a segment of a larger story. It is important to realize that students' concepts of historical causality, and additional concepts of otherness, are still quite primitive."[12]

3. It is not until well into their senior high school years, if then, that students become *formal* thinkers, develop a "craving for generality," a need to begin imposing order on the complex and fascinating world around them.[13] Up until this stage students are not inclined to think in terms of systems. Now they become interested in investigating the general laws by which the world works.[14] They are more likely at this level to become interested in general schemes that explain historical, psychological, social, or natural processes.[15] At this stage they are better able to connect abstract knowledge.

These developmental stages in the thinking of school-age young people have some important implications for course and program planning at the elementary and secondary levels, and suggest that teachers should:

1. Make every effort to adapt subject matter to the developmental levels of their students, and not hesitate to leave out subject matter that is inappropriate for the age group.
2. When organizing subject matter for early elementary school children, think about the subject in the categories used by a young child: basically emotional and moral categories, for example, opposing forces of good-bad, big-little, brave-cowardly.[16]
3. In selecting course activities and materials for students through middle adolescence, make plans that utilize the story form as often as possible to help convey meanings.
4. Unless working with groups of cognitively mature senior high students, avoid teaching units that contain mostly abstract concepts and generalizations, and avoid putting pressure on children or early adolescents to size up external reality in large chunks.

5. Emphasize the experiential in designing new learning for adolescents and expose them to many other realities (e.g., other customs), allowing as much firsthand exposure to "otherness" as possible (e.g., guest speakers, field trips).

6. Plan course activities to allow adolescent students a great deal of opportunity for verbal and creative self-expression. Recognize that, in exploring external realities, they want to know how they relate, how they match up, how they are fitting into the scheme of things.

7. Enable and encourage students to learn in as many ways as possible—through visual forms of expression, through simulations, role-play, and play-acting.

Real-Life Themes To make the various sections of your course more appealing to students, ensure that the course topics explain the rationale for what they will be learning. Each teaching unit should have an identifiable focus or major thrust that suggests a real-life application.[17] Here are some examples of major topics with thematic emphases from several different subject areas:

Mathematics. "Formulas: how mathematics saves time."
Home Economics. "Nutrition: how to be and stay healthy."
Language Arts. "Sentence structure: making your language talk."
Chemistry. "Matter and energy: building blocks of the world around us."
History. "The Roosevelt Era: A new direction for the United States."

Each subject area has its own specific requirements, of course. A teacher designing a program in literature might decide, in devoting a unit to the study of Julius Caesar, to have this unit focus on the theme of human ambition. Julius Caesar would provide the basic content for the unit, but the emphasis would be on the concept of ambition and what it can lead to. In choosing relevant themes for the group of learners with whom you will be working, it is important to try to pick themes of current interest or relevance to that particular age group. In this high school literature class, other appropriate themes for a unit on Julius Caesar could include betrayal, loneliness, frustration, or political assassination.

Thematic Curriculum Organization Many teachers have come to feel the need for a more thorough reorganization of curriculum. Finding that the customary teaching of the separate disciplines does not help their students make coherent sense of the world they live in, or help them to understand who, and what, and why they themselves are, they see the fragmentation of knowledge in present arrangements as a factor in student disengagement from and resistance to school learning, a contributor to psychological, and all too often physical, dropping out. A leader in the move toward curriculum integration points to another possible result of the program of "diagramming complex sentences, memorizing the names and routes of European discoverers . . . the same arithmetic year after year with no particular connection to [students'] lives," namely, its "deadening effect on the lives of many teachers." He wonders whether, "had they known that this would be the routine for 30 years or more, they would not have chosen a different line of work."[18]

A number of concerns are common to various forms of curriculum reorganization, ranging from the very limited ones mentioned in the previous paragraph to multi- or interdisciplinary approaches, thematic teaching, or wholesale integration:

1. Keeping a constant connection between what students are doing and learning in school and life and work in the "real" world, the world outside school.
2. Helping students gain increasing knowledge and understanding of themselves and others in that world.
3. "[Addressing] multiple intelligences by providing complex experiences within which students can use their individual intelligences (expanding into other types of skills and modes and benefiting from other people's intelligences)."[19]

Another contributor in the same journal writes not of our capacity to become "well-rounded" but of our capacity to develop "broad intelligence," a seamless combination of the various intelligences Gardner perceives us all to have.[20]

The combining of history, geography, civics, and so on in Social Studies is one example of early *intra*-disciplinary reorganization; Whole Language, and combined math/science courses are more recent developments. In a *thematic* approach, one or more teachers in an elementary school might make a theme of high interest such as Dinosaurs the focus of work for a week or longer. Social studies would be called on to describe when and where they flourished, and why they disappeared; math would concern itself with their relative weights, and size; science with where they fit in the evolutionary chain, how they lived, what they ate, and how we know. Art would be involved in portraying the beasts and the world they inhabited. *Full integration* entails either teachers, or teachers and students deciding on a major theme or problem to investigate and then together, over as long as a semester, using information and skills from whatever fields are needed to bring enlightenment and, possibly, to suggest solutions and forms of action. Integration gives teachers the chance to work together as a team in helping students to organize their work, and lesson planning thus becomes a cooperative process.[21]

The approach has exciting possibilities both for teachers and students, and it seems particularly attractive to teachers who see computers and educational technology in general as enabling students to delve purposefully into areas of knowledge for themselves, and to spend much of their time discussing and organizing what they learn rather than sitting listening to the teacher. The problem for teachers in this entirely new situation is not so much to provide students with information as to be equipped to help them make sense out of the almost infinite amount of information they can access and the contacts they can make direct via the Internet, the World Wide Web, and e-mail. What students need are teachers who can suggest frameworks, ask the difficult questions, provide direct help on occasion, or bring individuals and groups together to share their findings and to decide what the next steps need to be. Like any truly educational experience, becoming involved in any of these new contexts is almost inevitably difficult and challenging, but the rewards, both personal and professional, can be very significant. To be a member of a team comprising experienced teachers can do much to ease the problems mentioned in Chapter 1. You will not be alone, your experience with groups of young people will be shared, the teaching will tend to be less abstract, and you can hope to gain the support, encouragement, and approval of seasoned professionals.

Course Planning to Facilitate Learning Readiness In working with young learners, an essential part of the instructional task is to attempt to connect with students' interests and frames of reference as a way of helping them move into the more concentrated or abstract portions of a particular subject that will often require them to adopt slightly, or sometimes even entirely, new frames of reference. So in organizing a sequence of major topics and activities for a course you plan to teach, it is generally advisable to structure learning events to move from the familiar to the unfamiliar, from the known to the unknown, from the experiential to the conceptual, from the practical to the theoretical. There are several things you can do at the level of course organization to promote student readiness for the progression of learning activities they will encounter, including:

1. Provide sufficient time at the beginning of a new semester to lay a thorough groundwork for the course activity that is to follow. Deliberately plan introductions to the subject that will ease students into the course framework. This is especially important when you are teaching a subject with a reputation among students as being difficult, uninteresting, or obscure. Be thinking of "advance organizers" you can use to help students perceive the essence and scope of the subject or the nature of the class activity (e.g., major course subdivisions, central questions to be answered, the student's role in the learning). In some cases you may want to use an initial unit to do ground-breaking or perception-building activities for the subject.

2. As you do course planning, try to lead off a new semester or school year with subject matter that is likely to be most familiar, manageable, and motivating for your students. Plan to use interesting and experientially accessible topics as a bridge to the unfamiliar and initially less interesting content. For example, in sequencing main topics for a secondary-level art class, an introductory unit on Looking at Old Artwork Through New Eyes is likely to be a better interest and confidence builder for students than an initial unit on Perspective, Structure, and Composition (although some art teachers might consider the latter unit a better choice). In a junior high English class, early units that plunge students into actual writing and self-expression will generally turn out

to be better motivators and indicators of where further instruction is needed than initial units on sentence structure and formal grammar.

3. In planning for a subject that involves abstract ideas, build in activities that will serve to expand student's perceptions and experiential bases before they are required to conceptualize and generalize within your subject. Allow them to have encounters with new realities (through field trips, lab experiences, discussions, media reports, simulations, films, videotapes, Web sites, games, etc.) before focusing on verbal and textbook knowledge. Work first from *experience* objectives (see Chapter 3) that allow students opportunities to explore, to talk about, and to free-associate, as a means of setting the stage for more organized and formal learning.

4. As you are putting together a course of study, design it to unfold in a manner that will leave some sense of open-endedness in the minds of students. Provide early opportunities for students to plan activities and learning focuses with you. Make question raising and problem solving a foundation of the learning experience regardless of the subject. Resist any inclination to make the class a canned learning experience. Attempt to promote student interest by building variety, inquiry, and possibilities for serendipity into the course.

Deciding Time Frames

When you have completed the work of organizing and sequencing course content, the last major step in your large-scale planning is to decide the amount of time to be spent on the various topics in the sequence. This step is essential to ensure that the various portions of the course receive the attention they deserve. Failure to make firm time allotments often results in teachers spending disproportionate amounts of time on early topics, then having to rush through the last weeks of the course because of time limitations. A common mistake of U.S. history teachers, for instance, is to spend too much time on the earliest periods in the country's development and fail to give sufficient attention to crucial happenings within the last century.

Here is an example of unit divisions for a physical science course, indicating the number of weeks to be alloted to each unit:

1. Introduction to Physical Science; Air (four weeks)
2. Water (two weeks)
3. Fuels (three weeks)
4. Forces (four weeks)
5. Chemicals (six weeks)
6. Plastics (three weeks)
7. Sound (two weeks)
8. Light (three weeks)
9. Electricity (three weeks)
10. Earth Science (one week)

11. Astronomy (eight weeks)
    Review (two weeks)

For someone beginning a career in teaching, externally prepared curriculum guides and courses of study can be helpful in suggesting not only course topics and sequences, but also the amount of time to be spent on individual units—but they can also become addictive and be used as a substitute for a teacher's own thinking and decisions about what and how to teach.

◆◆◆ APPLICATION EXERCISES ◆◆◆

1. Prepare a one-paragraph statement of general aims for a course (or program) you might teach at the secondary or elementary level. Identify the grade level for which this course would be designed. As you review this statement of course goals and intentions, does it appear to include affective as well as cognitive learning goals? Does it reflect a sensitivity to the learning needs and interests of the students for whom it is intended? Does your description of course aims indicate a concern to have this experience relate to students' lives beyond school? Rewrite as necessary to produce a more comprehensive or balanced statement.

2. Choose appropriate major topics (approximately seven to ten) to represent units of instruction for the course you have described in the previous exercise. Determine the best logical order for teaching these units. Does the sequence of topics you have arrived at take into consideration prerequisite skills or understandings that might need to be developed before it would be advisable to proceed to other learning topics? What are some other reasonable options for topic selection and unit sequencing as you begin organizing this course?

3. Consider the particular group of students for whom you are designing the course in the previous exercises. Take time to sketch some main ideas for how you would like to see this course develop, taking into consideration the sorts of learning and developmental patterns to be anticipated in students at this age group. What kinds of course introductions, early experiences (e.g., exploratory opportunities, field trips), or unit sequences would help to promote interest and meaning for students at this level?

Unit Planning

Beyond initial course-level organization, it is important for you to preplan each of the various units of instruction that make up a year or semester of teaching. A unit can be thought of as a series of interrelated lessons, placed in a certain order so individual lessons can build on one another. Unit planning helps you avoid the fragmentation of learning that often results when teachers get into a pattern of planning lessons a day at a time. Without the unit plan to aid in organizing ideas and approaches, teaching is likely to lack cohesiveness, continuity, and relevance. Regular unit planning also eases the burden of having to prepare new lessons for each day of teaching. Having worked your way through the process of course planning, preparing a unit of instruction should be an extension of important foundational work you have already accomplished. To a large extent, it involves elaborating or spelling out instructional ideas you began to develop during your initial course organization. It allows you to convert generally stated learning activities and outcomes into specific objectives and lessons.

You should begin your unit planning with a consideration of the major goals of the unit together with a listing of the content you will be teaching. Unit goals and content should actually be developed together because your stated objectives should have a bearing on what you teach, whereas unit subject matter is the context from which learning will derive. You will likely find that the more closely you examine your teaching objectives, the more insight you will have for organizing subject matter. By the same token, the more precisely you are able to specify the learning content you will be working from, the better sense you will have of appropriate objectives.

With these things in mind, the work of unit planning should consist of the following basic steps:

1. Identifying the main goals of the unit
2. Producing a content outline for the unit
3. Determining types of learning outcomes to be promoted
4. Selecting teaching strategies and activities

Identifying Unit Purpose

As you begin planning a unit of instruction, you will want to identify the main goals and purposes of this particular segment of teaching: Essentially what is it you want the students to learn from the unit? It is important to take time here to identify the main thrust of this block of instruction within the larger course or program. Being able to summarize the major purposes of the unit in a brief paragraph or to list unit goals in a succinct manner gives you a foundation from which to organize the unit and helps you to establish its main boundaries. A teacher of eighth-grade U.S. history, planning a unit on Westward Expansion, might begin with a concise statement of aims such as this:

- Students will develop a feel for the largely undeveloped nature of this country during the early nineteenth century. They will learn of the explorations, settlements, new forms of transportation, and land acquisitions that brought the United States to its present boundaries. An effort will be made to have students identify with the adventure, hardship, violence, courage, determination, and, in some cases, ruthlessness that accompanied Westward Expansion. They will also gain an appreciation for the native American cultures that were largely destroyed during this expansionist movement.

Alternatively, this teacher could directly list four or five major goals that will constitute the basis for the unit.

Students will:

1. Understand the various factors that allowed the American West to become opened to travel, fortune seeking, and new settlements.
2. Understand the ideas that caused American leaders to want to extend the existing boundaries of the United States beyond the Mississippi River (e.g., Manifest Destiny).
3. Become acquainted with some of the important personalities of the period—including native Americans—who demonstrated exceptional leadership, bravery, or "rugged individualism."
4. Become acquainted with important details of pioneer life in the western United States, including a feel for the excitement, adventure, and hardships involved in frontier exploration, the California Gold Rush, and wagon trains.
5. Be made aware of the treaty violations and forcible acquisition of Indian lands that took place during the Westward Expansion of the United States.

As another example, a sixth-grade language arts teacher, designing a unit on Thematic Writing, could decide to use the following statement of purpose as a basis for further planning:

• This unit will focus on basic techniques for developing coherent written compositions on selected topics. Students will get practice in communicating their written ideas logically and persuasively. They will be encouraged to brainstorm manageable human interest topics, and to develop their ideas using techniques that will capture and hold the attention of the reader. While one main purpose of the unit is to help students achieve cohesiveness in their writing, it will also emphasize creative self-expression. Students will have opportunities to share their writing with classmates and to engage in peer editing, and to publish what they have written in some format within the school, or via the Internet and World Wide Web.

As an alternative, this teacher might have chosen to describe the instructional intent of this unit by summarizing the main goals as follows.

Students will:

1. Come up with original and manageable topics for their writing.
2. Show a continuing interest in and demonstrate their powers of creative self-expression.
3. Demonstrate their ability to write thematic compositions that are both technically (i.e., grammatically and syntactically) and logically coherent.

4. Show that they know how to engage and hold the interest of the reader.
5. Point to effective thematic techniques in the writing of others.

The important idea here is to establish anchor points for the unit, statements of aims that are broad enough, yet sufficiently descriptive, to provide a solid basis for this series of class sessions. The learning goals you produce at this stage in your unit planning will normally be intermediate ones (see Chapter 3), specific enough to help establish the boundaries of the unit, but not yet precise enough to serve as focuses for individual lessons.

Outlining Unit Content

In conjunction with your efforts to define the main purpose of the unit, you should take time to outline the concepts or ideas that are to form the framework of the unit. As an example, the U.S. history teacher planning a unit on Westward Expansion might produce a content outline that consists of the following topics and subtopics:

I. Causes of expansion
  A. Adventure
  B. New land and new life
    1. "Rugged individualism"
  C. Manifest Destiny
II. Land exploration and acquisition
  A. The wilderness road
    1. Daniel Boone
  B. The Land Ordinance of 1785
  C. The Louisiana Purchase
    1. Lewis and Clark Expedition
  D. The Northwest Ordinance
  E. Pinckney's Treaty
  F. Manifest Destiny
  G. Violations of treaties with native Americans
    1. Jackson's Indian policies
      a. The Indian Removal Act
III. Early settlements
  A. Native American cultures
    1. Nomadic lifestyle of the Plains Indians
      a. No concept of private land ownership
  B. Fur trappers and traders
  C. Miners
    1. The California Gold Rush
      a. John Sutter
  D. Cattle ranchers
    1. Cowboys

    E. Pioneer farmers
       1. "Squatters"
          a. Squatter's rights
    F. Settlers
       1. Brigham Young
       2. John Bidwell
IV. Frontier life
    A. Pioneer homes
       1. Clearing the land
       2. Building the home
    B. Food
       1. Hunting and farming
       2. Food preservation
    C. Clothing
       1. Spinning and weaving
    D. Tools and supplies
    E. Health and illness
    F. Education
       1. Traveling teachers
       2. Rote learning
       3. Practical skills
    G. Law and order
       1. Frontier justice and lawlessness
       2. The myth of the cowboy
    H. Social activities
       1. Corn-husking contests
       2. House-raisings
    I. The clash between native American and traditional European life-
       styles
       1. Divergent concepts of land rights
       2. Unstable coexistence
       3. Disintegration and destruction of native American cultures
       4. What survived
 V. Transportation
    A. Wagon trains and early trails
    B. The Erie Canal
    C. Railroads
       1. The beginnings
       2. National network before the Civil War
       3. Transcontinental Railroad

As is the case when preparing any outline, it becomes necessary to identify
central concepts and to distinguish these from subordinate or supporting elements within your content outline. You will normally have important choices
to make in determining what content gets emphasized and what is omitted or

relegated to extensions of main ideas. Students' interests and enthusiasm should play a significant part in this process.

Determining Types of Learning

Having identified main objectives and content boundaries for the unit, you should begin thinking in more precise terms about the specific kinds of learning you will want students to derive from this unit. You will ordinarily have considerable leeway here. Although the content of a particular subject area may be fairly prescribed, what you do with that content is not likely to be laid down. The basic question you should ask yourself is: "What is it that I want my students to know, feel, and be able to do as the result of this teaching unit?" By taking time to focus on this question at this point in your planning, you help to ensure that the teaching strategies and activities you select for this group of lessons will be consistent with the learning you hope to achieve.

In some subject areas cognitive learning will be the primary focus, in other teaching areas the development of physical skills of one sort or another will be the normal emphasis, and in certain subjects and levels of teaching it will seem appropriate to give special attention to the development of student attitudes and appreciations. However, it will usually be necessary for you to specify learning focuses more precisely. Cognitive learning could mean simply the memorization of facts or it might involve the formation of concepts and generalizations. On the other hand, it might also involve the development of various kinds of thinking skills (e.g., analysis, evaluation). If learning in the affective and psychomotor domains is added in, we realize that teaching lessons might focus on one or more of at least five different varieties of learning: facts and information, ideas (concepts and generalizations), physical and manipulative skills, thinking and reflecting, or attitudes, appreciations, and dispositions.

In neglecting to identify appropriate learning focuses during your unit planning, you may end up teaching understandings when you ought to be teaching proficiencies, teaching factual material when the topic calls for concepts or thinking skills, or teaching physical skills when the primary need is for perceptual and attitudinal development. Teachers may spend inordinate amounts of time trying to transmit information, when the student's prime need is to be able to *do certain things* (e.g., in writing classes or in the gymnasium). In other instances, the failure to adequately think out just what a student needs to know may cause teachers to feature performance skills prematurely or at the expense of important understandings (e.g., in physical education or industrial arts). It is also quite common, and disastrous, for teachers to attempt to force cognitive or skill learning when the initial focus should be on affective learning, that is, helping students get to like, feel at home with, become interested in, and to understand and accept the need to learn certain subject matter (e.g., in math, history, or physical education).

Thus, taking into consideration unit purposes, unit content, and student levels, the following are some of the kinds of things history teachers might want their students to know, feel, and be able to do in connection with the developing unit on Westward Expansion:

1. *Know facts*, for example:
   - Lewis and Clark explored the Oregon Territory in 1804
   - Native American inhabitants were the first true Americans
   - Pinckney's Treaty settled a conflict with Spain in the Southwest
   - Farmers were granted title to land through "squatter's rights"
2. *Form big ideas*, for example:
   - Rugged individualism, nationalism, Manifest Destiny (concepts)
   - The transcontinental railroad was a major factor in opening the U.S. West to travel from the east (generalization)
   - The life of the Western frontier helped form certain American character traits that continue to endure (generalization)
   - Events of the Westward Movement caught international attention and contributed to European immigration to the United States (generalization)
3. *Develop attitudes and appreciations*, for example:
   - This was a fascinating time in U.S. history
   - Many of the men and women who helped settle the West were unusually brave and hardy people
   - We owe a great deal to those early pioneers and explorers who helped extend our country to its present boundaries
   - Along the way some of these early Americans did things to the native Americans and other countries that were cruel and barbarous
4. *Practice higher thinking skills*, for example:
   - What kinds of people would have been interested in joining a wagon train?
   - How did Jacksonian democracy contribute to the spirit of the Westward Movement? (cause-and-effect analysis)
   - What were the most favorable outcomes of the Westward Movement in U.S. history? What negative effects were connected with it? (evaluation)
   - How might U.S. history have been different if the Erie Canal and the Transcontinental Railroad had not been developed? (synthesis or divergent thinking)
   - What factors led to the Civil War? (convergent thinking)

It is apparent that the lessons in this unit center on one or more types of cognitive learning. Units in other areas may be aimed primarily at the development of skills or language arts), although skill learning always has an important cognitive base. Sensitivity to such distinctions is important because these different types of learning require different teaching techniques and strategies in order to achieve the intended learning.

Selecting Teaching Methods and Activities

The topic of teaching methods and models is a large and complex one.[22] As a beginning teacher, what is essential is that you think of teaching as encouraging and promoting learning, an activity whose long-term effectiveness depends in large measure on the willing cooperation of the learner. There are a number of ways of going about teaching, and you need to be aware of and equipped to use a range of basic techniques and strategies, which you can and should extend and add to as your career moves along. A summary of principles for lesson organization by two eminent researchers is useful to keep in mind in this process. They sum up their findings by writing that

> Achievement is maximized when teachers not only actively present material, but structure it by beginning with overviews, advance organizers, or review of objectives; outlining the content and signaling transitions between lesson parts; calling attention to main ideas; summarizing subparts of the lesson as it proceeds; and reviewing main ideas at the end. Organizing concepts and analogies helps learners link the new to the already familiar. . . .
>
> Overviews and outlines help [students] to develop learning sets to use. . . . Rule-example-rule patterns and internal summaries tie specific information items to integrative concepts. Summary reviews integrate and reinforce the learning of main points.[23]

As you set out to decide on the best teaching methods for a series of lessons, there are two basic questions that call for continuing consideration: namely, (1) "What techniques should I use to promote specific types of learning?" and (2) "Should I use a direct or indirect teaching approach?"

Matching Teaching Techniques to Types of Learning It has been emphasized that the teaching of physical skills requires different teaching techniques than the teaching of factual understandings, that the fostering of student attitudes and values will call for a different teaching approach from that used to promote thinking and problem-solving skills, and so forth. The following are some concise guidelines for goal-directed teaching in five main areas of learning:

Teaching Facts

1. Organize the material into a maximum of four or five chunks, or learning units (e.g., spelling words, foreign language dialogues, historical events, lines of poetry or music) per learning encounter.
2. Help the students see relationships between the new information and what they already know.
3. Organize complex material into appropriate sequences of component parts.

4. Arrange for students to make use of new information in practical contexts over an extended period of time with provisions for immediate feedback.
5. Give students opportunities to independently evaluate the adequacy and accuracy of the new information they acquire for themselves.

Teaching Concepts and Generalizations

1. Establish the level at which students are able to grasp the concept (i.e., concrete or formal levels).
2. Teach students a strategy for distinguishing between examples and nonexamples of concepts (students functioning at concrete cognitive levels will attend to perceptible properties, formal thinking students to defining attributes).
3. Provide sequenced sets of examples and nonexamples in teaching and testing.
4. Emphasize the defining attributes to enable students to understand the concept.
5. Establish the correct terminology for the concept and its attributes.
6. Provide feedback for student responses to these new ideas.
7. Provide opportunities for students to apply newly learned concepts in understanding principles and solving problems.

Teaching Thinking and Problem-Solving Skills

1. Provide opportunities for students to engage in ways of thinking such as explaining, predicting, comparing, generalizing, hypothesizing, and evaluating in each unit.
2. Stress students' abilities to be sensitive and discriminating observers as the foundation on which all their other thinking skills are based.
3. Make regular use of questions that encourage reflective thinking in the classroom.
4. Develop patterns of content learning that sometimes require students to progress from factual, to analytical, to creative levels of thought, and other patterns that require the same levels but in reverse order.
5. Help students identify, and define solvable problems.
6. Give students initial help in analyzing and synthesizing information they would use in problem solving.
7. Promote basic forms of self-expression (mathematical, verbal, physical) as a means of fostering divergent thinking and creative ideas.

Teaching Physical and Manipulative Skills

1. Analyze the skill in terms of the learner's abilities and developmental level.
2. Provide a good demonstration of the skill to be acquired.
3. Provide instructions, or a plan, for carrying out the sequence of actions.
4. Arrange for students to practice tightly organized skills (e.g., diving) as a whole; loosely organized skills (e.g., football, baseball) as components.

5. Make the conditions of practice as close as possible to the conditions under which the skill will actually be used.
6. Make practice periods relatively brief, but distribute them over a good number of days at short intervals (except where fatigue is a factor).
7. Provide informative feedback and correct inadequate responses.

Teaching Attitudes and Values

1. Provide exemplary models for students to emulate.
2. Provide for pleasant emotional experiences in connection with the school situations for which attitude changes are sought.
3. Arrange for students to receive accurate information about persons, objects, or situations toward which attitude changes are sought.
4. Use group techniques (e.g., role playing, group decision making) to facilitate commitment to group-held attitudes and values (particularly effective at the elementary level).
5. Arrange for appropriate practice opportunities within the classroom, school, and community environments.[24]

Direct and Indirect Teaching In each of the preceding areas, the question is always whether learning will best be achieved by direct, largely teacher-directed methods, or by way of a more learner-centered, discovery-based approach. *Direct teaching*, sometimes referred to as expository or didactic teaching, is primarily a teacher-centered approach in which the teacher does most of the talking and performing. It tends to be thought of as the easiest type of teaching for those beginning their teaching career, and although it is frequently overemployed, especially when it is used primarily as a way of transmitting facts or as a means of control, it has considerable utility in the following situations:

1. When you want to introduce students to material that is quite unfamiliar, difficult, not readily available in written or visual materials, or not immediately inspiring. Your teaching in this mode can be made more effective by well-timed and focused use of film, videocassette, or computer-generated display. As good software becomes more available, and classes become increasingly diverse "direct teaching" may mean that the computer does the actual "instruction" and the teacher functions in the more complex roles of organizer, instigator, collaborator, individual tutor, and evaluator of learning rather than as that of straightforward teller.
2. When students need careful, detailed, and extended explanations (see Chapter 7 on techniques for providing these).
3. When you need to provide an introduction to a learning task or activity that you are going to teach by a more indirect method.
4. When your aim is to help students see connections between new ideas and situations, and between what they already know and new information.[23]

5. When you want to demonstrate how something works (as with friction, or air pressure, for example), or how students should act (as with some athletic skill), or how to achieve a certain result (as in art, shop, or music).

Indirect teaching places primary emphasis on students acquiring knowledge and understanding rather than on teachers inculcating them. Cooperative learning (see Chapter 8), pair or small group discussion, individual or group projects, and the interactive, inquiry method, which are examples of this approach, are all based on the premise that questions and perceived problems should properly precede answers in the learning process.[25] The teacher's functions are vital—but different—from those outlined for direct teaching. For this strategy to be effective, the teacher needs to give careful thought to establishing a framework flexible enough to allow students considerable choice and independence, but firm enough to ensure that significant learning is taking place in the appropriate area, and that results actually, in some form, demonstrate this (see more on evaluation in Chapter 10). Once the students are engaged in the process, the teacher has to be able to act as a resource, as "the guide on the side," as a troubleshooter when the students encounter difficulties, whether cognitive or affective, that they don't seem to be able to resolve by themselves.

These indirect ways of promoting learning are more difficult both to set up and to keep on track, but since they recognize the reality that students, people, have to *construct* knowledge and develop skills (rather than merely absorb information), it is important that you yourself develop the skills that are called for, while recognizing that building them up will almost certainly have to be a gradual and piecemeal process.[26] In general, indirect teaching is especially valuable:

1. When you are particularly concerned with higher-order thinking skills (see discussion on page 66).
2. When students need to work at their own pace, and/or on topics or in fields that they have been able to select.
3. When a learning objective calls for students to engage in problem solving.
4. When your goal is student interaction and social development.
5. When you sense that students need a change and are anxious to get on under their own steam.

Your Developing Style While you are working to achieve a base of confidence and security as a beginning teacher, you will most likely find a direct style of teaching to be most frequently suitable to your developing needs and abilities (see Chapter 5 on getting established in the classroom).

However, as you think in long-range terms about where you would like to be in several years as a teacher (see Chapter 12 on personal plans for professional growth), the ability to perform well in an indirect teaching mode is something to shoot for. As a general approach in teaching young learners, it is essential to work from where they are to where you want them to be insofar as new learning is concerned. This means being able to use indirect or learner-centered techniques to advantage in many of the things you teach. Chapter 6, which discusses motivation, suggests ideas for getting students involved in new learning that utilize students' existing perceptions, interests, and experiences as starting points. Also, Chapter 8 provides guidelines for communicating with students in an interactive mode, interactive communication being the basis for an indirect teaching style.

Even within lecture formats, it is quite possible to talk *to* and *with* students as opposed to talking *at* them about things you want them to know or do. Chapter 7 deals with strategies for providing students with sound and meaningful explanations, essentially a teacher-centered activity. It suggests ways of providing learner-paced, understandable explanations as another basic skill for classroom teachers.

Selecting Unit Activities   The final phase of unit planning is to select and organize the learning activities that students will engage in during the course of the unit. What will you and your students be doing from the beginning to the end of the unit to bring about the desired learning? Depending on the subject, the students, and your own inclinations, there are many kinds of activities you can utilize to promote student learning in your classes, ranging from more conventional activities such as lectures, narrations, teacher-class discussions, films, lab exercises, and independent seatwork to valuable activities like debates, field trips, small group discussions, simulations, guided imagery sessions, story form, visits from outside speakers, creative writing assignments, and so forth.

In some teaching areas, the pattern of learning activity will be fairly well established by the nature of the subject. Following introductory lectures or demonstrations, industrial arts and technology teachers at the high school level, for example, generally have students working on individual projects for the bulk of the learning time. Physical education units, mathematics units, and certain teaching units at the elementary level that draw heavily on programmed materials (e.g., reading) also fall into this category. In most teaching areas, though, you can expect to need to make choices as to appropriate activities for your classes.

Here are some general guidelines for selecting and sequencing learning activities within a typical teaching unit:

1. Have a deliberate progression of activities, a scheme for how the unit is to unfold, that is, a beginning stage, a developmental period, and a culminating phase. Either plan this with your students or help them understand the developmental plan of the unit from the beginning. Try to make sure students can see that they are working toward a clear goal for some intelligible reason. When possible, have them involved in ongoing projects or investigations related to the unit.

2. Allow ample time for an introductory or exploratory period at the beginning of the unit. Use these early sessions to arouse students' interests and to find out what present knowledge and abilities they may already possess related to the topic. Whenever possible, give students opportunities at the beginning of the unit to suggest projects and activities for succeeding meetings.

3. Vary activities from lesson to lesson to maintain variety and play into different styles of learning. If you plan a teacher-centered activity for one session, arrange to have a small-group or independent-learning project for the next. Avoid falling into a pattern of sameness with your activities. Keep students interested by challenging them to suggest and attempt constructive new activities. Keep an active file of learning activities that you have used successfully, and others that have been recommended and you intend to try.

4. Consider whether to use any kind of audiovisual aid. Before deciding to do so, be clear what benefit you intend students to gain from seeing or hearing it. Why will you be using this particular videotape, film, CD-ROM, or videodisc? As a "grabber"? As a reinforcement of a concept? As a dramatization of some episode? As a source of information? As a provoker of questions? Will you use all of it? Which part(s)? More than once? When you are satisfied that the tape (or laserdisc, or computer projection) will serve a definite educational purpose and won't just be a substitute for teaching, you will want to consider whether to give the class any guidance in what to look out for, or prime them with a question or two to be answered as a result of the experience.

5. Give careful attention to how you want to end the unit and to the sorts of activities that will provide good closure. Plan culminating activities that will give students opportunities to size up what they have learned from the unit and to report on any special projects on which they have been working. Select evaluational activities that are good logical conclusions to the unit and that students will perceive as extensions of the unit activities.

6. In designing any learning activity, be sure to give careful thought to what the student is to do during that session. Try to have a minimum of activities in which the students' role is to simply attend to someone else for long periods of time. Once you feel confident in your ability to control the class, find constructive activities that will regularly get students out of their seats. In math classes, for example, where physical movement is often minimal, sending students to the board in rows can give them a chance to work in a different way, give rise to good-natured competition between the rows, and make it possible for you to see how students are progressing.

7. In designing activities for units that involve skill development, be mindful that skill learning of any sort requires sufficient practice. Whether the focus is physical skills, math skills, writing skills, or concept development skills, it is important to build ample practice periods

(with feedback) into your lesson sequences. Remember also to provide adequate opportunities for students to conceptualize and visualize skill operations before they are expected to practice them.

To illustrate the kind of activity planning and sequencing that should constitute the final stage of unit organization, the following is a ten-day activity plan for the sample unit on Westward Expansion.

Day 1 (Large-group discussion) Initiate the unit with a teacher-led discussion centered on a large wall map of the United States. Discussion will revolve around the drastically changed boundaries of the United States as we move from the late eighteenth to the middle nineteenth centuries. Invite students to speculate on how this large-scale national expansion could occur in such a short time historically. Ask students to share what they may already know about U.S. expansion as an informal pretest of existing knowledge and interest. Ask students to begin thinking of a topic or question they might investigate on this subject. Provide some examples.

Day 2 (Film discussion) Show a film or tape depicting the exploration and territorial advances into the Western United States in the eighteenth and nineteenth centuries. Follow up with a teacher-led discussion of significant points from the film.

Day 3 (Small-group activity) Have students work in groups of three or four to come up with reasons why there was so much sentiment for western expansion at this time in our history. Assign students textbook reading to compare their group inferences with the views of historians.

Day 4 (Teacher-centered presentation) Prepare a teacher presentation that sketches as graphically as possible some of the landmark events of western expansion, for example, war with Mexico, the Donner Party, the Gold Rush, the completion of the Transcontinental Railroad, and so forth. Assign textbook reading that asks students to acquire more pertinent detail about these events.

Day 5 (Guided-imagery lesson) Conduct a large-group guided-imagery session in which students are helped to imagine and to feel what it would be like to travel west on a wagon train, to live in a mining camp, to be involved in a battle with native Americans, and so forth. Demonstrate and assign students a simulation activity for the next day.

Day 6 (Simulation activity) Have small groups of students simulate (or dramatize) some of the frontier events or situations that were the subject of yesterday's guided-imagery session.

Day 7 (Videotape discussion) Use a documentary videotape to portray today's cowboy and life on the range in the modern West. In a follow-up discussion, have students compare conditions today with those of the nineteenth century.

Day 8 (Large-group discussion) Conduct a large-group discussion that asks students to consider the moral standards of this period in U.S. history. Were some of these early Americans ruthless in the pursuit of their own passions and interests? How should we view our treatment of the Indian nations and of their sometimes violent reactions during this period? What examples of noble and honorable behavior can be cited?

Day 9 (Small-group and large-group reports) Have students give feedback on a topic or question they have been investigating. Have them share their findings in groups of three to four students, then have each group select one report to be shared with the whole class.

Day 10 (Evaluation activity) Do an evaluation exercise that asks students to (1) identify noteworthy personalities of the period and to indicate what their main contributions were; (2) detail a progression of main events or accomplishments that contributed to the opening of the U.S. West to settlement; and (3) describe an event or life condition that struck them as particularly exciting, challenging, or unusual and have them discuss how they might have responded to that situation had they been living then.

◆◆◆ **A P P L I C A T I O N   E X E R C I S E S** ◆◆◆

1. Select a suitable topic for an instructional unit within a program or course you expect to teach. Write a summary description of the unit, indicating the main goals and purposes of that particular block of teaching. As you examine this summary, are your goals descriptive enough to qualify as intermediate-level objectives? Does your statement provide for a range of learning outcomes, affective as well as cognitive? Rewrite if necessary to make your description more appropriate.

2. Produce a content outline for the unit of instruction you have described in Exercise 1. Follow standard outline form in specifying main ideas in relation to subordinate or supporting ideas. Having completed this content outline, analyze it to determine whether it represents a proper logical sequence of learning topics. Rearrange as necessary to make the topical order more appropriate.

3. Reexamine the content outline you produced in Exercise 2 in relation to your description of unit objectives from Exercise 1. What main types of learning outcomes would you be seeking to produce if you were to teach this unit to students at the level you expect to work (i.e., facts, concepts and generalizations, thinking skills, psychomotor skills, attitudes, and values)? What are some of the specific teaching strategies you would employ to promote these particular kinds of learning?

4. Describe a sequence of learning activities you might use to teach the unit under consideration in the previous exercises. As you attempt to

specify activities and sequences for this series of lessons, make an effort to apply appropriate logical and psychological criteria for organizing learning experiences at the grade level you will be teaching.

Lesson Planning

Having done the initial work of preplanning at the course and unit levels, many necessary decisions and much of your basic lesson structure should already be in place by the time you get to the lesson planning stage. Lesson planning should be a practical, highly concentrated activity. Besides being an opportunity for you to pinpoint the specific objectives, activities, and teaching strategies you will employ, a lesson plan should include key reminders to help you stay organized and focused during a lesson. As a beginning teacher, your lesson plans will probably need to be more highly structured than they will after you have taught for several years. The actual format of written plans though, may vary depending on the subject, the nature of class activities, and the kinds of students you are working with (one general model is presented later in this section). Some schools systems may require new teachers to use the system's lesson plan form, particularly when being evaluated by supervisors. However, for your own purposes as a developing teacher, the format of the lesson plan is less critical than the quality of your planning and the practical value you derive from it.

One of the most important functions of lesson planning is to get you to think through a lesson before you actually teach it. On beginning a class period, most competent teachers have mental images of how the lesson should unfold. They have a mental script to follow. Creative teachers are flexible enough to be able to modify that script as situations might require, but their ability to do a simulated "walk-through" before teaching a lesson helps to keep them on track once the class period begins. Some experienced teachers are able to rely on these internal plans to carry them through a lesson with a minimum of written reminders. Most early-career teachers, on the other hand, find it necessary to supplement their internal rehearsing with written plans.

Another practical reason for doing regular lesson planning is so you will be able to work effectively within the time constraints of a single lesson. By working out ahead the approximate amount of time to be devoted to various classroom events, you stand a better chance of being able to fit essential teaching activities and necessary classroom tasks together into what may have to be one short class period.

Some of the more important elements that should be included in a functional lesson plan are (1) a statement of the lesson goal and objective; (2) a concise description of lesson activities and teaching procedures in the sequences they will occur; and (3) reminders of things, external to the lesson itself, that need to be accomplished before or during the class period.

Pinpointing Lesson Goal

Your unit plan should have provided a solid foundation for the series of lessons with which you are presently involved. Now, as you begin to concentrate on activities for a single class period, it is important to be able to identify as specifically as possible the learning goal for this particular lesson. There are good reasons for taking time to do this. For one, some lessons are designed to promote measurable understandings or performance skills. These lessons need to be directed toward particular objectives. Also, a common tendency of new teachers is to try to do too much in a single class period. Their lesson concentration is often too broad as well as being too deep, in the sense that it tries to include excessive detail. Having a precise lesson objective not only defines what you want students to get from the lesson, but it helps you to keep your learning topics manageable for both you and your students. As an example, if a unit-level objective for a U.S. government class is to have students "know the function of the administrative branch of our government," this intermediate objective will likely need to be reduced to one more suitable as a lesson objective, which might be for students to "be able to enumerate the various powers of the presidency."

Although it is important to have an identifiable learning focus, it may not always be necessary to state your lesson objective in measurable terms. Of course that will depend on the subject matter and on your own teaching goals. For some lessons, the learning focus—the goal—may be deliberately broader than for others. As mentioned in Chapter 3, there are learning situations in which it will be counterproductive to prespecify intended learning outcomes in performance terms. When your intent is for students to have exploratory or perception-building experiences, these occasions may call for experience objectives rather than tight performance objectives.

Mapping Class Activities and Teaching Procedures

The heart of your lesson plan should be a concise description of lesson activities in the order they will occur. This progression of teaching events should be based on the same kinds of logical and psychological criteria that apply to course and unit organization. Generally, a well-organized lesson proceeds in three stages: a beginning or introduction, a main body, and a closing phase. Your effort should be to have the lesson unfold in a way that maximizes student interest and involvement.

In addition to being a time for attendance taking and other initial chores, the beginning stage of a lesson sets the tone for the teaching and learning that will take place during that class period. The way you begin a lesson often has a big effect on the success of that lesson. Your lesson introduction (or "set") should be designed to get students into an appropriate frame of mind for the learning that is to take place. This introductory set provides an appropriate focus for the lesson. It may consist of references to a previous lesson, a current event, or a relevant problem the lesson will address. An interesting object, photo, or story could also be an effective "grabber"—the actual attention-getter—at the beginning of a class session. For a skill- or performance-based lesson, appropriate beginnings may entail efforts to motivate students to carefully attend to the skill items they will encounter. In contrast to conceptually oriented lesson introductions in science or history, effective lesson sets in music or physical education might involve getting learners fired up to seek perfection in their performances or projects. See Chapters 5, 6, and 9 for additional ideas on initiating learning in your classes.

At some point in this introductory phase, it is often effective to provide the class with what is generally referred to as an "advance organizer," mapping out at the beginning of a unit or lesson what lies ahead in the way of ideas, experiences, and activities.

The central activity of the lesson should constitute the main body of your lesson plan. In a content-based lesson in which the approach is direct instruction, teacher presentations and explanations often predominate in this portion of the lesson. If the class session is to be performance- or activity-centered, the middle part of the lesson will ordinarily be devoted to practice periods or student projects (following initial teacher explanations or demonstrations), in which your main role will be to work with individuals or groups of students, and to check on their progress. In either case, it is important to preplan the succession of steps in the learning activity. With a teacher-centered lesson, it will be necessary for you to give primary attention to the specifics of the content you are presenting and the route you will take to solidify student understanding. When there is subject matter to be thought about or mastered, this portion of the lesson plan should contain not only a brief outline of content to be covered, but locatable reminders of key teaching maneuvers you intend to employ. You will find it worthwhile to have thought out and noted down *key questions* to ask and to mark points in the lesson where deliberate transitions or changes of approach are in order. Chapters 7, 8, and 9 provide more detail on teaching strategies and tactics that have special relevance for lesson planning.

In planning daily lessons it is also highly advisable to give deliberate attention to the wrap-up activities ("closure") that will round out a particular lesson segment. Instead of allowing the clock or the bell to end a lesson, it is important to conclude it with summary activities, plans and assignments for succeeding lessons, or some other form of deliberate closure. As the teacher you may have comments or summary remarks to make at the conclusion of a lesson, or you may decide to elicit pertinent comments or summaries from students. It is important that your planning allows for time at the end of a class period to achieve effective closure on lesson activities.

Incorporating Noninstructional Agendas

A final aspect of purposeful lesson planning is to be able to combine instructional activities with necessary managerial and support tasks within a crowded classroom schedule. There will often be materials to be procured, announcements to be made, students to be contacted, paperwork to be completed, and so forth, or there may be behavior management moves you want to make with a particular class (e.g., a new seating arrangement). It is important to be able to work these preliminary or extrainstructional elements into your class sessions so they flow along with rather than interfere with your teaching (see Chapter 9 on classroom management). By preplanning how you will incorporate these noninstructional items into your classroom activities, you help to ensure they get proper attention, while remaining subordinate to your lesson.

◆◆◆ **SAMPLE LESSON PLAN** ◆◆◆

INTRODUCTORY ALGEBRA

Goal: Solving simple equations with one variable using four operations.

Objective (if applicable): Students will be able to solve simple equations by subtraction, division, addition, and multiplication.

Set: "You need to know about equations because they are used in all sorts of situations, for example . . . " Or, better, provide an example of an equation being used in a familiar setting.

Advance Organizer: "Today we're going to start work on equations using four operations you are already familiar with: addition, subtraction, multiplication, and division."

Procedure
A. Comparing Equations and Balances
  1. Use a small weighing balance to represent the two equal sides of an equation—show an equation to be like two weights on a balance (five minutes).
B. Solving Simple Equations
  1. Using balance analogy, show how you can perform like operations (subtraction, division, etc.) to both sides of an equation without disrupting the balance. (five minutes).
  2. Work several examples of each operation with student participation (ten minutes).

Subtracting
$$3x + 2 - 2 = 11 - 2$$
$$3x = 9$$

Dividing
$$\frac{3x}{3} = \frac{9}{3}$$
$$x = 3$$

Adding
$$x - 6 = 18$$
$$x - 6 + 6 = 18 + 6$$
$$x = 24$$

Multiplying $\frac{1}{4}x = 5$

$$4 \times \frac{1}{4}x = 4 \times 5$$

$$x = 20$$

Combining (use this exercise)

$$\frac{2}{3}x - 4 = \frac{1}{4}x + 6$$

3. Have students independently solve practice exercises involving all four operations (ten minutes)
4. Send students to the board in rows to solve given examples using all four operations (fifteen minutes)
5. Combining the operations

Closure: Select students to summarize the four operations.

Evaluation: Observation of student progress during practice exercises and more formal check of tomorrow's homework.

Reminders

1. Lesson materials: weighing balance, overhead transparencies.
2. Makeup tests: Cheryl, Philip.
3. Send home notices for Back to School Night.
4. See custodian about broken chairs.

NOTE: This lesson could be taught more indirectly by using teacher questions at key points to promote a more inductive or guided-discovery route to this new skill.

◆◆◆   **A P P L I C A T I O N   E X E R C I S E S**   ◆◆◆

1. Identify an appropriate topic for a one-day lesson in a subject you would be qualified to teach. Having selected the lesson topic, prepare a lesson plan featuring a direct mode of instruction and containing the following elements:
   a. A learning objective that describes the lesson focus in nonambiguous terms
   b. A description of an original learning set for initiating the lesson
   c. A brief outline of lesson content together with a sequential sketch of main procedures to be employed in teaching that content

   d. A description of the intended means for bringing the lesson to a close
   e. Miscellaneous reminders of evaluation plans, necessary materials, time allotments, or other pertinent items
2. Consider the changes that would be required in the lesson plan if you decided to employ indirect or guided-discovery strategies rather than direct instructional techniques in teaching this lesson. What lesson elements would remain essentially the same? Which portions would require substantial changes or additions? What would be the role of teacher questions in the new lesson plan? Would time allotments for the various lesson segments need to be changed? Rework the lesson plan you developed in Exercise 1 to make it a plan for indirect instruction, possibly incorporating the use of computers by the students.

Planning for Individual Differences

As a classroom teacher, your instructional plans will ordinarily be group-based, designed to accommodate the learning needs of the average student in a typical class. A common frustration for beginning teachers is the early realization that what they consider their well-designed lessons often fail to engage students with learning and emotional needs that depart significantly from the norm. Some students always seem to be ahead of the game when it comes to understanding lesson content and completing assignments, and take a genuine interest in what they are set to do, while others consistently lag behind the rest of the class, and are inattentive or bored. This is not a new problem, of course, but increasingly teachers have been trying to find answers for the instructional problem caused by individual differences.

No plan, however well thought out, will ever be able to meet all the educational needs and interests of all students all the time, but there is much you can do in your planning to deal with the inescapable fact that, even in a class official tracked "homogeneously" there are students with widely different abilities, interests, and motivation. The need to develop strategies that effectively deal with what has always been the real situation in classrooms has been greatly increased by recent changes in the law and interpretations of the Fourteenth Amendment to the Constitution. Since the passage of the Individuals with Disabilities Education Act of 1991 (IDEA), schools are required to "assure to the maximum extent appropriate [that] disabled children are educated with children who are not disabled." They must limit the teaching of students in separate classes to cases "when the nature and severity of the disability is such that education in regular classes with the use of supplementary aids and services cannot be achieved satisfactorily." Several subsequent court decisions have laid it down that children *with* disabilities or without must be taught in the same classrooms unless those with a disability either cannot derive any academic or *social* benefit or are so disruptive that they interfere with the learning of the rest of the class.

Inclusion and Inclusive Classrooms

The implementation of IDEA, by means of what have become known as *inclusion* and *inclusive classrooms*, makes differentiated direct teaching (sometimes known as adaptive instruction)[27] and indirect teaching virtually essential. The former means that, within a general plan, the teacher arranges components that give extra help to those who need it and extra opportunity and challenge to those who need and can handle them. The latter is briefly described above. Neither of these is easy in classrooms in which the academic ability level already differs considerably, and the quality of attention and behavior may be equally varied. In addition teachers now have to be prepared to meet the needs of students with a variety of learning disabilities, of children with Down syndrome or cerebral palsy, of young people who may be blind, deaf, or wheelchair-bound. Many schools have worked to create integrated, inclusive classrooms in which all students can feel at home and function. They have often achieved this by arranging for the teacher with special education qualifications to work in the same classroom as the "regular" teacher, but two specialists in the area make it clear that major changes will need to be made in the future:

> In inclusive schools, the roles and responsibilities of general and special educators must change in fundamental ways. In addition, a shift has to occur in how educators collaborate—from conferring only about individual students' problems to making the curriculum available to a diverse group of students, including those with disabilities.[28]

Whatever the situation in the school at which you start your teaching career, the following basic strategies will stand you in good stead:

1. Find opportunities to work with individual students. As you develop workable classroom routines, the ability to attend to individuals during the course of a lesson can become a well-integrated part of your total teaching pattern. Make what can be brief personal exchanges occasions for offering encouragement, constructive criticism, correction, and inspiration. Taking time to look over students' papers, to comment on their progress, and to suggest possible avenues for improvement almost always encourage any and all students.

2. Arrange for students to work on various tasks individually or in small groups under your guidance. In such a setting, one group may be working in a corner of the room on a simulation. A second group might be working in another part of the room to prepare a report. One student might be tutoring another, and at the same time, individual

students be involved at their desks on special projects. Others might be reading, or clustered around a computer discussing what they see, and making plans. Group students according to interests, abilities, or special needs. For example, allow students with similar interests and goals to work together to solve a particular problem or to pursue a certain type of research. Keep your grouping patterns flexible to avoid creating a stratified social system. Allow grouping patterns to change, or intervene inconspicuously to change them, in keeping with the evolving interests, problems, and needs of students.[29]

3. Provide differentiated assignments. For example, in a mathematics class you may assign slower or less able students fewer problems. Or, in history and literature classes you might provide differentiated reading materials, based on demonstrated reading levels of students.

4. Design instructional packages that allow students to work independently, with or without a computer, on course units. These are sometimes referred to as learning modules. Each module or instructional package should include (1) an objective; (2) a set of directions and suggestions for proceeding through the unit; (3) materials for study; (4) frames of programmed material in which students proceed in small steps to apply what they have learned, thereafter receiving immediate feedback on their progress; and (5) a final mastery test. Students who meet the standard are then allowed to proceed to the next unit. Those who do not pass are given remedial assignments until they are able to meet the criterion.

5. Encourage students to help one another. Students often learn very effectively from each other. Take advantage of this fact by having students who have mastered a concept or skill coach other students who are experiencing difficulty. This kind of assistance will free you to give your attention to other individuals. It also allows students to share their talents and to practice communicating their ideas to others. It helps them as well as the beneficiaries to learn the subject more thoroughly.

6. Use a variety of materials. Provide reading and other instructional materials that are suitable to the various interests and ability levels represented in the class. Make sure these materials are available when individual students need them.

 ## A SUMMARY OF GUIDELINES FOR INSTRUCTIONAL PLANNING

1. Your instructional planning should proceed from long-range to intermediate to short-range plans. The planning you do at each level should be an amplification of the next longer-range plan of which it is a part.

2. Course-level planning involves identifying course content and goals, then organizing and sequencing the content to make it most teachable.

3. Subject matter for instruction should be organized logically to make it internally coherent and psychologically to take into account the learning styles, preferences, and abilities of students.

4. Regular unit planning allows you to bridge the gap between course organization and daily lesson planning. It involves structuring groups of lessons around a central topic or project, thus providing system to your teaching.

5. Having determined the objectives and content boundaries for a particular unit, the remaining task of unit planning is to prescribe lesson focuses, learning activities, and teaching strategies for that series of lessons.

6. As an extension of previous unit planning, lesson planning should be a highly practical activity that allows you to structure the sequence of activities for single class periods. It should be an opportunity for you to define in precise terms the focus of particular lessons and to rehearse what you intend shall happen.

7. A main consideration in unit and lesson planning is the adoption of teaching methods that will help the particular group of students you are working with. Two central questions are important here: (1) What teaching strategies will best promote given categories of learning (e.g., facts, concepts, mental and physical skills, attitudes), and (2) would it be best to use a direct or indirect approach in teaching a proposed lesson to a particular group of students? Will you incorporate audiovisual material?

8. Resolve to plan in detail as you start your teaching. Spontaneous ideas often come to the minds of experienced teachers as they are teaching because they have a wide familiarity both with the subject matter they are teaching and with students in classrooms. These may occur to you, too—but plan as if they won't!

9. Make a consistent effort to take account of individual differences in students as you do your instructional planning. Although there are no simple answers to the problem created by individual student differences, there are a number of strategies you can adopt that can help with this increasingly difficult challenge.

◆◆◆ SUGGESTED ACTIVITIES AND QUESTIONS ◆◆◆

1. What are some important things that all good lesson plans have in common?

2. Although it is generally held that sound planning is essential to effective teaching, some educators would maintain that *lesson plans* are made to be ignored. How would you deal with this apparent contradiction?

3. What are some of the most important decisions that a teacher makes in planning for instruction?

4. Discuss similarities in planning for teaching and planning for a vacation trip. What are some main differences?

5. What is the difference between the logical and the psychological organization of content for teaching? Discuss the main importance of each type of organization.
6. For what kinds of teaching situations are lesson plans most important? Are there times when formal planning may be less essential? Discuss.

Notes

1. Richard Kindsvatter, William Wilen, and Margaret Ishler, *Dynamics of Effective Teaching*. White Plains, N.Y.: Longman, 1988, p. 60.
2. George J. Posner and Alan N. Rudnitsky, *Course Design: A Guide to Curriculum Development for Teachers*. White Plains, N.Y.: Longman, 1986, p. 2.
3. Some would recommend that large-scale planning start with the determination of central course topics, after which learning goals are derived from a consideration of main understandings, skills, and attitudes that are to result from the study of these major concepts or themes. As you will likely find in your own planning, learning content and learning goals tend to be two sides of the same coin. For conscientious planners, it is difficult to think of one's subject matter without thinking of what you want students to learn from it. And vice versa, it is usually difficult to stipulate goals for teaching apart from considerations of the content that one will be teaching. As you gain experience in planning, you will be able to decide which approach works best for you.
4. This list of sample topics and the subsequent arrangement for "clustering" and sequencing them are from Posner and Rudnitsky, *Course Design*, pp. 113–14.
5. Posner and Rudnitsky, *Course Design*, p. 116.
6. Richard Hamilton and Elizabeth Ghatela, *Learning and Instruction*. New York: McGraw-Hill, 1994. See Chapter 6, "Piagetian and Neo-Piagetian Theories of Cognitive Development," pp. 206–251.
7. Kieran Egan, *Educational Development*. New York: Oxford University Press, 1979, p.7.
8. Egan, *Educational Development*, p. 15.
9. Egan, *Educational Development*, p. 18.
10. Egan, *Educational Development*, p. 31.
11. Egan, *Educational Development*, p. 47.
12. Egan, *Educational Development*, p. 45.
13. Egan, *Educational Development*, p. 52.
14. Egan, *Educational Development*, p. 51.
15. Egan, *Educational Development*, p. 56.
16. Egan, *Educational Development*, p. 26.
17. The idea of providing basic themes when specifying course topics and several of the topic examples that follow are from Kenneth H. Hoover, *The Professional Teacher's Handbook*, 3rd ed. Boston: Allyn and Bacon, 1982, pp. 13–14.
18. James Beane, "Curriculum Integration and the Disciplines of Knowledge," p. 618. See also James Beane, "The Middle School: Natural Home of Integrated Curriculum." Both articles are in *Educational Leadership* 49 (October 1991). The entire issue is devoted to the theme, "Integrating the Curriculum."

19. Renata Nummela Caine, "Maximizing Learning: A Conversation with Renate Nummela Caine." *Educational Leadership* (March 1997): 14–15
20. John Abbottt, "To Be Intelligent." *Educational Leadership* (March 1997): 7.
21. On the whole subject of thematic teaching, see James A. Beane (Ed.) *Toward a Coherent Curriculum: 1995 ASCD Yearbook*. Alexandria, Va.: ASCD, 1995. For examples of interdisciplinary teaching, see Terry Deal Reynolds, "Courting Controversy: How to Build Interdisciplinary Units." *Educational Leadership* 51 (April 1993): 13–15; Sasha A. Barab and Anita Landa, "Designing Effective Interdisciplinary Anchors, pp. 52–55; Tim Peters, Kathy Schubeck, and Karen Hawkins, "A Thematic Approach: Theory and Practice at the Aleknagik School" *Educational Leadership* 53 (April 1995): 633–636.
22. Every beginning teacher should become familiar with the most thorough account of what research shows about effective teaching. See Maynard C. Reynolds (Ed.), *Knowledge Base for the Beginning Teacher*. Oxford: Pergamon Press, 1989. For an in-depth treatment of various models of teaching, see Bruce Joyce and Marsha Weil, *Models of Teaching*. Englewood Cliffs, N.J.: Prentice-Hall, 1972. Also, for another comprehensive approach to the subject of alternative teaching strategies, see Paul D. Eggen and Donald P. Kauchak, *Strategies for Teachers: Teaching Content and Thinking Skills*, 2nd ed. Englewood Cliffs, N.J.: Prentice-Hall, 1988.
23. J. Brophy and T. L. Good, "Teacher Behavior and Student Achievement." In M. C. Wittrock (Ed.), *Handbook of Research on Teaching*, 3rd ed. New York: Macmillan, 1986.
24. The groups of teaching guidelines in this section were adapted from Herbert J. Klausmeier, *Learning and Human Abilities*, 4th ed. New York: Harper and Row, 1975, Chaps. 10–14.
25. John Dewey's, *How We Think* (Boston: D. C. Heath, 1933) is a classic description of inquiry learning. See also Jerome Bruner, *The Process of Education*. Cambridge: Harvard University Press, l960; and Lee Shulman and Evan Kesslar, *Learning by Discovery*. Chicago: Rand McNally, 1966.
26. The view of education that informs much of the preceding is best summed up by Resnick: "As cognitive psychology has elaborated a theory of the human being as an active *constructor* of knowledge [and not just a *receiver* of information], a new view of learning has begun to emerge—one that describes changes in knowledge as the result of learners' self-modification of their own thought processes and knowledge structures. This in turn means that *instruction must be designed not to put knowledge into learners' heads but to put learners into positions that allow them to construct well-structured knowledge*." L. B. Resnick, cited in M. C. Wittrock (Ed.), *Handbook of Research in Teaching*, 3rd ed. New York: Macmillan, 1986, p. 102.
27. D. B. Strother, "Adapting Instruction to Individual Needs: An Eclectic Approach." *Phi Delta Kappan*, 67 (January 1986): 308–311.
28. Cynthia L. Warger and Marleen C. Pugach, "Forming Partnerships Around Curriculum." *Educational Leadership* (February 1996): 62.
29. Virginia Roach, "Supporting Inclusion: Beyond the Rhetoric." *Phi Delta Kappan* (December 1995): 299. The issue contains a special section on Inclusion. *Educational Leadership*, December 1994, is entirely devoted to "The Inclusive School." For some thoughts on "The Role of the Classroom Teacher," and on "Curriculum and Instruction," see Ray Van Dyke, Martha Ann Stallings, and Kenna Colley, "How to Build an Inclusive School Community." *Phi Delta Kappan* (February 1995): 477–478.

CHAPTER 5

Becoming Established with Student Groups

Planning for the First Days of School

As a new teacher you will no doubt approach the beginning of school with mixed feelings of anticipation and anxiety. You will want to make these first days and weeks as a teacher as successful as possible. In preparing to meet classes for the first time you are apt to find yourself musing over such questions as: How should I present myself to my students? What is the best kind of relationship to develop with these young people? Will I be able to keep them interested and cooperative? What should I be doing at the beginning to build a solid foundation for the rest of the year? These are pressing concerns for most entering teachers. A good beginning generally depends on realistic images of the situation facing you as a classroom teacher (see Chapter 1). It is important to have an initial perception of the leadership role you will assume with your classes and to begin firming up some of the group process strategies you will want to employ.

This chapter provides ideas and suggestions for developing an appropriate group climate in your classes, for establishing productive relationships with students, and for helping your students learn to work effectively together as a group. It offers suggestions for getting an early handle on classroom routines and for weathering the inevitable ups and downs of those first days in your own classroom.

Setting an Appropriate Tone

In an occupation in which personality and style are important, the things you do during the first days and weeks of school will set important precedents for what is to follow. The pattern of rules and expectations you instill, the kind of relationships you establish with your students, the learning atmosphere you foster—these are foundational to your classroom system, and are conditions that you actively build up in your early contacts with your students. Your ability to set an initial tone for your classes will go a long way toward determining the kind of year you will have with a particular group of students.[1] The way you greet students as they enter your classroom, the interest you exhibit as you call the roll for the first time, the enthusiasm you convey toward opening activities, will all serve to create a class atmosphere.

Your role as a climate-setter is fundamental to everything you do as a classroom teacher. In most lasting groups of whatever size (including families), there will ordinarily be those who take responsibility for keeping the group energized and productive and others whose basic agendas do not include group-maintenance tasks. In the confines of your own classroom you are clearly in the former role. You are the single most important factor in determining whether students approach your class with interest and anticipation, whether they show initiative and enthusiasm toward class activities, or simply go through the motions while waiting for the class period to end. The group climate you foster at the beginning of the school year will be the one you and your students are destined to live with during the many hours you spend together.

Groups of school-age young people cannot be expected to settle into a harmonious and workmanlike classroom pattern without deliberate and sustained efforts on your part to bring it about. The younger the students, the more likely it is that minor distractions and preoccupations (e.g., an untied shoe) will distract the group and prevent it from getting down to work until skillful leadership intervenes to capture their interest and attention. At the high school level, students will regularly enter your class carrying residues of hall conversations and preceding lessons, mental and emotional baggage that must be quickly set aside if they are to effectively concentrate on the business at hand. A large part of your task as a group climate-setter is to work as a counterforce to those elements within the school environment that tend to compete with the learning atmosphere you are seeking to develop.

If you are to create student interest in your class you need both to be, and to appear to be, enthusiastic. Studies describe the enthusiastic teacher as "one who conveys a great sense of commitment, excitement, and involvement with the subject matter,"[2] and also, it needs to be added, to and with the students since enthusiasm with only the subject matter *can* lead the teacher into being a thorough bore. A teacher's enthusiasm, unlike that of a scholar in a particular subject matter, should be primarily invested in promoting student learning, and evoked by achievement of learning.

Starting with Well-Laid Plans

Students will enter your classroom on the first day of school with certain preconceived notions of what to expect. Regardless of how long they have been in school, they will bring initial attitudes—positive or negative, eager, apathetic, or even hostile to some or all school subjects and school classrooms. However, because they have found teachers to vary widely in their approaches to instruction and class management, most students will be feeling some initial uncertainty and apprehension about what you might have in store for them. They will usually be extraattentive on the first day of school. Students want to know what your class will be like—whether it will be interesting or boring, comfortable or threatening, lenient or demanding. You should take advantage of this initial concern by immediately establishing the kinds of classroom patterns that will allow you to work effectively with these young people. Specifically, it is recommended that you[3]:

1. Set aside time on the first day for a discussion of rules.
2. Take a systematic approach as with any other teaching objective.
3. Begin by involving students in easy tasks to promote early successes.
4. Use activities that have a whole-group focus for the first few days.
5. Do not assume students have learned class procedures after one trial.

You need to be especially well organized for your first meeting with a new group of students. You will want to make a concentrated effort to foster a learning climate and expectation system that is businesslike and interesting. You can also expect the first day of school to be rather hectic. On opening day you can anticipate students will be nervous and highly social. Some will be hunting for classes and making last-minute schedule adjustments. These are all reasons to be particularly well-prepared for the first day of classes.

The following are practical suggestions for things you can do during the first few days of school to begin establishing a positive and productive learning climate in your classes:

1. Take time to *visualize* what you want to have happen in your classroom, the sorts of learning and behavioral patterns you would like to have in place after several weeks of school. Picture students carrying out assigned tasks. How, exactly, do you want them to respond as a group when asked to pass forward a homework assignment? How, precisely, are you going to have them break into smaller groups? Use these preliminary images as a basis for planning your introductory sessions with new groups of students.
2. Have a good first-day activity and an appropriate early assignment which you have carefully designed as impression builders, interesting and capable of being done with a high degree of success. Be deliberate and emphatic in introducing classroom procedures. Plan early activities that require students to give careful attention to teacher directions. Find opportunities to walk them through simple procedures as a means of bringing the group into sync with you.
3. Show a sincere interest in your students as individuals—their names, their appearances, their personalities. Welcome students as they enter your class. Make it plain you are glad to have them with you. Students

will be more likely to show an interest in your class and its activities if you demonstrate a genuine interest in them.

4. Let them see your enthusiasm for learning right from the start. Nothing dampens the interest and initiative of students quicker than a teacher who appears simply to be going through the motions.

5. Take early opportunities to stress the need for personal responsibility and individual choice. Make it clear that individuals in the class are responsible for their own behavior; for example, people speak only for themselves, people choose their attitudes toward the class and toward one another, people choose to represent themselves proudly or sloppily in the work they do.

6. Take time to review your overriding objectives for your teaching (see Chapter 3). When feeling confused, ask yourself what it is most important to achieve during these first days with a new group: "What are my most important priorities as a teacher?"

Aiming for Effective Organization

Classrooms are inevitably complex, busy places because of the number of diverse people schools try to accommodate and the number of agendas they seek to accomplish. During a typical class period you will need to effectively manage administrative chores, learning activities, materials and equipment, student behavior, and clock time. Under the circumstances, a premium gets placed on managerial efficiency—the ability to keep things moving, to attend to several agendas at the same time, and to maintain a goal-directed emphasis in your approach.[4] This aspect of teaching usually has a profound impact on new teachers:

> Once class starts, it's definitely show time. You've got to be ready to perform. There's really a lot to do in a short space of time. In a way this makes teaching kind of exciting for me.
>
> I'm not quite sure how to describe the work of managing an elementary classroom. Someone compared it to the job of an air-traffic controller in a large airport. I can imagine how hectic that would be. But teaching can also overload your brain. You need to be able to move quickly in order to stay on top of all the activity.
>
> For me the most challenging part of teaching is managing time. During the first few weeks I never seemed to have enough class time for all I wanted to accomplish. I was always leaving out important things. Now I'm learning to use my time better. I still have a ways to go though.

You need, then, to have worked out well in advance, and be ready to use an effective system for checking attendance, for getting students quiet and attentive, for distributing and retrieving materials, for giving directions and monitoring compliance, for executing transitions, and for handling interruptions.

Competent teachers are able to maintain an instructional pace that reduces "dead time" and keeps students actively involved with learning activities.[5] You will want to develop a style of classroom management that moves students through activities with a minimum of fuss and wasted time (see Chapter 9). Research on effective teaching has concluded that "teachers' ability to manage smooth transitions and maintain momentum is more important to work involvement and classroom control than any other behavior management technique."[6]

The following are some recommendations for streamlining your class routines to make them as efficient as possible in order to foster learning and reduce behavioral problems:

1. Make your directions and explanations crisp and succinct. When asking students to perform a task, tell them precisely what you want them to do and check carefully that they do it; for example, "Please pass your papers forward . . . quickly and quietly. That's fine" (or "there's too much noise, try again").

2. Learn to pace class activity appropriately. Generally, you should arrange for groups to do such things as getting in and out of the room, passing materials, and making transitions from large- to small-group activities as quickly and efficiently as possible. It is equally important, however, to alter the pace when promoting reflective thinking or other learning processes in which concentration and deliberation are essential.

3. Work to avoid slowdowns that disrupt the momentum of a lesson. Slowdowns can be caused by spending too much time on a minor aspect of a topic or through fragmenting an activity by working with individuals one at a time when you really ought to be concentrating on the whole group.[7]

4. Seek to maintain momentum in your teaching by learning to attend to two tasks simultaneously ("overlapping"), for example, admitting a latecomer without disrupting the flow of the lesson, or directing the activity of a small group while monitoring the work of the larger group.

5. Make effective use of your class time by overlapping administrative tasks with learning activities when possible. For example, start class by assigning students a short task while you are taking attendance. This is not only a good utilization of time, but a technique that gets students into an appropriate frame of mind at the beginning of class.

6. Work to achieve smooth transitions when moving from one activity to another. This is best accomplished through well-established routines, clear directions, and completing one task before beginning another.

7. Have prepared materials ready so you do not have to use class time to organize them. Avoid taking class time to write extensively on the board with your back to students. Substitute the overhead projector (and prepared transparencies), or duplicated materials for the chalkboard whenever possible.

Chapter 9 is devoted to a more in-depth treatment of classroom management strategies.

Establishing Sound Teacher-Student Relationships

As you look forward to spending your working hours in the classroom with groups of young people, it is important to know something about teacher-student relationships and the kinds of leadership and association patterns you want to develop with your students. Should I be warm and friendly, you may be wondering, or should I remain somewhat distant from my students at the outset? Should I consult with students about classroom policies or should I be more directive in the beginning? What type of teacher-student relationship will provide the best learning environment in my class? These sorts of questions are likely to be of special concern to you as you assume this new leadership position with student groups.

There are several main types of leadership you could conceivably adopt as a classroom teacher, and three of them will be examined, those that have been called, respectively, the autocratic, the permissive, and the democratic leadership style.

Authoritarian Leadership

You may resolve to be stern and businesslike in your relations with students, emphasizing strict attention to subject matter and classroom ground rules. This approach is generally referred to as the autocratic or authoritarian leadership style. Its first priority is the establishment of teacher authority. As a beginning teacher, seeking to achieve control and predictability in your relations with students, you may find yourself gravitating to this largely if not entirely top-down style of classroom leadership. A main problem with autocratic leadership, however, is its reliance on external pressure to motivate students. Autocratic teachers seek to control by imposing their will on the class, by what William Glasser has dubbed "boss management."[8] Although they may generally be able to force student compliance at a surface level, their methods often engender resentment and rebellion, resulting in bad morale, resistance to learning, and a habit of looking at authority as coercive and negative. There is a strong tendency for nothing to get done unless the teacher specifically requires it, and then only in the minimal degree.

Permissive Leadership

You might, on the other hand, decide to take a much less structured approach and start out loose and tolerant, allowing classroom rules and regulations to derive from group process as the need arises. This leadership style has been labeled the permissive or laissez-faire approach. It is based on the assumption that students will respond more genuinely and cooperatively to a teacher who gives them maximum freedom to make decisions and solve problems as situations require. If you are a new teacher with residual tendencies to identify with the student role, you may find yourself emotionally inclined toward permissive leadership. It may seem more natural to feature yourself as "one of the group" in your early encounters with students. However, the permissive style tends to leave students confused and frustrated, bereft of any authority beyond that of the group or of their own whims and passing desires, and it can very easily and rapidly lead to chaos.[9]

Democratic Leadership

A third leadership style attempts to avoid the extremes by combining the best intentions of the autocratic and permissive approaches. This pattern shares the assumption of the autocratic model that students need order, limits, and the firm hand of the teacher as a basis for productive class activity (the adult guidance function).[10] It also assumes, along with the permissive approach, that to develop personal initiative and responsibility, young people need a good amount of involvement in decisions that affect them (the decision-making function). This approach to teacher-student relationships is generally referred to as a democratic leadership model. Democratic teachers attempt to capitalize on the intrinsic motivation of students whenever possible. They allow students more freedom to decide on their own behavior on the understanding that they will be held accountable for the consequences. In contrast to authoritarian teachers, democratic teachers aim to achieve group decisions whenever possible, and are constantly open to discussion and to suggestions. They are not, however, afraid to make decisions, even unpopular ones, in which the welfare of the class is at stake, or in which adult experience clearly indicates the need for students to do or think what they might well not do or think were they left to themselves. It has been found that teachers who are able to work along these lines are apt to have classes in which the members are more satisfied, more cooperative, less hostile, and better able to follow through on group projects without constant surveillance and with a minimum of prodding.[11]

Although a democratic leadership pattern has important advantages over the autocratic and permissive approaches to teacher-student relations, it is a style that ordinarily takes time to develop. It requires a high level of organization and interpersonal sophistication on the part of a teacher and needs to be worked toward gradually and carefully.[12] Nevertheless, the early investments you make in this more participative, balanced, and reasonable approach to class decisions and relationships will result in a better environment for teaching and learning.[13] It is, of course, also much more geared to the development of people who have the appropriate dispositions and abilities for membership in our kind of society, an outcome that is one of the fundamental purposes of education in American schools. The interactive teaching techniques presented in Chapter 8 will be helpful in your efforts to develop a democratic leadership style with your classes.

Student Attitudes Toward Teachers

The first few days of school will be a "psyching out" time for students, during which they will be trying to decide what kind of teacher you are going to be. They will ordinarily make every effort to like and accept you, in the hope that your class will turn out to be something special. In fact, you can usually expect to enjoy a "honeymoon" period with your students for the first few days, or perhaps even a week or two. Students during this early stage can be unusually tolerant and cooperative, even inclined to give you the benefit of the doubt if your behavior should be somewhat puzzling or inconsistent. Depending on the grade level, the feelings of students toward teachers can be quite intense. Usually, the younger the students, the more emotion they will invest in the relationship.

When in the beginning you encounter student attitudes that seem particularly positive or negative, you can usually anticipate an eventual leveling-off of these feelings. With older students especially, you can expect the honeymoon relationship to lose its edge once you have begun to correct misbehavior, or to give tests and grades. It is not unusual for adolescent students to show a complete reversal of attitude toward a teacher or a particular class over a short span of time. For no apparent reason, students may rapidly or even suddenly go from honeymoon behavior to attitudes of disenchantment with class activities and/or teacher leadership patterns. Some students run hot and cold, one day amiable, the next day aloof. Some of this changeable behavior you will be able to attribute to what is happening in a student's life outside school or to mood swings typical of children or teenagers. Much of it, however, will be explainable in terms of advancing stages in group development, a topic considered in a later section of this chapter.

Some Practical Suggestions

In the final analysis, there are no simple formulas for arriving at the kind of teacher-student relationships that will be most appropriate for the conduct of your classes. Developing positive and productive human relationships is more of an art than a matter of prescription. Although a consideration of leadership styles provides an initial framework for looking at classroom relationships, there remains the need to devise practical strategies for one's early meetings with students. In this regard, there are some central principles that should guide your behavior as you begin interacting with the young people in your classes.

In the first place, you need to be mindful that you are an adult with groups of young people. You qualify by virtue of your superior knowledge and maturity to be in this leadership position. For you to have credibility with them, students need to perceive you this way. During the time you are becoming established in the classroom, it is essential for students to see you as an adult both mentally and emotionally.

Following from this requirement, it is also important for students to view you as being in control, as operating from an established set of guidelines for the conduct of classroom activity. Students will look to you for confident and consistent judgment. They will depend on you as the ultimate arbiter, and as the one responsible for keeping things together.

Finally, it is critical that students see you as a teacher who is there for the right reasons. They need to perceive you as a fair-minded person who is interested in them as individuals, as someone who will not sacrifice their best interests for the sake of the system or for your own personal advancement. Students must find you approachable, a person who is not so caught up in the formalities of teaching and learning that you ignore individual needs and differences. From these basic guidelines we can proceed to offer a number of suggestions for establishing solid working relationships with the students in your classes. They include:

1. Start with a few simple ground rules around which classroom procedures revolve. Work to be firm and consistent, but not rigid, in upholding these basic rules.

2. Be relaxed and informal around students when it is appropriate, but firm and businesslike when the situation requires it. The more open and self-disclosing you are able to be with students, the less inhibited and guarded they are apt to be in your presence.[14] Attempt to earn students' respect through the authority that comes from their perception of you as someone who has knowledge and understanding of the subject matter, of the world outside the classroom, and of them as individuals, rather than through mere power or position.

3. Develop the capacity to draw the line between a friendly, relaxed teacher-student relationship and a peer-level relationship with your students. When searching for a way to address a class of students, "you people" is much preferable to "you guys." Also, allowing students to address you by your first name can easily give the wrong message.

4. Do not allow yourself to overreact when things do not go exactly as you would like. Avoid projecting an image of yourself as a complainer or as one who is easily irritated by minor problems and inconveniences.

5. Work to maintain predictability in behavior and temperament in your interactions with students. Try to avoid abrupt variations in your moods, policies, and responses to classroom situations.

6. Show understanding of, and patience with, the evolving feelings of students toward you and your class. Expect highly positive or negative emotions to become more moderate once students have had enough time to experience your system of operation as fair, reasonable, and effective. In the meantime, aim for moderation in your own feelings toward your students, being careful not to get annoyed when student sentiments toward you are unrealistic.

7. Make a consistent attempt to recognize students as individuals. Whenever possible, greet students as they enter class. Show appreciation for their idiosyncrasies and special talents. Make efforts to acknowledge students in the halls, the lunchroom, and at extracurricular events.

8. Respect the inner life of your students. Let them know that their thoughts and feelings are important by listening and responding to them on an individual basis (see Chapter 11). Whenever appropriate, consult with them in matters that affect them. Make the development of individual self-expression an overriding goal in your work with these young people.

The Dynamics of Group Development: A Maturation Process

Beginning a school year with one or more classrooms of students is both an adventure and a challenge. The adventure part stems from the fact that all classroom groups are both unique and changeable. Veteran teachers will testify to the fact that each set of students is different from every other group of students and will tend to take on a distinct personality. Some groups will develop a collective warmth and will seem especially receptive to your influence. Others will seem distant and hard to reach. On balance, though, all student groups of whatever grade or ability levels will exhibit periodic changes in moods and tendencies. Some days they will be inclined to get down to work with a minimum of persuasion. The next day, for no apparent reason, the group mood will be abnormally restless or feisty. Beginning teachers are often dismayed by the unpredictable fluctuations in student temper:

> I've given up trying to predict the kind of mood my students will be in. One older teacher told me it had a lot to do with the weather. He said to watch out when the north wind is blowing. Students can be expected to be especially lightheaded on those days. I'm not sure how true that is, but I do know one thing: you've got to expect some wide variations in these kids' behavior patterns. I can't remember if I was that flighty when I was in school.

Making allowance for the changing dispositions of students is one of the things you must learn to do if you are to avoid being constantly unnerved.

Another part of the teaching challenge is to get this collection of individual students working together as a cooperative and productive group. Class cohesiveness and the skills and attitudes necessary for fruitful group interaction cannot be expected to develop by chance. They will generally be the result of a long-term effort on your part. The normal tendency is for classes to remain disjointed and inefficient at cooperative tasks until teachers take deliberate steps to help them develop into coherent working groups. Although some students will have been together socially or in previous classes, they will still need to learn to work together on group activities in the context of your classroom.

Stanford[15] has found that effective classroom groups share the following main characteristics:

1. The members understand and accept one another.
2. Communication is open.
3. Members take responsibility for their own learning and behavior.
4. Members cooperate.
5. Processes for making decisions have been established.
6. Members are able to confront problems openly and resolve their conflicts constructively.

Group development has been likened to the progression from infancy to mature adulthood. As with the human developmental process, groups must learn to cope with new problems and must generate new abilities in response to these problems.[16] Just as many human beings fail to grow up socially and emotionally, many classes also fail to develop into effective working units. You will feel a sense of genuine accomplishment when you have been able to take an assemblage of new students from a raw, entry level of group development to the point at which they can work skillfully and trustfully together on group learning tasks. This process normally takes place in several identifiable stages.[17] It will help you to know what these stages are and to have some appropriate strategies for bringing classes to the mature level of group performance.

The Orientation Stage

As suggested earlier, you can expect the first few days of school to be a feeling-out period for the students in your classes. They will usually come into the class full of questions: "Will there be a seating chart?" "How much homework will we have?" "What will we need to do for an A?", and so on. The more precise information you can give them about some of what is going to go on in the class, the sooner you can quiet their anxieties and apprehensions.

Students will also be concerned to find out who else is in the class. They will typically scan the room to see if they have friends in the group, at the same time hoping there will be no one who might embarrass or intimidate them. This process of trying to determine what the class is going to be like and the nature of the social environment is likely to continue until students begin to feel comfortable with one another and with the situation. Some students will adapt very quickly. They will have no trouble finding friends in the group. At the same time, there will usually be students who feel strange and uncomfortable in the new class surroundings. These students will resist interaction with classmates, tending to wait for others to break the ice with them. Some groups of students will take little initiative to learn one another's names or to interact socially. The getting-acquainted process can be aided considerably by a teacher who recognizes the need for students to feel socially comfortable and accepted as a necessary first step in group development.

Here are some things you can do to help students make a successful adaptation during the orientation stage in group development:

1. Start the first day with a brief sketch of what students can expect to be doing in this class. Give clear and precise information about the sorts of things they will be studying, the activities they will be involved with, the type of homework they can anticipate, and the approach you will take to evaluation and grading.
2. Take the lead in encouraging social openness and self-disclosure by including a brief description of yourself in your course introduction. Give students insights into you as a person by mentioning significant things about your formative experiences: hobbies and interests, immediate family, and so forth.
3. Use structured, low-threat, get-acquainted exercises to help students get to know one another. For example, (1) Allow the whole group to

mingle freely with the stipulation that each person take the initiative to interact briefly and share an interest with everyone else; (2) have students wear name tags for the first few days of school, and attempt to learn as many names as possible; (3) run a contest at the end of the first week, offering prizes to those who learn the most names; and (4) pair students and have them share something significant about each other with the class.

4. Make an early effort to show the interpersonal attitudes and behaviors you intend to have students acquire in your classes. In practice this could mean learning student's names, interests, and special qualities as quickly as possible, giving the same amount of attention to slower and possibly less able students as to academically advanced students, and displaying equal concern and appreciation for each student no matter what their background.[18]

5. Make the physical organization of the class reflect your interest in promoting fairness and equality. Use circular, semicircular, or horseshoe-shaped seating arrangements when appropriate to allow students to be face-to-face with one another. When breaking the class into subgroups, make sure that students frequently get to work with different people.

6. Allow shy or reticent students time to adapt to the class environment. Be careful not to prejudge students who initially appear uninterested or distant, and be prepared to accept genuine expressions of fear and doubt in new students.

The Formative Stage

After the first few weeks together most groups of students begin to feel freer and less inhibited with one another. It is important at this stage for you to take note of these emerging patterns of influence and participation within the group. Friendship circles will start to become apparent, and you will start to notice "spheres of influence" within the classroom. Some students will establish themselves as more influential than others in helping the class with learning tasks, or in keeping the class functioning as a group. Other students may show signs of developing into class clowns or teacher baiters. You need to come to grips with students like this right away. Sometimes giving them responsibility of some sort does the trick: taking preliminary attendance, distributing materials, keeping tabs on supplies such as pencils and books, cleaning the board, and so on. With other students, making it clear as calmly and firmly as you can from the outset that you aren't going to accept behavior from anyone that interferes with learning may be called for, and may in fact be just what the student actually needs, a sense of a situation that is in control. Moves like these are likely to help you build up the kind of student-teacher relationship in which "discipline," in the best sense—goal-oriented, other-regarding, self-control—develops.

One of your main concerns during the pattern formation stage in group development should be to promote broad involvement in class activities, thus avoiding the dominance of a small minority of students, and to stimulate free-flowing communication within the group.[19] Your ability to induce active two-way communication between teacher and students and among students will lead to more active involvement and interest within the class.[20] To facilitate genuine dialogue with and between students, the following basic communication techniques are especially useful[21]:

1. *Paraphrasing*. Paraphrasing is a matter of restating what you think another person has said, but in your own words. It is a communication skill that shows a concern to accurately understand the other person's message and to be corrected if you have misunderstood. A paraphrase usually begins with a lead-in such as, "I hear you saying that . . ." or "I understand you to say . . ."

2. *Behavior description*. This technique involves describing what you see another person doing without attempting to attach motives or meanings to it (a common cause of friction and miscommunication). The intent is to simply describe what you have observed (perhaps something troublesome) without attributing bad intentions or personal weaknesses—"I noticed you didn't have anything to say in class today," or "Several people are still talking while Debby is trying to make her point."

3. *Descriptions of one's own feelings*. The ability to communicate your own feelings directly about a situation tends to promote honesty and understanding within a group. By directly describing feelings and impressions, people can bring problems or likes and dislikes to a head in a precise way, and thus avoid misunderstandings. Members of the group show openness and sincerity when they are able to say, "I feel embarrassed" or "I feel angry." Similarly, telling people about one's positive feelings—"I enjoy your sense of humor" or "Mary certainly knows how to make a point!" helps everyone enjoy being in the group.

4. *Perception checking*. This is similar to paraphrasing except that it involves interpreting feelings and internal processes rather than the words and behavior of the other person. A perception check aims at getting the other person to talk directly about his or her feelings by describing in a tentative fashion what you think you are noticing, as for instance, "I get the impression you're angry with me. Are you?" and "You look bored with the work! Am I right?" When using this technique, you should avoid implying disapproval at least until the other person has said something.

Another of your main aims during this formative stage of group development should be to give students practice in group-centered as well as teacher-centered activities. Although the class will have made significant advances socially, they may still be relatively unsophisticated as a *working group*, unless, of course, they have already been trained in cooperative learning in earlier classes (for more on cooperative learning, see Chapter 8). If they have not had this experience, they will most likely lack the skills and attitudes necessary to carry out subject matter tasks as a *cooperative* unit. For example, if you assign them subgroup projects, they will typically tend to stray from the task without close teacher monitoring. They will ordinarily be ineffective when it comes to establishing appropriate divisions of labor which allow and require everyone to contribute, to resolving differences of opinion, and to getting proper closure on the group assignment. If you intend to have a class that does more than listen to the teacher and take notes, but which does not just waste its time in what can be for many students largely worthless "group work," you will want to establish some fundamental group process goals during the first several weeks of school. The following six elements are considered foundational to productive group interaction[22]:

1. *A worthwhile task.* The group's task should be sufficiently extensive, difficult, and complex to require cooperative work.
2. *Group responsibility.* Everybody contributes to the work of the group; leaders emerge from the group itself.
3. *Responsiveness to others.* Members listen attentively to one another and attempt to combine their ideas to form a group product.
4. *Interdependence.* Members cooperate to achieve goals rather than competing with one another.
5. *Decision making through consensus.* The group aims to arrive at decisions acceptable to all, rather than imposing the will of the majority on the minority.
6. *Confronting problems.* Disagreements are faced rather than ignored, and solutions are actively sought.

It is apparent, then, that there are a number of things you can do during the formative stage of group development to help students learn to function cooperatively and productively together. These include:[23]

1. Using indirect techniques to stimulate student participation. Besides employing mirroring techniques (paraphrasing, perception checking, behavior description), it is important at this stage to use questions that invite students to share thoughts and impressions and to be as accepting as possible of students' feelings and ideas (see Chapters 8 and 11 for further discussion of these communication skills).
2. Working to stimulate effective two-way communication between members of the class. You can do this by letting them see you paying close attention to what is said (see Chapter 8), by allowing only one person to talk at a time, and by giving students small-group tasks that require active listening and sharing.
3. Providing opportunities for the class to discuss and understand group functions and processes. Help them to appreciate the kinds of communication skills necessary to arrive at decisions and solve problems in, and by means of, a group process.
4. Making a conscious effort to keep classroom communications as open and free-flowing as possible. Stress the importance of widespread con-

tributions to the group process. Find ways to help groups tone down members who tend to dominate group interaction, without appearing to muzzle their peers, for example, by limiting the number of times any one member may speak before some one else gets a chance.

5. Encouraging group-based responsibilities. Shift from teacher-centered to group-centered activities. Focus student attention on group tasks to be completed, defining clear results for these tasks and frequently grading the whole group rather than, or as well as, individuals.

The Conflict Stage

Student groups that spend extended periods of time together are bound to experience some conflict and disagreement. In fact, as group members become more open, responsive, and group-centered in their attitudes and behavior, it becomes more likely that some friction will occur. It may be manifest in increased bickering and complaining among students or in a student challenging teacher authority. Conflict within a group that has begun to demonstrate cohesiveness and task-level competence should be considered a sign of growth rather than regression.

A period of intragroup discord is often a natural result of widespread participation and occurs when a broad spectrum of opinions, values, and personal styles are allowed expression. Also, your success in getting students to confront rather than ignore problems often initially increases their dispositions to be critical of one another and of the teacher. Another underlying reason for conflict in a developing group is the need on the part of students who are beginning to feel constrained by the group atmosphere to assert themselves as individuals. Grumbling or even outright hostility may reflect a temporary need for students to challenge peer influence or teacher authority in a group that has begun to come together as a working unit. When you sense that a classroom group is going through a normal conflict stage in its development, the following are some measures you can take to help students deal constructively with this period of instability:

1. Help students to understand that group conflict can be an indication that positive rather than negative things are happening and that it is not something that should be avoided or suppressed, because it is usually a sign that group members care enough to be direct and honest with one another.

2. Provide support and reassurance for students who become nervous about the increased group friction or about perceived challenges to teacher authority. Give them time to understand you have the situation under control and that you see this as a normal phase in the group process.

3. Do not react defensively and become more authoritarian. The imposition of tighter limits at this point will not solve the problem students are experiencing. Instead, resolve in your own mind to help students learn constructive ways of coping with group conflict.

4. Show that you are listening to and thinking about what is going on to assure students you are hearing and understanding their concerns (see Chapter 11). It is important that you understand and accept the feelings that underlie the surface complaints or criticisms students are expressing.

5. Be able to conduct "airing-out" sessions with the class in which the topic is *the group itself* and its progress as a productive unit. Have a procedure for allowing students to express grievances reasonably, with self-restraint guided by an awareness of and regard for others' feelings. Use these sessions to practice the kinds of problem-solving skills you want the group to master.

The Productive Stage

As you take a classroom of students through the normal phases of group development, you will often be amazed at the changes occurring in the group as the weeks and months go by. Once a group has reached a mature stage in its growth they can be especially enjoyable to work with. It will make the energy you have invested in group development well worth the effort. At the productive level students are not only able to interact effectively when involved in learning activities, but they can also deal with disagreement and intragroup conflict in constructive ways. One of the central characteristics of mature groups is their ability to effectively resolve their own problems.[24] At this level the students are ready to work effectively in subgroups or as a total body. Although such classes can at times be noisy places, and interpersonal tensions can arise unexpectedly, student interest is typically high and a good deal of learning that would otherwise be impossible takes place.[25]

When you are successful in reaching this level with a group of students, you will very likely notice increased closeness among students and between yourself and the students.[26] The ability to confront and clear the air of shared problems tends to bring groups of people closer together. Stanford points to the deepening relationships that characterize the productive stage in group development. In this connection, he suggests teachers need to be prepared to deal with two common types of problem. First, students often have difficulty knowing how to deal with the stronger feelings that accompany closer relationships with their peers and their teacher. In addition, there is the frequent tendency for students at this advanced stage of group development to want to concentrate more on their intragroup relations than on subject-matter tasks. When this happens, teachers have to take steps to right the balance.[27]

As a teacher, it is good to have some strategies for helping students maintain their productive edge once they reach this level of group development. The following are some suggestions:

1. Be prepared for temporary regression (e.g., disorganization, lack of participation, conflict). This often happens when a short vacation or special event interrupts the normal routine. Regression to earlier group patterns can also occur after students have been working for extended periods of time in smaller groups or on individual projects.

2. Take measures to help the group maintain its skills. This may involve periodic class discussions aimed at getting students to see the need for skill maintenance. Often simply identifying and talking over the problems students are having is enough to get the group back on a productive track. If it isn't, structured practice sessions may be required to reacquaint them with the group process skills they are beginning to neglect.

3. Expect students to want to alternate between working on learning tasks and working on their interpersonal agendas. Try to arrive at an appropriate balance between subject-matter learning and the social-emotional learning that accompanies deepening peer relations. When possible, try to devise learning activities that link students' personal concerns with content-related skills.

4. Retain your prerogative to set limits to student power, but first give the group an opportunity to deal with its own problems.

Coping with the Normal Ups and Downs of the Job

Teaching is the kind of occupation in which the moods, abilities, and cooperative efforts of other people can have a large bearing on what gets accomplished on any given day; thus it is realistic to expect there will be times when everything seems to fall in place and other days when nothing goes right. This tendency to experience a pattern of ups and downs, for example, several good days followed by a series of bad days, is a more acute problem for beginning teachers than for veterans. It is more likely to happen during the early days of a new job, before you have had an opportunity to establish a system and to become stabilized in your teaching pattern. The following samples from the diary of a first-year teacher of seventh-grade social studies dramatically illustrate the vacillating feelings and impressions that arise when a person is introduced to the rigors of full-time teaching:

> *September 7*—I have the feeling that I am really going to enjoy teaching, and am very anxious to get at it! I'm surprisingly not nervous (yet!). None of the students seem particularly rowdy. There are a few dominant personalities and some very quiet individuals.

> *September 10*—What a day this turned out to be! . . . Much of my former eagerness suddenly left me. . . . My main fear was that in going over the material after the test, I was going to seem unsure of myself. . . . The kids were testing me, for sure. Third period took a good five to seven minutes to quiet down. Lots of students getting up to sharpen pencils (for longer than necessary). Several boys in the back of the class found the whole thing hilarious and kept others from hearing.

> *September 16*—A great day in classes today! . . . This was the most valuable experience I've had so far with the students. They asked

for my help and I felt glad to give it to them. They showed obvious respect and appreciation, and the whole thing was very healthy for our mutual relationships. . . . Today I left school feeling like it was all O.K. and had a very optimistic attitude.

September 22—Today I gave the class a very short quiz on vocabulary and spelling. . . . Everyone moaned and groaned about how third grade it was, but not many scored all that well. . . . I've felt a lot of frustration in dealing with the class when they act this way. They don't see me as an authority figure, partly, I'm sure, because I don't see myself this way. I don't really know what I can do to change this.. . . I go home in the evenings and give myself little pep talks on how to deal more effectively with the students, then the next day it never seems to make a difference. I get awfully nervous when the class misbehaves.

October 3—Today we played a game that all the class seemed to like. . . . I really enjoyed the students in lots of ways. . . . I want to make next week a turning point in my teaching. I want it to be the best teaching job I've done, and I want each week after that to be even better. I'm feeling pretty good about teaching right now.

October 11—Well, considering that this was supposed to be the best week of the semester, it turned out to be right up there with one of the worst weeks of my life. Just when you think things might be looking up, there you are—face down again. . . . I am only glad that I didn't have a ton of lesson planning to do, because I was so emotionally distraught that I don't think I could have done it. . . . I spent a few days doing some serious thinking about whether or not I really should pursue this course in my life after all.

October 23—This week seemed to go fairly smoothly. . . . I am trusting the students to behave better and it seems that they are more comfortable also. . . . I'm finding I am enjoying the classroom experience much more. . . . I still have some high ideals that I'd like to see through to the end.

Understanding What Is Happening to You

Unless you have prepared yourself to deal with the normal succession of good and bad days that characterize early-career teaching, you may start to wonder whether you'll ever be able to get used to the inconsistency and unpredictability. It helps to have some idea of what you are going through and why, in the event you should find yourself on an emotional roller coaster during those first days and weeks of the job.

For one thing, you may have inadvertently set yourself up for disappointment. You could be hoping for more initial success than it is reasonable to expect. It may be that some of your long-standing images of day-to-day teaching need revising (see Chapter 1).

Second, your emotions are likely to be running on high during your first few days of teaching. The profound enthusiasm and exhilaration you feel after a satisfying session with your students leaves you susceptible to a corresponding low when this experience is not repeated the next day. One of your personal projects during the first weeks of teaching will be to get your emotional equipment stabilized, to learn to adjust more effectively to the highly changeable circumstances of this kind of work.

You are also, as a beginning teacher, likely to experience alternating good and bad days because you have not yet had time to devise a teaching pattern that reduces such fluctuations. Once you have developed a reasonably stable and consistent set of classroom procedures, you are not as apt to allow externals, for example, student moods and inclinations, to upset your teaching day.

In the meantime, here are some suggestions to help with the kinds of ups and downs you are likely to experience as an early-career teacher:[28]

1. Do not allow yourself to dwell on the negatives of the job. Find effective ways of clearing the slate after a bad day (e.g., meditating, or taking your favorite form of exercise). Do something you enjoy. Work on something constructive and relaxing (e.g., hobbies, reading).

2. Recognize that in a character-dependent activity, such as teaching (see Chapter 2), there are built-in obstacles to be overcome. The patience and confidence to deal with minor problems and setbacks are characteristics every good teacher must cultivate, but they take time to develop, so be patient with yourself and your students.

3. When you are ready to view the situation more rationally and less emotionally, attempt to figure out what you may or may not be doing that would help to account for these early problems. Review basic teaching strategies or management techniques that would relate to the problem you are experiencing, and plan to make the necessary alterations. This process can in itself be enheartening as you find an approach or new materials that you *feel sure* will work.

4. Learn to reframe problems to get a look at them from a different perspective. What was it that actually happened in school today? Was it really all that serious? Is it possible I overreacted or misconstrued the situation as a reflection on me and my competence, when in reality it didn't arise out of anything *I* did (or didn't) do?

5. Find supportive people you can regularly talk to about your teaching. Keeping a personal journal (or diary) in which you note significant school happenings along with your thoughts and feelings can also have therapeutic value.

6. Look for an outside-school teachers' group (some areas have Teachers' Centers) with whom you can regularly discuss and share ideas. If you are already connected to the Internet, look around for such groups, for other individual teachers, and for Web sites that provide ideas and materials for teachers to use in their classrooms.[29]

◆◆◆   SUGGESTED ACTIVITIES AND QUESTIONS   ◆◆◆

1. Picture yourself as a teacher about to begin a school year with a group of students in an area you are qualified to teach. Mention three or four orientational items you would want to be sure to discuss with your students on the first day. What are some things you would do to make this introductory session most effective?

2. How do you anticipate handling the matter of seating as you begin organizing for the first day of school? How will you arrange the chairs and desks/tables? Discuss some of the pros and cons of each of these possible approaches: (1) allowing students to sit where they wish, (2) assigning seats alphabetically, or (3) seating students according to size or special problem, for example, short students or those with vision or hearing problems in front.

3. What is your attitude toward allowing students to be involved in the planning of classroom rules and procedures? Are there some areas of classroom life where joint policy planning would be appropriate? If so, what are some other areas where you believe it would not be advisable to give students a hand in developing group guidelines, and why not? How would the grade level affect your views on this issue? Elaborate.

4. What kinds of leadership roles have you had occasion to play in your life? What previous situations have you been in where you were called on to be a prime organizer or climate-setter for other people, young or old (e.g., family, military, athletics)? How do you perform in situations where the task falls to you to bring energy, enthusiasm, and positive direction to a shared project or cause?

5. What degree of formality will seem most natural to you in relating to students at the grade level you intend to teach? What do you anticipate will be your preferred mode of addressing students in group settings (e.g., "boys and girls," "you kids," "you folks," "you people")? Will you feel comfortable calling students by their nicknames (e.g., Cal, Steph)? Would there ever be occasions in which you would allow students to be on a first-name basis with you?

6. Consider each of the leadership styles discussed in this chapter: autocratic, permissive, and democratic. Analyze each approach in terms of its main advantages and disadvantages. Does one or another of these styles seem most suited to your own personality or philosophy of teaching? Should these be the criteria to base your decision on which to adopt? Should the length of time a teacher has been teaching have a bearing on one's leadership approach? Discuss reasons what it is about democratic classroom leadership that calls for more skill than the autocratic or permissive varieties.

7. Identify veteran teachers who are able to consistently bring positive energy and enthusiasm to their classes. Find opportunities to discuss with these teachers their strategies for remaining vital and upbeat on a day-to-day basis. Attempt to obtain insight into techniques they employ to help them bounce back after a bad day in the classroom.

Notes

1. Kevin Ryan, ed., *The Roller Coaster Year: Essays by and for Beginning Teachers.* New York: HarperCollins, 1992. The firsthand accounts of 12 beginning teachers are vivid and informative. The final chapter by Ryan is full of practical advice.
2. Phi Delta Kappa, *Practical Applications of Research.* Bloomington, Ind.: Newsletter of PDK Center on Evaluation, Development, and Research, vol. 3, no. 4 (June 1981): 2.
3. Myron H. Dembo, *Applying Educational Psychology in the Classroom*, 3rd ed. New York: Longman, 1988, p. 259.
4. Jacob Kounin, *Discipline and Group Management in Classrooms.* New York: Holt, Rinehart and Winston, 1977, pp. 92–97.
5. Ibid., pp. 102–105.
6. C. M. Charles, *Building Classroom Discipline*, 3rd ed. New York: Longman, 1989, p. 33.
7. Kounin, *Discipline and Group Management*, see Chap. 5.
8. William Glasser, *Quality School: Managing Students Without Coercion.* New York: Harper and Row, 1990, p. 25. He sees replacing boss management with *lead management* (see 3. above) as the critical feature of educational reform "because it limits both the quality of the work and the productivity of the worker. See also Charles, *Building Classroom Discipline*, p. 72.
9. Richard A. Schmuck and Patrick A. Schmuck, *Group Processes in the Classroom.* Dubuque, Iowa: Wm. C. Brown, 1971, p. 29.
10. Charles, *Building Classroom Discipline*, p. 73.
11. Richard C. Sprinthall and Norman A. Sprinthall, *Educational Psychology: A Developmental Approach*, 3rd ed. Reading, Mass.: Addison-Wesley, 1981, p. 549.
12. Charles, *Building Classroom Discipline*, p. 86.
13. Schmuck and Schmuck, *Group Processes in the Classroom*, p. 29.
14. Joseph Morris, *Psychology and Teaching: A Humanistic View.* New York: Random House, 1978, p. 84.
15. Gene Stanford, *Developing Effective Classroom Groups.* New York: Hart, 1977, p. 26.
16. Ibid., p. 27.
17. The approach to group developmental stages presented here is adapted from the work of Gene Stanford, *Developing Effective Classroom Groups.*
18. One study found that students in classes where they felt class members were treated equally and had little hostility toward one another had higher academic achievement (H. J. Walberg and G. J. Anderson, "Classroom Climate and Individual Learning." *Journal of Educational Psychology* 59 [1968]: 414–19).
19. Schmuck and Schmuck, *Group Processes in the Classroom*, p. 121.
20. Schmuck and Schmuck, *Group Processes in the Classroom*, p. 121.
21. Schmuck and Schmuck, *Group Processes in the Classroom*, p. 97. On the value of dialogue in general, see the very valuable work of Nicholas Burbules, *Dialogue in Teaching: Theory and Practice.* New York: Teachers College Press, 1993. Burbules describes what he calls "the communication virtues" as "tolerance, patience, and openness to give and receive criticism, the inclination to admit one may be mistaken, the desire to reinterpret or translate one's own concerns in a way that makes them comprehensible to others, the self-imposition of restraint in order that others may have a turn to speak—and often neglected as a key element in dialogue—the willingness and ability to listen thoughtfully and attentively" (p. 42). He goes on to point out that "making such personal qual-

ities into *primary* [his emphasis] educational objectives . . . has enormous implications for the organization of classrooms, [and] our assumptions about curriculum and instruction" (pp. 45–46).

22. David W. Johnson and Roger T. Johnson, "Social Skills for Successful Group Work." *Educational Leadership* (December 1989): 29–33. Also Mara Sapon-Shevin, Nancy Schniedewind, "If Cooperative Learning Is the Answer, What Are the Questions?' *Journal of Education* 174, No. 2 (1992): 27–28.

23. Some oppose this practice. Johnson states his belief that "for achievement gains to occur, positive *goal* interdependence has to be present. Group *rewards* are optional." Cited in Alfie Kohn, "Don't Spoil the Promise of Cooperative Learning." *Educational Leadership* 48 (February 1997): 94. Stanford, *Developing Effective Classroom Groups*, pp. 77–78.

24. Stanford, *Developing Effective Classroom Groups*, p. 29.

25. Schmuck and Schmuck, *Group Processes in the Classroom*, p. 122.

26. Schmuck and Schmuck, *Group Processes in the Classroom*, p. 122.

27. Stanford, *Developing Effective Classroom Groups*, p. 253.

28. Ryan, *The Roller Coaster Year*, pp. 249–259.

29. Some "hot sites":

ART

Kennedy Center http://artsedge.kennedy-center.org/artsedge.html (K–12 art resources)

Favorite Lessons http://www.in.net/~kenroar/lessons.html

Getty's Artsnet http://www.artsednet.getty.edu/ArtsEdNet/

BILINGUAL EDUCATION

Bilingual Education Resources
http://www.edb.utexas.edu/coe/depts/CI/bilingue/resources.html

National Clearinghouse For Bilingual Education
http://www.ncbe/gwu.edu/

ENGLISH AS A SECOND LANGUAGE

Internet TESL Journal for Teachers of ESL http://www.aitech.ac.jp/

ESL Resources for Learners
http://schoolnet2.carleton.ca/~kwellar/esl-sne/slinks.html

FOREIGN LANGUAGES

National K–12 Foreign Language Resource Center
http://www.educ.iastate.edu/ currinst/nflrc/nflrc.html

HEALTH EDUCATION/PHYSICAL EDUCATION

Pennsylvania State Association for Health, Physical Education, Recreation, and Dance http://astro.temple.edu/~phete/psahperd

National Association for Sports and Physical Education http://www.aahperd.org/nnaspe.html

LANGUAGE ARTS

Web Resources for English Teachers http://nickel.ucs.indiana.edu/ ~lwolfgra/ english.html

Purdue Online Writing Laboratory http://owl.trc.purdue.edu/

MATH

Activities Integrating Mathematics and Science http://204.161.33.100/

Eisenhower National Clearinghouse http://www.enc.org

Math Forum http://forum.swarthmore.edu

MUSIC

Music Educator's Home Page http://www.athenet.net/~wslow

K–12 Resources for Music Educators http://www.isd77.k12mn.us/ resources/staffpages/shirk/ cindys. page.k12.link.html

SCIENCE

Online Educational Resources http://quest.arc.nasa.gov/OER/

Franklin Institute Science Museum http://sln.fi.edu/

Science Teacher's Resources http://198.110.10.57/Chem/EastSciRes.html

SOCIAL STUDIES

Center for History and New Media http://web.gmu,edu/chnm

National Council for Geographic Education http://multimedia2.freac.fsu.edu/ncge/

From Revolution to Reconstruction and What Happened Afterwards http://grid.let.rug.nl/ ~welling/usa/revolution

SPECIAL EDUCATION

Special Needs Ed Network http://schoolnet2.carleton.ca/~kwellar/

Gifted Resources Home Page http://www.eskimo.com/~user/kids.html

Internet Resources for Special Educators http://www.mordor.com/wader/sped.html

PROFESSIONAL ORGANIZATIONS

http://www.nsta.org (National Science Teachers Association)

http://www.nctm.org (National Council of Teachers of Mathematics)

http://www.ncte.org/ (National Council of Teachers of English)

http://www.ncss.org/ (National Council for the Social Studies)

http://www.ascd.org (Association for Supervision and Curriculum Development)

http://www.aahperd.org (American Association for Health, Physical Education, and Dance)

http://www.cec.sped.org/ericec/links.htm (Council for Exceptional Children)

DISCUSSION AND RESOURCES

Teacher Talk http:///www.mightymedia.com/talk/working.html

Use of WWW in Education http://kl2. cnidr.org:90/wwwedu.html

Focus on Urban Education http://eric-web.tc.columbia.edu/

Websites and Resources for Teachers http://www.csun.edu/~vceed009

ERIC Documents http://ericir.syr.edu

Childaware (Preschool Information and Resources) http://inetcom.

School Networking Projects http://sunsite.unc.edu/cisco/edu-arch.html

Cyberspace Middle School http://www.ascri.fsu.edu/~dennisl/CMS.html

Homework Help http://www.tpoint.net/~jewels/homework.html

K–12 Curriculum And Instruction Materials http://calvin.cc.ndsu. nodak.edu/

Website for Busy Teachers http://www.ceismc.gatech.edu/BusyT

Technology, Teaching, and Learning http://www.ehhs.cmich.edu/~rlamb/

Web66 Schools on the Web http://web66.coled.umn.edu

Education Virtual Library http://www.csu.edu.au/education/all.html

http://www.union-city.k12nj.us/virtual_tour/

CHAPTER 6

Drawing Students into Encounters with Learning

It is remarkable how often educators use the word motivation *when what they mean is* compliance.

Alfie Kohn

The Motivational Task

Before you can teach students subject matter, you must first be able to engage them productively in classroom learning. Yet, because of the formal nature of most school learning, students often fail to perceive its relevance to their own lives (see Chapter 1). As a result, you can usually anticipate some initial indifference or resistance toward the subject matter and skills you have in mind to teach. This places a premium on your ability to approach new learning in ways that engender active interest and involvement on the part of your students. Veteran teachers often cite motivational skill as the main key to successful teaching:

> It all comes down to keeping them interested. On days when they happen to be jazzed on the lesson, my discipline problems are nonexistent. But when they're bored, they will always look for something extraneous to occupy them. That's when my problems start. If I had it to do over, I'd minor in psychology and make motivation my specialty.

> You've got to be able to motivate them in order to reach them. It's as simple as that. In fact, we should call the job motivation rather than teaching. Once you're able to get students really involved in a subject, they'll pretty much learn it on their own. But if they're not personally involved, you can talk about your subject until you're blue in the face and they won't hear you.

> Today's kids have too many other distractions. Most school learning bores them to death because it can't compete with what's going on around them. My advice to anyone starting out in teaching would be to collect all of the techniques you can find for making your teaching stimulating.

Resourceful teachers are able to arouse student interest in their classes without having to rely on threats, grade anxieties, or strong social pressures to get them to learn. They are able to draw students into meaningful encounters with the subject by appealing to their present interests, their previous experiences and understandings, and their innate tendencies to want to resolve problems. This requires some knowledge of how, and under what circumstances, students learn best as well as effective strategies for helping them to do so. This chapter is designed to help you understand what it will take to involve students actively and meaningfully in classroom learning. It will offer a brief introduction to the psychological processes involved in productive learning, including a discussion of some of the obstacles that must be overcome if you are to foster in-depth learning in your classes.

Avoiding the Path of Least Resistance

Formal or nonsituational learning is inherently abstract, that is, removed from its normal life context. It is thus less easy for students to perceive the meaning and significance of what they are learning in school than in what they learn in the give-and-take world outside school. To compensate for this limitation in formal schooling, you will need to develop techniques to reduce its abstractness and to help students find meaning and purpose in school learning. In order to accomplish this you will need to overcome certain forces within the school system itself that tend to foster superficial learning.

As discussed in Chapter 2, the pressures and distractions of modern teaching can threaten to keep you preoccupied with organizational matters, and tempt you to look for shortcuts and routines to make the job less burdensome. In the process of trimming teaching to fit into bureaucratic requirements, you run the risk of making learning more artificial and less meaningful to students. This has become a serious problem in U.S. schools at all levels.[1]

Many teachers are attempting to cover more material in a given period of time. They are making less effort to ground new learning in the experiences, perceptions, and existing knowledge structures of students. At the secondary level, particularly, teachers are more than ever attempting to instruct by telling rather than by setting up situations and introducing materials that enable students to learn through active participation, with the teacher often acting in a variety of ways as an intermediary. On the whole, school learning has become more verbal, more subject-centered, and more remote from students' life experiences. The resultant alienation many students feel toward school tends to increase discipline problems and to decrease the satisfaction teachers derive from their work.[2]

To avoid taking the path of least resistance and falling into a largely mechanical and routinized pattern of teaching, your first and continuing imperative has to be an unshakable determination to help your students acquire knowledge, skills, and attitudes that *they* can see mean something, and in ways that give them a sense of satisfaction. Knowing what it takes to help students understand and value what they learn, and having a firm resolve to continue developing the capacity to promote this kind of substantive learning in your own classroom are essential prerequisites to becoming a good, and possibly eventually even an excellent, teacher. If you succeed in achieving this difficult goal, at least from time to time, you can hope to experience the deep and unique satisfaction that comes from real teaching. This experience can be so powerful that it keeps teachers in classrooms despite so much that is difficult and problematic in working to help young people individually develop into maturing adults, despite the fact that most of the time you have to deal with them in groups.

Requirements for Meaningful Learning

A school's emphasis on learning by way of words rather than through actual experience is apt to be particularly evident in academic subjects such as science, math, English, and social studies. Even such classes as art, shop, physical education, and music normally depend on the student's ability to handle verbal information as a basis for skill learning. There are two basic ways in which students can deal with what they see and hear in classrooms, *reception* and *construction*.

Receptive learning is what occurs when students add to their existing stock of assorted facts via rote, drill, and practice exercises. This process of pure repetition and *memorization* produces the ability only to give back the material in the form it was memorized or in response to exact cues such as multiple-choice questions, or "essay-type questions" that permit reproduction of fixed strings of information generally, but not necessarily, without much comprehension (a process students often refer to as "spitting back"); it may have utility if quick recall or easy and possibly lasting access is all that is required. David Perkins refers to the various types of "knowledge" that this kind of learning produces as either "inert," "naive," or "ritual." It is "inert," lifeless, because it is remembered only when a student is directly quizzed, and is not, and cannot, be used elsewhere or otherwise. It is also frequently "naive" because the new facts, perhaps about the roundness of the earth, for example, make no actual difference to a young student's belief that it is actually flat. And it is often "ritual," a part of "the school game that students learn," which produces "schoolish performances [that] make little connection to [a student's] intuition about the way things are."[3]

Constructive learning can occur in two different ways. One takes place when students incorporate new material into an existing framework; they learn with understanding. In this process, material is *remembered* and what is still thought of as *the* world is seen somewhat differently, as though through new spectacles, "in a new light." This is the staple diet of any good classroom. Information is turned into knowledge so that what starts out as mere data, or facts becomes manipulable and applicable in new forms in different situations.

However, besides the learning that can come from this additive process, there is a second kind of constructive learning that is sometimes referred to as *transformative*, or *generative*. In this process, what is learnt entirely changes or completely replaces a mental structure or frame of reference—new worlds come into sight, literally, through such instruments as microscopes, or metaphorically by use of the imagination, in either case leading to a complete scientific or symbolic change of outlook technically known as a "paradigm" shift. This is an occasional and marvelous occurrence, often quite unpredictable even by teachers who have been in the classroom for years. Duckworth calls it "the having of wonderful ideas," in her inspiring book of that name.[4] Even beginning teachers however may experience such a shift in a single student, or even in a whole class, and the exhilaration of the experience is so powerful that it is a major reason why true teachers stay teaching despite the unique discouragement all teachers undergo from time to time.

As an example: a student may just learn the bare fact that water is also known as H_2O, but he or she *may* then move on to the knowledge that water is a colorless liquid with certain physical characteristics and properties, and to the understanding of how those can change, eventually, to knowledge of water (and thus the world as a whole) as teeming with invisible life, or the source of vast energy, or to a perception of water as symbol of birth and rebirth.

The latter two kinds of learning, additive—that which is fitted into a student's existing mental framework, and transformative—that which changes the framework itself,[5] absolutely require that students be given the opportunity to work with the words they hear or read, or with the visual symbols they see, so that they can actively incorporate them into their thought processes, and not just let them wash over their ears and eyes.

It is thus clear that constructive learning has clear advantages as compared with learning that is merely receptive. Since the latter brings with it no comprehension, the only performance supported by it is verbatim repetition. Information learned "by heart," and not assimilated into a student's existing knowledge framework, is of little practical value (outside school), and is apt to be quickly forgotten. When the significance of the knowledge is understood and appreciated by the student, it is far likelier to be incorporated and so to be available for use in varied situations, and in further learning.

What Does Understanding Involve?

Like the word *learning*, the term *understanding* is often used loosely in educational circles without serious attention to its meaning. It is not uncommon for teachers to ask students, "Do you understand?", when they have not thought through what it really means to understand something, or how students themselves would know for sure whether they did or not. Dictionary definitions include words like *comprehend, embrace, grasp,* and *seize* to convey the notion that understanding is a process of reaching out, gathering in, ordering, and connecting, and in general making sense out of individual items. As a learner is able to pull together items of information under an umbrella of existing knowledge, understanding begins to take shape. Grounded understanding involves the establishment of *mental relationships*. When teachers ask students, "Do you understand this?", what they are really asking is, "Are you able to connect this new information with what's already there?"

As learners, we begin to comprehend the meaning of a word like *fascism* when we are able to conceive of it as a type of *government*, a term with which we are already familiar. Our understanding is further enhanced when we are able to compare and contrast fascism with *communism* and to see them both as being forms of *totalitarianism*. If we have read accounts and seen film of fascist dictators and life under their regimes from the World War II era, we have yet, other, more concrete, references with which to connect the idea.

We have the potential to understand why heavy steel ships are able to float on the sea if we can relate this phenomenon to the general principle of flotation that is already anchored in our minds. The essence of understanding is the pulling together of particulars under one previously established generalization or "big idea" for which these particulars are an extension.

A second requirement of grounded understanding is for a learner to be able to perceive an application of the new learning. Students take a big step toward understanding any object, process, or fact when they see how it can be used to fulfill some purpose or goal. As soon as they perceive what something is for, they understand it to some degree. Thus, learning that can be seen to have some practical use is much more likely to be internalized than that which is encountered simply as an academic exercise.

To have a solid understanding of a historical concept such as imperialism, students need not only to comprehend it in the abstract as a particular variety of aggressive and acquisitive behavior of one country toward another, but to recognize how the concept is used in our present world. Students' understanding becomes firmer as they realize how the term is employed by the leaders of some countries to label and judge the activities of certain other countries.

For understanding to be functional, then, a learner's ability to see relationships among concepts, generalizations, and facts needs to be complemented by a perception of the purpose, or personal significance, such as interest or enjoyment, that is served by this formal knowledge. It turns out that understanding is best achieved when the learner can perceive a value or a use for that which is to be learned. This is an absolutely crucial reason for teachers to see that motivation and understanding are integrally related.

Teaching for Understanding

The ability to understand what is seen and heard requires considerable skill on the part of a young learner. It is a skill that takes a good deal of practice even for students at the formal operations level, those who have attained the ability to deal with abstract thought.[6] It requires the ability to call up relevant background knowledge and to make appropriate connections between this existing knowledge and new information as it is being received. Within the school setting, learners must be able to do all this fast enough to keep pace with the incoming flow of new knowledge. If the information is coming from fast-paced teacher talk, it is easy to see how a student may fall behind and give up trying to understand.

When students are continually presented with abstract information that they are unable, or unwilling, to assimilate because of inadequate knowledge backgrounds or lack of perceived relevance, they will be inclined to turn off their mental processors and resort to passive memorization. In other words, they will stop trying to understand and instead will devote their mental efforts to storing and recalling material in which they see no significance, purely for purposes of the test. The frequent student question, "Will it be on the test on Tuesday?" is an indication that students recognize when, and *how*, they need to "learn" material to satisfy what teachers regard as important. Although there is a definite skill involved in the accurate memorization of arbitrarily associated bits of information, receptive learning is essentially a mechanical process with limited utility in helping students develop the capacity to learn for themselves, and by themselves. It does not require nor provide practice in logical or reflective thinking, operations that are fundamental to independent learning.

Unfortunately, many students get far more practice during their school careers in memorizing verbal material than assistance in learning how to understand it. Were it the case that these skills were complementary processes or that skill in memorizing information could lead to or serve as a prerequisite to skill in understanding, we might begin to justify this heavy emphasis on learning without concern for meaning in so many school subjects. For the most part, however, it is a dead end. Unassimilated learning is not only quickly forgotten, but it works counter to the development of understanding because it deprives students of much needed practice in thinking things out. It also tends to put students off learning, possibly even for life.

When introducing new learning, there are a number of steps you can take to assist students to deal effectively with what they are being taught:

1. Provide what are termed "advance organizers," outlines, preferably graphic or visual, in some simple, easily grasped, and memorable form that give a preview of the topic that is about to be explored, clearly pointing to logical relationships among the various elements of the learning content.
2. Attend carefully to the pacing of instructions or explanations you provide students. Allow adequate time for them to assimilate new information as it is being received.
3. Take an active interest in how students are dealing with the information you are teaching. Organize your lessons to accommodate the learning needs of students at their particular stages of conceptual development.
4. Have students attempt to talk through the mental operations they are using to discover gaps or "sticking points" in their information-processing patterns.
5. Be clear in your own mind when it is important for students to understand new material (generally) and when it is appropriate for them to

memorize information (occasionally). Be sure you have a good reason for the latter choices.

6. When introducing students to large segments of new knowledge, subdivide it into separate meaning units, each representing a skill element able to be assimilated (see Chapter 7).

7. Offer students helpful strategies for approaching assignments, recognizing that different subject matter (math, say, and literature) is likely to call for very different kinds of thinking.

◆◆◆ A P P L I C A T I O N   E X E R C I S E S ◆◆◆

1. Design a note-making strategy that you might offer students to help them organize new material in a subject you plan to teach. Make this note-taking procedure exemplify basic guidelines for the *constructive learning* of new information.

2. Identify a cognitive process that could be the focus of a unit or lesson in your teaching area (e.g., dividing fractions, or reading for main ideas). Analyze this cognitive operation from the standpoint of the component mental skills it would require (e.g., the ability to multiply fractions, the ability to recognize logical relationships between main ideas and supporting points). Based on your task analysis, outline a strategy for teaching this cognitive skill that takes into consideration the suboperations students would need to be able to perform.

3. Select a concept (expressible in one or two words) that could be the focus of a unit or lesson in a subject you teach (e.g., animals). Brainstorm a number of related concepts that represent larger categories, uses, needs, and extensions of this main concept. For example, the concept "animal" calls to mind the concepts "dog," "mammal," "reptile," "living thing," "food," "shelter," "pet," and so on. Use your list of concepts to prepare a concept map, a graphic form of organizer, showing relationships (links) among these various ideas, with the targeted concept at the center. Think of ways concept maps can be useful to you in your efforts to apply an information-processing model of learning. For a more extended treatment of the subject of concept mapping, *Learning How to Learn*, by Novak and Gowin, is highly recommended.[7]

Encouraging Inner-Self Processes in Young Learners

The human personality, like fruit, can be thought of as having an outer, social layer, a skin, as it were, covering and hiding all that lies within, the personal core. The inner recesses of the personality contain the attributes that make a person distinctively human. Here lies our potential to think deeply, to believe, to love, to care, and to hold values. It is the basis of our capacity to take initiative, and to act—as opposed to simply being acted upon. It is in this dynamic center of our personhood that lie our powers of self-expression and of decision making, together with our creative capacities.[8]

We are able to depend on the external layer of our personalities to perform tasks that require little attention or emotional involvement. Our *outer-self* is usually the only part of us that is active when we are doing busy work, being polite, or waiting in line to buy groceries. It is the part we are most likely to show strangers or to retreat to in situations in which we do not feel comfortable enough to be "the real us." It is also the part of our self that is involved when we are inclined just to go along with the crowd. Our outer-self does nonetheless have some important functions. Besides its ability to serve as a protective shell for our more sensitive and vulnerable *inner-self*, it allows us to "run on cruise-control" as we encounter tedium or routine in our daily lives, situations that do not require inner-self involvement.[9]

There is, however, a serious problem in allowing our outer-selves to take over life functions that properly belong to the inner-self. There is little chance for us to develop our potential to think, create, value, and relate to others if we continually allow this external layer of our personalities to represent our whole being.[10] In an increasingly impersonal society like our own, there is a distinct danger that a person's dynamic center, their real self, will remain inactive and underdeveloped. Unless we are regularly able to be in situations that stimulate dynamic-self involvement, this vital core of our personalities is likely to remain weak and inaccessible.

Young people in today's schools are greatly in need of learning encounters that challenge their inner selves if school is to be a true growth experience and not just a meaningless game. For education to be genuine, it must work to stimulate the dynamic-selves of young learners. To be effective, it has to activate and cultivate those inner qualities that help a person become their best self.

Teaching to the Inner Self

As a teacher, you have an important role to play in the inner-self development of students. The way you begin lessons, the lead-ups you use in approaching assignments, and the rationales you offer for school learning will determine whether you encourage dynamic-self or simply outer-self involvement in learning.

When a history teacher opens a lesson by showing a picture of a famous historical personality and asks, "What do you see in the facial features of this person?" he or she is appealing to the perceptions, imaginations, and human interests of the students. When a teacher of literature begins a new lesson segment with the question, "What would you have done had you been confronted with the same dilemma as the main character of this story?", that teacher is appealing to the students to think themselves into the inner life of another person and to apply their own experiences, values, and problem solving abilities to the situation. Similarly, when a science teacher asks students to design through brainstorming techniques a lab experiment that would illustrate the process of oxidation, that teacher is presenting a challenge to the higher thought processes of these students.

In each instance, students are being invited to get in touch with a part of themselves that, at this stage in their lives, is likely to be largely undeveloped. They are being asked to think, to feel, and to care at deeper levels than they are ordinarily accustomed to doing in their fast-paced interactions with the world around them. The teachers are seeking to activate inner processes that constitute the growing edge of the student's personal development, his or her maturing as a human being.

Unfortunately, as Chapters 1 and 2 point out, there are powerful forces at work in many of our schools that tend to discourage teachers from arousing students' interest in learning. An emphasis on getting through material, on "covering the curriculum," and on learning material that can most easily be tested, measured, and graded tends to be at cross-purposes with the inner-self development of students. Harried classroom teachers often find it more expedient to rely on external pressures such as threats of punishment or promises of reward to get students to learn. Feeling the pressure to meet the bureaucratic demands of the organization, teachers often begin lessons by invoking students' grade anxieties or competitive instincts rather than their dynamic-self processes. Openers, such as "You people need to pay close attention here today because there will be a test on this material on Friday" or "We need to speed up the pace on this unit because the sixth-period class is already a day ahead of us," are common forms of extrinsic appeal. They take the focus off meaningful learning and instead center the student's attention on the need to submit to the school system.

Extrinsic approaches focus on the more instinctive and mechanical layer of the student's personality. They attempt to get students to learn by playing on their fears, insecurities, and urges to conform. When widely used, they keep students focused on deficiencies—what the student doesn't know, can't do—rather than on their possibilities for growth. They convey the notion that learning is something you do merely to avoid the stigma of failure or to be able to hold your own in a competitive society. They do nothing to promote the realization that learning can have interest and value in and of itself. If we believe the school experience should enhance a young person's capacity for self-initiated learning, these kinds of manipulative appeal do a serious disservice to a student's potential as a lifetime learner.

As you seek ways of teaching that will maximize the personal involvement of students in their own learning, the following general strategies are recommended:

1. Encourage new learning by invoking students' intrinsic rather than extrinsic motivations to learn.
2. Avoid communicating to students a feeling of urgency just to get through lessons.

3. Respect learning rhythms by allowing sufficient time for the "romance" stage of learning before moving to the "precision" stage.
4. Work to develop a learning atmosphere that promotes confidence, trust, and reflection on the part of students.

Tapping Intrinsic Motivation to Learn

Teachers sometimes give up rather quickly on efforts to stimulate intrinsic interest in subject matter, and fall back on external motivation because they feel it is more effective and reliable (and a lot easier). If, as is quite likely, students do not come to class feeling initial enthusiasm for the subject matter, a reminder of the need to pass or to please the teacher generally acts as a convenient motivator, as many teachers have found. When teachers resort to this approach, it is often because they have not made a strong enough attempt to link what they are setting out to teach to students' interests, concerns, and purposes.

The time and mental energy that teachers invest in tapping into intrinsic motivation are well worth the effort for practical reasons as well as human development benefits. They are also highly desirable from political and moral perspectives in schools that exist to maintain and improve our free and democratic society. Learning that activates the inner-self processes of students is not only higher-quality learning, but it is also self-sustaining. Students do not need to be continually prodded to "stay on task" when they are engaged meaningfully in classroom learning projects. As a result, the teacher's need to be a disciplinarian is considerably reduced. Moreover, students who have developed an intrinsic interest in learning activities are more genuinely involved and more enjoyable to be around. It makes the long hours spent with student groups a great deal more satisfying.

With experience and careful reflection, you will gain a sense of what will work, first to draw students into active involvement with a particular lesson or project, and then to keep them thus engaged.

Student *curiosity* is one potential motivator you can build on. As indicated in Chapter 4, students at the concrete operations level will ordinarily have a lively interest in nonabstract realities that strike them as extreme or extraordinary. Young people at this stage can be found to exhibit a sudden fascination with the extremes of what exists and what is known.[11] They are often attracted to knowledge sources such as *The Guinness Book of World Records* with its accounts of the biggest, the smallest, the fastest, the highest, the furthest, and so on. You can take advantage of this developing interest in external reality when it comes to designing "grabbers" for initiating new learning.

Another internal stimulus to learn derives from the *mental challenge* involved in dealing with mysteries, puzzles, conflicts, discrepancies, and problems of one sort or another. Most people have an inborn desire to resolve incongruities and to get beyond sticking-points in their lives. When skillfully managed, students from middle elementary and on usually respond to invitations to address challenging problems or dilemmas, whether their own or someone else's. Inattentive students often sit up and take notice when a piece of new information conflicts with a personal belief or when the discussion turns to some interesting problem or predicament. Some particularly good teachers are able to employ a problem-solving frame of reference in approaching most any new learning activity, realizing its potential to arouse the intrinsic motivations of their students. There are other highly successful teachers who become known for their "devil's advocate" ploys to create cognitive dissonance. They feign disagreement or contrariness to give a sense of drama to classroom interaction, thereby helping to keep students interested.

Related to this internal urge to resolve problems, is a student's inner *desire for personal competence*. Most people feel the need to be good at one or more things. It is an extension of the desire for personal adequacy. This inner drive to become competent is thought to be self-initiating and unrelated to the need for social approval or economic reward. Some students of human motivation have considered it a primary incentive for learning. In her valuable survey of the sources of motivation, Stipek draws attention to the claim by some motivation theorists that, in addition to the need to feel competent, students have a need to feel self-determining. They want to believe that they are engaging in activities by their own volition—because they want to rather than to achieve some external reward or to avoid punishment.[12] Skillful teachers are able to build on these desires for personal competence and self-determination to draw students into encounters with learning, while taking pains to minimize irrelevant potential social or competitive overtones.

Avoiding the Misleading Challenge

You should take special care not to allow classroom learning to be equated with getting through a series of events. That is the attitude conveyed when a teacher says to students, "If you finish Chapter 8 by Wednesday, I'll give you some free time on Friday."

This sort of bargain[13] reflects the high priority teachers place on meeting their own content coverage deadlines. It implies that the quality of the learning is a lesser consideration. From an educational standpoint it turns out to be a misguided challenge because it appeals to students' desires to have a break from learning, not to any genuine desire to learn.

It is also a mistake to tell students that learning tasks will be either difficult or easy when giving assignments. To say to a student, "I'd like you to work on those problems—they're easy," is to represent the learning activity as relatively unchallenging, but something that needs to be done to satisfy the teacher. Similarly, to warn students that "this next assignment is an especially difficult one" is to suggest that although they may not have the ability, the important thing is to complete the assignment anyway, and it is equally ineffective. If you want to be a teacher, and not just an instructor, you have to begin to find more complex intrinsically challenging methods for engaging students in school learning. Students who are stimulated to apply their best resources to a particular learning task will experience the kind of inner satisfaction that people generally feel when they are deeply engaged in working at something that matters to them.

There will be occasions when your efforts to draw on intrinsic motivation simply fail to engage students. Particularly with younger students at the early elementary level, basic needs for security and belongingness will often override intrinsic interests in learning, requiring that you have some well-conceived forms of external motivation at your disposal.[14]

You will find it easier to understand the general, but by no means universal, decline in intrinsic motivation as students move up the grades if you know that research suggests that this may be because[15]:

1. Children's interest in engaging in tasks for the sake of developing mastery is replaced by an interest in obtaining external rewards, such as high grades.
2. Children's self-confidence in being able to master tasks encountered in school declines with age and experience in school.
3. School becomes more formal, more evaluative, and more competitive.

You can, nonetheless, do much to offset this drop in enthusiasm if you search out materials and techniques that at least reduce the need for external pressure. The following are some techniques you can use to promote students' intrinsic interests in your class and its activities:

1. Make individual self-expression a major priority in designing your teaching objectives. Consider self-expression to include initiative taking, caring, valuing, and problem solving as well as verbal and written performance. Provide ongoing opportunities for students to exhibit various forms of personal expression, and make success, at some level, possible for all students much of the time.
2. Design learning activities that are problem-based. By approaching learning from the standpoint of questions rather than answers, and incorporated in projects in which they have some choice, rather than set assignments, you help students recognize the practical value of organized knowledge in meeting human problems and needs.
3. Let them know that you are as concerned about *how* they arrived at an answer or a solution (the process) as you are interested in the outcome itself—and that there may be more than one solution in some cases (or possibly none, for sure).
4. Build a sense of drama into your teaching style. Use well-placed humor and devil's advocate ploys to maintain interest; and use indirect teaching strategies to produce unanticipated "learning payoffs."
5. Offer good-natured challenges to students' performance skills as a means of initiating and maintaining interest in class activities, for example, "Who would like to go to the board and try Problem 6," "How many think they'll be able to finish their projects by next Friday?"

6. Use frequent pair or small-group discussions in class. Shy or inhibited students often find their voices and reveal their personalities in close encounters with peers. This can serve to ease reticent students into greater involvement in the class as a whole.
7. Regularly share with students details of interesting reading you are doing, unusual personalities you have met, exciting trips you have taken, or strange events you have witnessed. Arrange low-key group sharing sessions during which students have opportunities to share something of their personal lives and experiences with one another. Use these occasions to promote respect and support for the individuality of students.
8. Make your teaching as concrete and visual as possible. Bring in, and encourage your students to bring in, relevant real-world material such as current newspapers and magazines, videotapes you or they have recorded, and things you have picked up in your travels (or they in theirs).

Respecting Learning Rhythms

The Period of "Romance"

Those who have developed an awareness of their own learning patterns may have noticed that learning tends to develop in recognizable, natural stages. Most of us learn best when we have first had an opportunity to play with ideas or objects for a period of time before narrowing our attentions to precise details or skills. During this early stage of learning we are allowing our intuitions, perceptions, and imaginations free expression. This is a time for exploration, free association, and arousal of interest. Too much narrowly focused thinking at this stage can serve to abort the process. A. N. Whitehead refers to this period of first contact with new learning as the *stage of romance*. This initial stage in the learning process is the period of first apprehension:

> The subject matter has the vividness of novelty; it holds within itself unexplored connections with possibilities half-disclosed by glimpses and half-concealed by the wealth of material. In this stage knowledge is not dominated by systematic procedure.[16]

The Precision Stage

The second stage of learning is a period in which romance gives way to the more controlled and concentrated study of facts and terms. This is the time for exactness and analysis of details. Whitehead calls this the *stage of precision*. He warns against the danger of introducing precision in learning before an extended period of romance with the new learning:

> In this stage, width of relationship is subordinated to exactness of formulation. It is the stage of grammar, the grammar of language and the grammar

of science. It proceeds by forcing on the student's acceptance a given way of analyzing the facts, bit by bit. . . . It is evident that a stage of precision is barren without a previous stage of romance: unless there are facts which have already been vaguely apprehended in their broad generality, the previous analysis is an analysis of nothing. It is simply a series of meaningless statements about bare facts, produced artificially and without any further relevance.[17]

The Generalization Stage

When learning proceeds in its proper cycle, the stage of precision is followed by a third phase that Whitehead labels the *stage of generalization*. Having had a chance to become acquainted with organized detail related to the subject under investigation, the learner attempts to see the new learning from a wider angle once again. The third stage of the learning cycle is in a sense a return to the romance stage, with the advantage of new information from the precision phase. It involves bringing the elements together in the form of new insights, and attempting to project relationships and applications.

With this learning cycle in mind, you should regard the introductory phase of learning as a time for building the context. At this stage you are attempting to help students become interested and intrigued enough to assimilate the new information that is to follow. Your main objective here is to make it possible for students to develop insight, and perspective, and thus to be able to see meaning in the forthcoming detail, and to look for more. Thus, in introducing a unit on the U.S. Civil War, the following types of statements and questions could be used to get students into the habit of speculation and inquiry:

> More Americans lost their lives in the Civil War than in World Wars I and II combined.
>
> The Civil War threatened to leave us with two separate countries instead of one.
>
> Many soldiers in the Civil War were fighting against their own fathers, brothers, or near relatives.
>
> How could such a destructive war have happened in this type of country?
>
> Can you imagine something like this happening today, where neighboring states like California and Oregon would be fighting one another across state boundaries?
>
> What would you imagine might have caused such an internal war of brother against brother?

It is important to allow students to spend long enough in the romance phase of learning for them to form questions and viewpoints that will carry over to the precision stage. Then, following their acquisition of details of the Civil War, students should be assisted at the generalization stage to consolidate their learning through the formation of new insights and projections, derived from questions such as these:

What factors were most responsible for causing the Civil War?

What would it have taken to prevent it?

Did the outcome justify the terrible suffering and loss of life?

Is any war ever morally justifiable?

Did any real heroes emerge from this war? How were they heroic?

Had you been alive and eligible, would you have been willing to fight for one side or the other in the Civil War?

What was the main importance of this war in our national history?

Do you think another civil war could or could not ever happen in this country? What might lead in that direction?

Have the effects of the Civil War ceased to affect the United States?

Maria Montessori pointed out to the fact that there are what she called "teachable moments." What she meant is that there are good, not so good, and downright bad times for teachers to introduce students to new material and new ideas. People who develop into good teachers learn to sense when students are ready and willing to grapple with unfamiliar facts and notions. Similarly, they develop the capacity to recognize when the time has come to review and to sum up subject matter that has been worked through. Competent teachers are keenly aware whether students are ready for fresh learning, and of what kind, and in what mode. As a result of careful observation and reflection on what they have done and its results, they have acquired a particularly acute sense of when to talk, and when, on the other hand, to arrange for students to become involved in interacting with materials, with each other, or with instruments and tools such as computers, microscopes, or musical instruments (or all simultaneously). They sense when it is a fitting time to send students to the library for information, for instance, or when the time may be ripe for a field trip.

The most common violation of learning rhythms in formal education is the widespread practice of introducing precision at the beginning of a lesson or unit with no effort being made to develop learner readiness by allowing opportunities for exploration. Consider the following key measures you can take in your own teaching to provide for sufficient romance in the learning process:

1. Take time at the beginning of new units to discuss with students their initial interests, questions, and perceptions relating to the area of study you are about to have them embark on.
2. Always prepare good introductory sets for your teaching lessons (see Chapter 4).
3. Allow for a good number of affective objectives as you design unit and lesson plans (see Chapter 3).
4. When constructing performance-based teaching units (e.g., writing, basketball, painting), allow students to experience the whole activity before requiring the mastery of individual skills.
5. Whenever possible, provide lab experiences, field trips, films, and other concrete experiences at the beginning rather than at the end of teaching units.

6. Provide students ample opportunities for intuitive thinking and free association of ideas without the immediate compulsion to produce data or conclusions.
7. Place as much emphasis on how students learn as on what they learn.
8. Don't try to hurry learning.

Providing a Facilitative Learning Climate

A main prerequisite for getting students to apply their best efforts to learning in the classroom is to provide an atmosphere that is both encouraging and stimulating. This means developing a learning climate that supports thought and exploration, one in which students feel secure and confident enough to throw themselves wholeheartedly into learning activities.

Making Learning Manageable

One way you can encourage students to become genuinely involved is to make learning tasks manageable for them. Students are more likely to give their best efforts when they know what they are up against, when they feel a sense of personal control over their own learning. The attitudes you demonstrate toward the content you teach will go a long way toward determining the confidence with which students approach this new learning.

Too often the subject matter contained in textbooks and teacher presentations seems mysterious to young learners. They don't see how the world of formal knowledge connects with their own experience. As a contributing factor, teachers often treat formal knowledge as obscure and impersonal, something that demands unquestioning acceptance and ritualistic consumption. Students thus see themselves as cast in the role of passive receivers of preestablished truths that stand apart from their lives and that make them feel small and insignificant in comparison.

When you are sensitive to the learning needs and perceptions of growing young people, you are less likely to teach your subject matter in ways that put up barriers between the student and the world of knowledge. You will be more inclined to emphasize the tentative nature of much that is found in textbooks, and to make it clear to students that textbooks present a very much simplified view of the way things are, or are thought to be, or to have been.

In addition to the attitudes you exhibit toward the subject(s) you teach, there are a number of things you can do to give students more confidence in their capacity to learn and a greater measure of control in dealing with new material. They include:

1. Make learning tasks as clear and explicit as possible.
2. Minimize technical language when introducing students to a new topic.
3. Work from where students are to where you want them to be (i.e., from a student-centered to a more subject-centered view of a topic).

4. Help students establish connections between new learning and the world outside of school.
5. Seek to provide early success for each student.
6. Make use of objectives that are challenging but attainable.
7. Give tests that enable students to do well, in part because they do not consist wholly of mere recall or recognition, as with most multiple-choice questions.
8. Encourage and assist students to learn on their own, or with others as often as possible.

Establishing Trust and Support

When you stimulate learning through interest and a sense of purpose you are asking students to invest a substantial part of themselves in school activity. For this to happen, you must have established a solid bond of trust and respect with your students. This condition is enhanced when students perceive you as your own person, someone who is responsible for his or her own decisions and actions. The teachers who succeed in getting the best out of their students are those who have earned student respect and confidence out of an authority that seems to come naturally. This means avoiding as much as possible the use of your official position as leverage to control students or to get them to learn. It means taking personal responsibility for what goes on in your classes. One of the things that helps to communicate a sense of natural authority is the use of *I-messages:* "I feel this is an important assignment and I'm going to ask everyone to do it" (as opposed to "All of the ninth-grade classes are doing this assignment. It's a departmental requirement"). Or "I'd like everyone to take a look at the problem I have here on the board" (as opposed to "Maybe we ought to get busy with our math so your parents don't think I'm wasting your time"). When you use authentic I-messages to convey your intentions, you indicate a willingness to accept responsibility for decisions that affect the behavior of students in your classes. You show a readiness to be personally accountable for your choices.

A student's willingness to become deeply involved in school learning usually involves risk. When students show strong feelings about a poem or demonstrate serious concern about a particular social or environmental issue, they leave themselves vulnerable to the resentment or criticism of those who are less involved or think otherwise. There is the potential for being perceived as too intellectual or too emotional. Some peers may regard such serious involvement as simply a ploy for a better grade. As a teacher, you must be prepared to support and reinforce students who respond positively to your efforts to appeal to students' deeper feelings and values. Here are some ways you could try to do this:

1. Make it clear during the first meeting that this is a class in which students need not be afraid to exhibit individuality, honesty, and a wide range of personal expression.

2. Share some of your own innermost thoughts and feelings with your students when you feel that it is appropriate.
3. Get used to listening attentively to students' ideas and commenting in ways that encourage further participation.
4. Let self-revealing students inconspicuously know how much you value and appreciate their openness.
5. Make a conscious effort to avoid being judgmental when students show a willingness to share their deepest thoughts and feelings.
6. Protect such students if students who are less open show resentment. Do this tactfully, of course, so as not to alienate those who need to be encouraged to become better risk takers.
7. Let students know when you are trying something new and exciting, and that you're not sure how it's going to work out (maybe its success depends on them).

Encouraging Reflection

Reflective teaching techniques are those which use the learner's frame of reference to encourage questioning, imagining, guessing, and hypothesizing. The ability to produce a reflective atmosphere is a key indicator of high-quality teaching.

There are some basic conditions that contribute to a reflective climate in a school classroom. One is a pervasive *spirit of inquiry*. The classroom where reflective thinking is promoted is one in which inquiry and discovery are valued. Teachers in these classrooms are able either to acknowledge uncertainty: "It's not at all clear how evolution works," or to let students know that there are often added or alternative possibilities: "I'm not sure about my interpretation of the poem—I continue to see other things in it." These teachers welcome intellectual challenges: "You're right in raising that issue—I need to rethink the matter." They continually convey their belief in the value of thinking and frequently demonstrate by what they do and say that education involves exploring the unknown as well as learning what is known.

A spirit of inquiry is also fostered by teacher-questioning techniques that probe students' thoughts, imaginations, and previous experiences in a personal yet nonthreatening way. Questions (referred to as "divergent") that appeal to each individual student's thoughts and feelings are particularly effective at doing this:

What do you anticipate would happen if . . . ?
What do you think the connection is between . . . and . . . ?
How would you account for . . . ?
Can you imagine a . . . ?
Suppose you were in a position where . . . ?
How would you feel if . . . ?
Have you ever seen a person who . . . ?
What do you think causes people to . . . ?

Another important attribute of a reflective classroom is an emphasis on problem *finding*. Normally, classrooms are places where answers are sought and solutions are valued. In a thinking-centered classroom, students are taught and encouraged to find problems, to wonder, and to speculate on what solutions or answers there might be. The teacher nurtures the problem-finding and problem-solving attitude by encouraging students to ask questions, not just to get answers, but often for pushing forward to see how the problem might be addressed: "Here are some data about voting patterns in the United States—what questions could we ask?" Or "We'll be studying family life in the Soviet Union—what questions would you like to have answered?"

A third condition that serves to promote reflective thinking in the classroom is a *deliberative pace*. Many classrooms seem to encourage impulsiveness—the teacher asks a question, expects an immediate answer, and calls on the first student who raises a hand. Although this practice may tell the teacher what that particular student knows (although it says nothing about what the other students know), promote rehearsal of facts, and prove student attentiveness, it is generally counterproductive when thinking is the focus. Teachers in a reflective classroom make it possible and comfortable for students to think about things without feeling hurried to produce answers. By allowing thoughtful pauses of several seconds at the end of teacher questions and at the end of student answers, teachers can help to promote this unhurried atmosphere. Teachers who avoid bombarding students with rapid-fire questions, but instead give students time to construct ideas, are showing their respect for the internal processes that produce meaningful learning.

◆◆◆ APPLICATION EXERCISES ◆◆◆

1. Call to mind a lesson you expect to teach in the near future. Describe a problem on which you will base the lesson (e.g., some conflict of values, prejudice, misconception, confusion, or lack of insight). Identify the general approach you will take in developing the lesson, including the set you will use, the central questions you will raise, and the main activity you will arrange.

2. Devise a creative introduction (set) that you might use to initiate a junior high school science lesson on air pollution. Compose an alternative opening for a third grade lesson on household pets and an original set for a senior high school lesson on study skills. Design each of these lesson introductions to appeal to some form of intrinsic interest. Identify the specific type of intrinsic motivation to which you are appealing in each case (e.g., competence, curiosity, control).

Addressing Individual Learning Needs

Multiple Intelligences

As you continue to work closely with groups of young people, you will soon be aware of very significant differences in your students' interests and abilities. Until very recently—and the view is still common—intelligence was supposed to be a kind of inborn, general mental excellence, a "giftedness," or "smartness," which each individual had in a greater or lesser, and largely fixed, amount as measured by "intelligence tests" and quantified as an "IQ." However, at least as far back as the early 1970s, some scholars were taking a different view: "that humans have diverse . . . distinct abilities . . . multiple intelligence systems,"[18] but it was Howard Gardner who finally put together what he called a "theory of multiple intelligences"[19] and this has become widely accepted and integrated into everyday teaching practices. According to Gardner, a student's "intelligence" can express itself in one—or almost always several—distinct capacities: linguistic, logical, spatial, bodily-kinesthetic, musical, interpersonal, and intrapersonal. In terms of "smartness," these translate roughly into word-smart, logic- and number-smart, picture-smart, music-smart, people-smart, and self-smart.[20] Practically, this means that you, as a teacher, both can and must continually try to help students learn by giving them opportunities to use *all* their intelligences and avoid teaching in ways that almost exclusively emphasize linguistic and logical capacities. Students tend to put their intelligences to different uses, too, as Sternberg has pointed out, some favoring analysis, others creation, and yet others practice.[21]

Research in the last 20 years or so has also confirmed what you have no doubt noticed, and perceptive teachers have always known, namely, that students differ greatly in how they deal with new experiences, and how they learn from them. This is not a matter of intelligence but of what has come to be called *style*. Some seem, as Bernice McCarthy put it, "to respond primarily by sensing, and feeling, [or intuiting] their way, while others think their way through [though] no one uses one response to the total exclusion of the other."[22] In processing information or experience, "some people are watchers first, others are doers first. The watchers reflect on new things, the doers act on new information immediately."[23] What this variation comes down to in practice is that some seem at any particular time and in any particular situation to be better able and more inclined to learn through listening and talking to and with teacher and classmates. They tend to enjoy and to profit from teacher presentations and student discussions in small or large groups. Others have an aptitude and preference for learning by seeing and looking—at words in a book, at images on a screen, at visual materials of any sort. Yet a third sort of student finds hands-on experience, any kind of physical performance (quite possibly feet, legs, arms, and all bodily-kinesthetic experience), especially but not exclusively in the area of physical education, particularly attractive and productive.

This being the case, teachers have a responsibility not simply to follow their own *teaching* preferences but to use (and it may be they first have to acquire) a variety of teaching approaches and of materials that will allow any group of students to learn in ways that they individually presently favor while making it necessary and reasonably agreeable for each of them to develop other ways of acquiring knowledge and skill, especially since all of them will need to be able to learn in varied ways throughout their lives. What one might call "cross-channel learning," the type that comes from activities that integrate the use of eyes, ears, and hands with reflective thinking, is also likelier to be more stimulating and productive than learning confined to a single channel required by the teacher or chosen out of habit (or as the line of least resistance) by the student. Since working with computers often entails the use of most of the multiple approaches to learning, and lends itself equally well to individual or group activity, developing ways of integrating computer-aided learning into one's teaching must be a high priority for the teacher who wants to get through to all students. (See Chapter 8 on the use of computers and Chapter 4 on planning for individual differences.)

Teaching Minority and Disadvantaged Students

It is important that you be able to adjust your teaching patterns to meet the often special learning needs of minority students and disadvantaged or "at risk"[24] youngsters in your classroom. These students are frequently alienated by the prevailing school culture. Their educational aspirations, their learning styles, and their social patterns are often significantly different from those of the typical middle-class white, American-born student, sometimes giving the false impression that they lack the potential for learning.

The following are some basic measures you can take in your efforts to adapt your teaching to the learning needs of educationally disadvantaged or culturally alienated youngsters in your classes:

1. Do as much as possible to foster collaboration and working within groups (cooperative learning). These students need opportunities to participate, to work collectively, and to practice critical thinking. Minority and poor populations are often more group-oriented and interactive than white, middle-class students who belong to a subculture that tends to stress and reward individualism.[25]
2. Build on the wide array of intelligences these students, just as much as any others, possess, and allow as much as you can for varying types of ability and learning style. Spend less time ranking students and more time helping them identify their natural abilities and gifts.
3. Attempt to provide some of the "emotional and cultural capital" that is often missing from the lives of disadvantaged students. The parents of many of these youngsters have often, for one reason or another, but above all because of poverty, not been able to give them the consistent personal attention, intimacy, and assurance that their more fortunate peers received. By making a deliberate effort to provide a reasonable and caring environment for these students, you can help to foster the

kind of confidence and positive outlook they will need to cope with school, and life in general.

4. Work to gain the cooperation and collaboration of parents. Efforts to improve home-school relations do not have to be highly structured (see Chapter 11).

If you have any doubt that all students can learn, do not go into teaching. When you have realistically high expectations for all of your students, you will foster an atmosphere that allows success to become the norm; that is, your expectation will tend to become a self-fulfilling prophecy. On the other hand, if you have low expectations, you will almost inevitably be promoting failure.

◆◆◆ SUGGESTED ACTIVITIES AND QUESTIONS ◆◆◆

1. What are the main differences between receptive and meaningful learning? What has to take place inside a learner before understanding has occurred?

2. Can you name school learning tasks for which you consider rote learning appropriate. Is it sometime unnecessary for learners to achieve grounded understanding in such areas? Why is that, do you think? Mention other kinds of school learning in which you believe meaning and understanding are crucial. What are some of the central advantages of meaningful learning?

3. Take the opportunity to learn more about associative learning as you encounter it in other contexts (e.g., educational psychology texts). What are some of the different varieties of conditioning or stimulus-response learning that have been identified by behavioral psychologists? How appropriate are these for teachers to employ in our society?

4. Make an effort to extend your knowledge of human learning by becoming acquainted with areas of human study such as cognitive learning theory, humanistic psychology, and existential philosophy. What common assumptions regarding human nature and human learning are shared by the aforementioned schools of thought?

5. What kind of inner-self development do you believe U.S. schools should be promoting in young people? What types of thinking skills will you be attempting to promote in your teaching?

6. What does it mean to have "learned how to learn"?

7. Will you be teaching subjects in which the perceived usefulness of the learning will be relatively apparent to students, or will you have to make special efforts to build this into learning activities? How will you do that?

8. Discuss some of the main techniques teachers can use to draw on students' internal motivations to learn. On what kinds of theories and assumptions regarding human motivation are these methods based?

9. What are some of the motivational techniques that good teachers should avoid if they are to depend on intrinsic rather than extrinsic appeals as their primary form of classroom motivation?

10. What are the differences between *romance* and *precision* in human learning? Mention general strategies you might use to build sufficient romance into the learning you will be promoting.

11. What are some of the important ways teachers can produce an atmosphere conducive to thoughtfulness and deliberation in their classrooms? Which of these methods have you seen used effectively by teachers in your own school career? Which do you feel confident you will be able to put into practice in your own teaching? What do you need to learn in this area, and how will you go about learning it?

12. How does a natural-authority relationship with students help teachers to better facilitate the inner-self development of these young people? How does a teacher acquire this kind of authority?

Notes

1. See John Goodlad, *A Place Called School*. New York: McGraw-Hill, 1984, especially Chaps. 6 and 7; Stuart B. Palonsky, *900 Shows a Year: A Look at Teaching from a Teacher's Side of the Desk*. New York: Random House, 1986, see Chaps. 3 and 7; Theodore Sizer, *Horace's Compromise: The Dilemma of the American High School*. Boston: Houghton Mifflin, 1984, and see Part 2 of this handbook.

2. Goodlad, *A Place Called School*, pp. 229–31.

3. David Perkins. *Smart Schools: From Training Memories to Educating Minds*. New York: Freedom Press, 1992.

4. Eleanor Duckworth, *The Having of Wonderful Ideas and Other Essays on Teaching and Learning*. New York: Teachers College Press, 1987.

5. Richard Hamilton and Elizabeth Ghatela, *Learning and Instruction*. New York: McGraw-Hill, 1994, pp. 214–217, 243–247.

6. Ibid., pp. 226–227.

7. Joseph D. Novak and D. Bob Gowin, *Learning How to Learn*. New York: Cambridge University Press, 1984.

8. Gordon W. Allport, *Becoming: Basic Considerations for a Psychology of Personality*. New Haven, Conn.: Yale University Press, 1969, p. 48.

9. Ibid., p. 63.

10. Ibid., p. 51.

11. Kieran Egan, *Educational Development*. New York: Oxford University Press, 1979, p. 31.

12. Deborah J. Stipek, *Motivation to Learn: From Theory to Practice*. Englewood Cliffs, NJ: Prentice-Hall, 1988, p. 44.

13. Sizer, *Horace's Compromise* (p. 180) suggests that an agreement between students and teacher may be a "conspiracy of convenience," a way to fill time with neither strain nor untoward effect, "a conspiracy of the least."

14. For a useful treatment of strategies for extrinsic motivation, see N. L. Gage and David C. Berliner, *Educational Psychology*, 4th ed. Boston: Houghton Mifflin, 1988, Chap. 15.

15. Stipek, *Motivation to Learn*, p. 49.

16. Alfred North Whitehead, *The Aims of Education*. New York: Macmillan, 1929, p. 28.

17. Ibid., p. 29.

18. Sheldon H. White, "Social Implications of IQ." In Paul H. Houts (Ed.), *The Myth of Measurability*. New York: Hart Publishing Co., 1977, p. 40.
19. Howard Gardner, *Frames of Mind: The Theory of Multiple Intelligences*. New York: Basic, 1983.
20. Thomas Armstrong, *Multiple Intelligences in the Classroom*. Alexandria, Va.: ASCD, 1994, p. 38.
21. Robert J. Sternberg, "What Does It Mean to Be Smart?" *Educational Leadership* (March 1997): 21.
22. Bernice McCarthy, "Using the 4MAT System to Bring Learning Styles to Schools." *Educational Leadership* (October 1990): 31–32. This issue was entirely dedicated to "Learning Styles and the Brain."
23. Ibid., p. 32.
24. The term *at risk* has become a popular expression for describing students who are in danger of dropping out of school or otherwise failing to achieve their educational potential as a result of their disadvantaged status, persistent underachievement, drug involvement, or other such serious problems.
25. M. Sandra Reeves, "Self-Interest and the Common Weal: Focusing on the Bottom Half." *Education Week* (April 27, 1988): p. 18, et seq.

CHAPTER 7

Explaining Things So Students Will Understand

The gap between what passes for understanding and genuine understanding remains great.

Howard Gardner

Something All Teachers Do

The ability to give clear and concise explanations is essential to a teacher's effectiveness in promoting student learning. Explanation is teacher talk designed to clarify any idea, process, or procedure that students have a need to understand, not just know, much less just have heard about. This means you are furnishing explanations any time you explain procedures for fire drills, discuss reasons for a particular assignment, or describe details of your grading system. More fundamental yet are the instructionally related explanations you will provide when you attempt to show the meanings of terms, the steps involved in certain processes, or the causes of particular events.

Whether the approach to new learning is primarily teacher-centered or more activity-based, teacher explanations usually constitute the starting point, if not the main body, of classroom instruction. You will also need to be able to provide explanations when students raise questions during group lessons or when they need help with individual work or independent projects. Given the central importance of verbal understanding in the learning of most school subjects, you are likely to be delivering explanations in all phases of your teaching. Explanation giving is as basic to the work of a teacher as the ability to use a hammer is to a carpenter.[1]

To achieve a sense of mastery as a classroom teacher, you will need the confidence and skill to be able to put together preplanned as well as spontaneous explanations for your students. It is a skill to which you will probably have to give some concentrated attention.

This chapter focuses on basic requirements for sound and intelligible classroom explanations. It presents main criteria for recognizing good explanations as well as guidelines for making your explanations clear to your students.

Explaining Ability Seldom Comes Naturally

If you are like most entering teachers, you have had considerable experience attempting to explain things to others before coming to teaching. You have had numerous opportunities to give directions, to clarify the meaning of language, and to offer reasons for actions or events. Unfortunately, this is no guarantee of proficiency.

In the normal give-and-take of life, there is a tendency for a person's explanations to be hastily formulated and delivered in a rather hit-or-miss fashion. Chances are you have been the recipient of off-the-cuff directions to some location while you were traveling, only to find yourself more confused by the explanation than you were beforehand:

> **YOU:** Excuse me sir, but could you direct me to the nearest gas station?
>
> **STRANGER:** Sure. There are two of them in this area. One is about a half-mile from here. The other is a little further away, but I like their gas better because their tanks are cleaner. I used to work there. But if you want cheaper gas, you might try the other one. I'll tell you how to get there first. I can't remember the name of the street, but you go north for about five blocks until you come to an intersection with a white building on the southeast corner. Make a right turn, and you'll go over a set of railroad tracks. Be sure to stay in the left lane.

Out-of-school explanations are frequently delivered on the run or in situations in which feedback on the adequacy of these explanations is seldom available. Consequently, few people have had occasion to become good explainers before entering teaching.

The ability to deliver clear and accurate explanations, and especially impromptu ones, does not come naturally to the majority of teachers. It is a skill that you need to deliberately cultivate if you are to become competent. Before entering the classroom, most teachers have received very little constructive feedback on their ability to explain, so it is easy for new teachers to assume they have greater natural proficiency than is the case. Thus, when you allow your classroom explanations to become simply extensions of long-term, previously unexamined language patterns, these explanations won't help students much, and may even leave them more confused.

This points up the need for you as a new teacher to begin perfecting your explanation techniques as you prepare yourself for the classroom.

Designing Logically Sound Explanations

A good explanation in teaching must satisfy three main requirements: (1) It has to be technically sound, that is, explain accurately and thoroughly what it is supposed to; (2) it must be intelligible to the students; and (3) it must be attractive, that is, it must engage the students' attention and interest. Explanations, however sound or intelligible, will likely fall on deaf ears unless the student sees some good reason, and *wants*, to understand.

Types of Explanations

To give explanations that are technically well-constructed and to be able to judge those given by students, you should be familiar with the main varieties of explanations,[2] be able to recognize when they are applicable, and know what they require to be considered sound. There are three main types of explanation, which are discussed below.

When teachers attempt to specify the meanings of terms such as *metaphor, percentage, propaganda,* or *aerobic exercise,* ("*what?*" explanations), they are presenting what are referred to as *interpretive explanations* because they are intended to clarify the meaning of a term. A sound interpretive explanation amounts to a good analytical definition of the concept. The task is to establish both the meaning and the boundaries of the concept. This requires identifying the class of things to which the term belongs and then showing its differentiating characteristics within that class. For example: A *tariff* is a form of tax imposed by a government on imports or exports for the purpose of raising revenue, protecting home industries, or coercing other countries into mutual trade agreements. A *meter* is a unit of length equal to 39.37 inches.

A second class of explanations (the "*how?*" kind) spells out the steps in a process or procedure, such as how to extract a square root, how a bill becomes a law, how sulfuric acid is made, or how a computer works. This type of explanation, *descriptive explanation,* usually involves showing the series of events, parts, or functions that come together to achieve some goal or end state. As noted, an interpretive explanation can be thought of as clarifying *what* something is, whereas a descriptive explanation is aimed at delineating *how* something occurs or is constructed.

A third main type, the *causative explanation* (the "*why?*" type), shows the relationship of some happening to a general rule, law, or human purpose. A reason-giving explanation attempts to explain why it is cold in winter and warm in summer in the Northern Hemisphere, why the United States entered the Vietnam War, why we use quotation marks in written English, and why Hamlet waited so long to kill Claudius.

Instructing as Explanation Whenever you are involved in direct instruction, you will likely be providing one or another (or a combination) of these three types of explanations. In fact, a teacher lecture is best thought of as an extended explanation, or series of explanations, in which the intent is to enable students to understand a particular concept (interpretive), process (descriptive), or causal relationship (connective). Although there are other purposes for direct teaching, as we have seen in Chapter 4 (e.g., inspiring, storytelling), most of your direct teaching should be aimed at explaining ideas or procedures of one sort or another. By thinking of direct instruction as explaining rather than simply information giving, you accomplish several important things.

In the first place, when your conscious effort is to provide a descriptive or interpretive explanation, this gives you a precise task focus. It becomes easier to draw deliberate boundaries around your teaching, and thus keep it from wandering.

An explanation approach to direct teaching also keeps you mindful of the need to make what you are saying intelligible. When you are explaining, you are always explaining something to someone; in a classroom situation, you are teaching to a group of individual "someones," each with their own differing powers of comprehension. You are more likely to have students' understanding as your goal when the task you have set for yourself is to clarify an idea or a procedure rather than to just pass on information.

Finally, an explanatory frame of reference carries some well-established guidelines for making your verbal presentations logically sound as well as meaningful for your students. These prescriptions for good teacher explanations provide the focus for the rest of this chapter.

Guidelines for Logically Sound Explanations

When judging the logical soundness of an explanation we are concerned with the suitability of the explanation to the situation, and with its thoroughness, coherence, and accuracy. The following are basic recommendations for designing classroom explanations that are technically and structurally appropriate:

1. *Know what you are trying to achieve before launching into an explanation.* Does your aim call for an illustration of a process or procedure (such as illustrating how to prepare an outline for an essay)? Does it involve showing a direct cause-and-effect relationship (as in the case of heat changing a liquid to a gas)? Does it entail showing the intent of an action or process (like explaining the role of primaries in the election process)? Does it require showing that a particular action is governed by a general rule or law (like explaining the need for protective glasses when using power tools)? Or does it involve classifying and showing the boundaries of a concept (as with identifying a mammal as an animal that is warm-blooded, suckles its young, etc.)?

   It is possible to combine the three kinds of explanations in one explanation sequence. When explaining how a bill becomes a law, one might well give reasons why certain steps rather than others take place, and explain the meaning of some of the terms involved. However, because each of the different kinds of explanations considered separately raises different problems, for purposes of analysis there is good reason to treat them as distinct.

2. *Recognize the potential ambiguity of the word "explain."* Find out what a student wants to know when he or she makes an unclear request such as "Explain the invasion of Normandy." It could be taken as an appeal for a descriptive explanation or for a reason-giving explanation. That is, it could be a request for an account of the major events of the invasion, or it could be a request to clarify the reasons for the invasion. Awareness of the ambiguity allows you to probe further to find out specifically what kind of explanation the student is asking for.

   A clear way to indicate that an interpretive definition is sought is to make explicit reference to meaning, as in "Please explain the meaning of sovereignty." The most common way to ask for a descriptive explanation is "Explain how . . ." The most dependable cue for a reason-giving explanation is the word "why": "Explain why the fuse blew," or "Explain why 'compelled' is spelled with two ll's." However, reason-giving explanations can also be requested in other ways, such as "How do you know that angle HEF is equal to angle EFD?" or "What accounts for the blowing of the fuse?"

3. *Do not allow synonyms and examples to become easy substitutes for interpretive explanations.* When we turn to a dictionary for the meaning of an unfamiliar word, we ordinarily find three kinds of definitions: synonyms, examples, and analyses of meanings. Each of these may help us to understand the new term better. However, the most conceptually useful type of definition is the analytical or classificatory one. Synonyms and examples are helpful when all we are looking for is a reference to the sort of thing for which a word stands. For example, a synonym for automobile is "car" and an example is "Ford Escort." While synonyms and examples provide us with familiar references for the word "automobile," neither of these brings us closer to an understanding of what constitutes an automobile. We need to look to a classificatory definition, such as "an automobile is a self-propelled land vehicle usually having four wheels, designed primarily to carry passengers, and driven by an internal-combustion engine." This kind of definition allows us to distinguish automobiles from other motorized vehicles.

4. *Try to avoid circularity when offering interpretive and reason-giving explanations.* One of the main problems with relying on synonyms to define terms is their tendency toward circularity: "A morally good man is one who acts virtuously." "Morally good" and "virtuous" are synonymous in this context, so the definition merely repeats the word that is being defined. Although synonyms may help to advance concrete understanding, they do not have the explaining power to be considered interpretive explanations.

   Circularity can also be a problem with reason-giving explanations. When in response to the question, "Why did she commit suicide?", someone gives the answer, "Because she had a death wish," we have a case of circular reasoning. The introduction of the term "death wish" has little explanatory value beyond that already implied in the original question.

5. *Take care to clarify and simplify the elements of a descriptive explanation.* The thing to be explained should be broken up into parts, which should be presented in a carefully chosen order depending on their relationship to one another. In explaining processes such as long division or the making of sulfuric acid this would ordinarily be chronological. In some explanations a choice must be made between presenting the parts in order of increasing generality or decreasing generality. In explaining the structure of the United Nations, for example, one must decide between starting at the top or starting at the bottom to show lines of authority.

6. *Make an effort to complete reason-giving explanations and encourage students to do the same.* It is quite common for students to offer incomplete explanations, as in the following examples:

TEACHER: Why are the two sides of the triangle equal?
STUDENT: Because the two base angles are equal.
TEACHER: Why is the ostrich a fast runner?
STUDENT: Because it is unable to fly.

In each of these examples the student has made progress toward a satisfactory explanation, but has neglected to complete it. In the first case the student has left out the general rule regarding isosceles triangles that allows him or her to make this claim ("In any isosceles triangle—a triangle with equal base angles—the two sides other than the base are equal"). In the second example, the student could have completed the explanation by indicating that the ostrich's ability to run reflects a natural survival provision that often gives animals with physical liabilities in one area compensating abilities in another.

◆◆◆   **A P P L I C A T I O N   E X E R C I S E S**   ◆◆◆

1. Identify the type of explanation—interpretive, descriptive, or reason-giving—that is called for in each of the following explanation requests. In cases in which more than one kind of explanation could be appropriate, rephrase the question to make clear that one or another type of explanation is being sought.
   a. What must a person do to get a driver's license?
   b. What makes a person's muscles twitch?
   c. What are animals?
   d. What were the circumstances of President Kennedy's death?
   e. What causes a thunderstorm?
   f. What are the effects of pollutants in the air?
   g. What is the process of preparing vegetables for a salad?

    h. Explain how to diagram a sentence.

    i. Explain the arrangement of material in a dictionary.

    j. Explain the purpose of firing pottery.

    k. Explain the need for protective glasses in the shop.

    l. Explain the meaning of the word "classical" in literature.

    m. Explain the entrance of the United States into World War I.

    n. Explain the structure of the court system in the United States.

2. Decide the adequacy of the following as logically complete explanations. Suggest any revisions or additions that would make them more sound.

    a. Physical fitness is a term used to describe people who are in good shape physically.

    b. The reason wool is worn in the winter is because it is warm.

    c. A democratic form of government is the type you find in the United States and Great Britain.

    d. A home is a place of residence.

    e. The reason for the president's inability to bring about social change was a Congress dominated by the opposite party.

    f. The reason why the classroom is well-lighted is because it has light-colored walls.

    g. No true believers were condemned because true believers were not heretics.

    h. You can screw a nut on a bolt tighter with a wrench than you can with your fingers because there is more mechanical advantage with a wrench.

3. Outline appropriately sequenced explanations to describe the following. Give reasons for the particular sequence of steps you have adopted in each case.

    a. The process we use in the United States to elect a president.

    b. A procedure for students to follow in preparing a special report or research project in a class you would teach.

4. Plan logically appropriate explanations to meet the following teaching situations:

    a. You wish to explain the concept of capitalism to a junior high social studies class.

    b. You need to explain the use of an exclamation mark in written English to a group of elementary school children.

    c. You are preparing to explain to a general science class the conditions that cause water to boil.

    d. You have undertaken to explain the concept of percentage to an elementary school math class before helping them learn to calculate percentages.

    e. You must explain to a group of high school juniors the general procedure for being admitted to college.

Giving Explanations That Students Can Understand

It is possible to give logically well-constructed, that is, accurate, explanations that students fail to understand. As a teacher, your explanations must also be *psychologically* appropriate.[3] In other words, they must convey meaning *to the students* in addition to being sound.

There are some important general guidelines to be followed in making explanations understandable for young learners: (1) center on what the student is likely to know and be able to comprehend; (2) do not provide more information than can be assimilated; (3) use techniques that enhance clarity and emphasis; and (4) check frequently to find out whether individual students are making sense of your explanations.[4]

Working from the Students' Frame of Reference

To make classroom explanations understandable to students, you must learn to work simultaneously from two standpoints. You will need to maintain a focus on the object to be explained, while remaining attuned to the learning needs, capacities, and dispositions of the students. Teachers who are especially well-acquainted with a particular domain of knowledge are often preoccupied with the subject matter, to the neglect of the student. Their knowledge has become second nature to them and they have lost sight of the route they took to achieve understanding. Thus, highly knowledgeable people aren't automatically equipped to be good explainers of what they know.

As a teacher, it is essential to remain mindful of what understanding requires for a learner. As discussed in Chapter 6, understanding involves (1) making a connection between new information and existing knowledge structures; and (2) seeing a use for new knowledge. These two basic requirements must be met in order for explanations to be meaningful to students.[5]

Building on Existing Knowledge   Skillful teachers are able to use explanation not just to give students new information but to enable them to *rearrange* and *extend* what they already know.[6] Students' existing knowledge and experience can be valuable resources for developing new knowledge. A major part of the teacher's task is to draw on this present knowledge by helping students see it in a different light and with some new labels. The following teacher-student exchange illustrates how a teacher can use a student's past experience to help explain a new idea:

> STUDENT: (on encountering an unfamiliar term in the reading): Can you tell me what "military punishment" means?
>
> TEACHER: Have you ever been in a situation where everyone in the class had to stay after school because of the wrong behavior of several students?
>
> STUDENT: Yes, and I thought it was unfair. I didn't think the teacher should have held everyone responsible for the problem. I

thought the teacher should have picked only those who were disrupting class.

TEACHER: This is an example of what is sometimes referred to as "military punishment." It's a case where a whole group is punished for the behavior of a few of its members. They sometimes do this purposely in the army to help develop group responsibility by showing that everyone is affected when one or two people make mistakes.

This teacher resisted the temptation to simply tell the student what "military punishment" is and be done with it. In this brief exchange the teacher was able to get the student to draw on his or her knowledge, personal thoughts, feelings, and values in order to understand the new term. This teacher wanted the student to do more than merely memorize a formal definition. A link to students' present understandings or past experiences, sometimes in the form of a well-placed question, can help establish reference points for what is to follow.

In attempting to foster insight into the process of multiplication with a group of elementary school students, a teacher undertakes to show that multiplication is actually a streamlined form of addition:

TEACHER: Can you think of a practical use for multiplication that all of us are familiar with?

STUDENT: Yes. It helps you to count your change more quickly.

TEACHER: O.K. That's one good example. What special advantage does multiplication give you here?

STUDENT: Well, if you had six quarters, seven dimes, and four nickels you could do some quick multiplication and a little adding in your head and come up with the total.

TEACHER: Otherwise, if you didn't know how to multiply, you'd have to do what?

STUDENT: You'd have to add each separate coin. That would take longer and you might need paper and pencil.

TEACHER: So multiplication is really a shortened way to do what?

STUDENT: To do addition.

TEACHER: Exactly. Let's take a closer look at this.

Again, this is an example of a teacher explanation that begins with what students already know and attempts to build on that existing knowledge to form a new understanding. It proceeds from the assumption that learning, as distinct from memorization, involves seeing new relationships rather than simply acquiring new pieces of information.

Centering on Ideas Rather Than Terms   The teachers in the previous examples avoided the use of formal language and monologue as the basis for their explanations, appealing instead to students' present levels of understanding in a language that was mostly conversational and familiar.

Teacher explanations often introduce too many abstract terms too soon; for example, "Today we're going to talk about photosynthesis. Photosynthesis is the process by which complex carbon compounds are manufactured in green plants with the help of light energy. The light energy needed for the process is absorbed by a green pigment called chlorophyll."

Beginning an explanation with formal terms, using abstract definitions to try to explain complex ideas, will cause students to lapse into mechanical verbalization (see Chapter 6). Their mental energies will be directed toward memorizing material without meaning to them. Too many ideas they can't digest will overload their short-term memory, and clog students' thought channels.

Students need to confront new ideas in their own language and at their own levels of understanding before they are ready to "own" textbook concepts. If you fail to allow this initial "romance" stage in learning (see Chapter 6), your explanations will not get through to students. The best strategy is to seek to ensure that students know what the concept means before attaching the labels. Although it may not always be possible to do this without using some formal language, it is important to avoid having students simply repeat terms and to give priority to their functional understanding of the new ideas.

Stressing the Function of New Learning It is important to stress the functional aspects of new learning so that students can perceive a use for new information or skills. Students will best understand explanations that have a direct bearing on something they are trying to do or do better. A good time, then, for a teacher's explanation is following an activity that has caused students to realize a need for new knowledge, and to have questions they wish to ask. Students are likely to benefit more from explanations relating to subject-verb agreement when they have had a chance to do some writing that matters to them, and sense that what they have written isn't quite right. Basketball players can be expected to be more attentive to a coach's demonstration of good defensive play following a scrimmage that showed their inadequacies in this aspect of their games. Taking advantage of these propitious moments for new learning will make explanations carry more meaning because they will be serving some real need.

When students don't see any usefulness in what they are learning, you should work to build the use of it into your explanations. The younger the students, the more need there is to make explicit the functional and operational dimensions of all new learning. Teacher explanations should tell students: "This is how it works," "this is what you do with it," "this is the need it helps us to satisfy." Always aim to have students perceive that what they are learning has an identifiable use.

Using Analogies to Bridge the Understanding Gap Teacher explanations in some subject areas may involve the introduction of new ideas or realms of study that require a mental leap on the part of the student. As an example, it is possible for students to talk about plant life from a concrete and experiential point of view, yet find a biologist's conception of "plant" to be obscure and incomprehensible; for example, "A plant is an organism of the vegetable kingdom which characteristically has cellulose cell walls, grows by synthesis of organic substances, and lacks the power of locomotion."

Analogies, metaphors, similes, representations, word pictures, and what are sometimes referred to particularly in the sciences as "conceptual models" (such as, for example, conceptual models of DNA or of the atom) are often effective and even essential in bridging the understanding gap and helping students gain insight into complex ideas or processes.[7] The inner nature of a plant becomes more transparent to biology students when they can relate it to a concept with which they are already familiar:

> Think of a plant as a factory that needs raw materials. To make a ship a ship-yard needs steel plates, rivets, wood for decks, etc. It also requires a supply of energy in the form of fuel or electricity for working cranes and other machinery. Well plants are nature's factory, and they also require energy and raw materials. . . . The sun provides the energy needed by plants in the form of light. . . . And what are the raw materials that make up a plant? . . . Suppose we took a plant, weighed it and then dried it in a warm oven. . . . So you can see that a large part of a plant is water.[8]

Although the understanding of teacher explanations can be considerably assisted by the use of good analogies, it is important to make sure your comparisons are appropriate. Poor analogies can oversimplify and trivialize explanations as can the misuse of synonyms and other forms of concrete reference. However, this should not discourage you from seeking good analogies to promote student understanding of complex ideas.

Focusing on Individual Units of Meaning

There is a limit to the amount of new knowledge students can make their own in a short teaching session. Particularly when dealing with abstract content, your explanations should be organized and paced to allow students to work on one idea at a time (individual concepts can generally be thought of as constituting distinct ideas, or single units of meaning, e.g., "energy," "government," "metaphor").

It is important for you to avoid a textbook type of presentation as the model for your explanations. Textbooks often present too much information per paragraph and at a level of abstraction that makes understanding difficult. The following passage from a junior high school world history text is an illustration:

> Like all other Greek city-states, Athens started out as a monarchy. However, about 750 B.C. some Athenian nobles, merchants, and manufacturers took over the government. After a time, fighting broke out between them and the

farmers and artisans over land ownership and debt. Since upper-class Athenians did not want the fighting to turn into revolution, they agreed to make reforms. To do this, they had to reorganize the government.[9]

This portion of content represents an attempt at descriptive explanation of events leading to democracy in ancient Greece. To make sense out of this sort of tightly compacted information, students would need time to focus on individual units of meaning before having to deal with succeeding points. The initial statement of the paragraph is a condensation of a lot of information about the Greeks. To appreciate its import, students would need to know and understand concepts such as "city-state," "monarchy," "revolution," and "government reform."

It would take considerable elaboration for them to grasp the significance of the political transition from a single ruler to the unsettled state of affairs and eventual revolutionary conditions that followed. For example, what does "took over the government" mean in terms of any activities and events that junior high students are familiar with? Was the takeover violent? How did the citizens get control? Did they use the army? Is there significance in the fact that the revolutionaries were nobles, merchants, and manufacturers rather than farmers, artisans, and military leaders? What were the human factors involved? Were the Athenian monarchs hateful and selfish? Were they involved in scandals like some present-day political leaders?

Most precollege students are going to have difficulty assimilating lifeless, highly concentrated information presented in this fashion. It fails to make contact with realities with which they can identify. The purpose of an explanation should be to unpack ideas for students, not to compress them so tightly that their inner contents are never revealed. It is not just enough to explain. As Brophy observes,

> Teaching involves inducing *conceptual change* in students, not infusing information into a vacuum [and this] will be facilitated by the interactive *discourse* during lessons and activities. Clear explanations and modeling from the teacher are important, but so are opportunities to answer questions about the content, discuss or debate its meanings and implications, or apply it in authentic problem-solving or decision-making contexts.[10]

When you feel you need to acquaint students with abstract subject matter through a teacher-centered presentation or assigned reading, you should take any measures you can to make it easier for them to grasp. There are several ways to accomplish this:

1. Be certain of what it is you want students to understand—a concept, a process or procedure, or a series of events with causal connections. This will normally point to the need for some kind of extended explanation. If you are simply presenting information to students with no clear focus on a what, how, or why question that they may have, and that will help

them answer it, you are very probably making it difficult for them to see any sense or appeal in it, and hence to learn it with understanding.

2. Provide students with advance organizers to help them anticipate the logical flow of the information they will receive, and "see that students know why it is important for them to know [this information]."[11] This should amount to a brief introduction that gives them an idea of how the lesson will proceed, and a framework into which to fit the new material.

3. Organize your explanations to allow students to deal with one idea at a time. Make an effort to help students separate complex ideas into separate meaning units (individual concepts or principles). This frequently involves providing explanations within explanations.

4. Identify points within the explanation that deserve special attention. Then determine the kind of elaboration these ideas are to receive in terms of illustrations, previous references, or human interest anecdotes.

5. In building explanations on abstract concepts to which students have previously been exposed, do not assume they are already familiar with—and understand—them. When new learning depends on students' abilities to handle concepts like "monarchy," "government," "revolution," and "reform" in the abstract, you should not take it for granted they understand and can work with them simply because they have encountered these terms in earlier lessons. At the very least, you should take time to do some reaching back to previous learning by means of questions, such as: "Who can remind us of the differences between a monarchy and an oligarchy? Can you recall why the Greek city-states were all monarchies at this time?"

Achieving Clarity and Emphasis

Making Explanations Visual Many high school seniors have not yet acquired the capacity of dealing with formal reasoning, that is, with thinking in terms of abstract concepts, and among those who have, there are many who have only just begun to be able to handle this kind of thinking. For both of these groups of students you will need to provide as many concrete, personal references, and hands-on experiences as you can. The more graphic you can make your explanations, the more meaningful they are likely to be for your students.

Certain kinds of teacher explanations are virtually impossible to get over in the absence of visual aids or demonstrations. For example, the most skillful teachers of beginning auto mechanics would have trouble explaining how a four-cycle engine operates if they had to rely exclusively on language. They would need at least a two-dimensional diagram to enable students to understand what they were describing. The ideal would be for them to make use of an actual engine or instructional model as a reference. Demonstration is the most effective form of representation teachers can provide when giving an explanation. It is often a necessary extension of descriptive explanations of processes and procedures in performance-based subjects and in science labs.

At the same time, there are teaching situations that depend primarily on a teacher's verbal skill to explain abstract concepts that resist concrete illustration. Interpretive explanations of concepts like "justice," "democracy," "culture," and "mental health" are not easily enhanced by visual or physical devices because they refer to intangibles such as forms of government, human behavioral tendencies, and patterns of human relationship. Skillful teachers may use techniques such as role playing to simulate the social behaviors that exemplify such abstract ideas as democracy and justice, but understanding of these complex ideas ultimately depends on symbolic—that is verbal—rather than concrete representation.

Whenever possible, however, you should avoid trying to make explanations solely by way of talk or written material. You should supplement your explanations by using whatever visual materials are available. You can use the chalkboard to good effect by drawing your own maps or graphic devices to show movement, connections, cause and effect, and much else. These can serve as advance organizers, illustrations of development, or forms of closure. Students can produce their own copies, or work on photocopied versions you provide. There are numerous other types of visual material, among them posters, pictures, overhead transparencies, physical objects, slides, films, videocassettes, videodiscs, and CD-ROMs. Projection devices for use with computers are still expensive, but their cost is bound to go down, and they will then be a very valuable resource, not least because they can be totally controlled by the teacher.

There are also increasing numbers of software applications available that now make it possible for the student, either as one of a class, or as an individual using the material in the format of computer assisted instruction (CAI) to, as it were, *see* explanations happen—equations transforming themselves in cyberspace, "objects moving in frictionless Newtonian ways we rarely encounter in the world,"[12] biological systems in action up on the screen.

Besides using actual visual materials to illustrate your teaching, you can make your explanations more intelligible and memorable if you can provide lucid and, if appropriate, dramatic verbal descriptions of objects, events, processes, and personalities. For teachers in areas such as social studies and English, it is especially important to be able to enhance explanations with appropriate narrative accounts and descriptions. Stories that involve people most readily appeal to young people (as they do to people in general—witness the perennial popularity of sitcoms). Explanations in these teaching areas need to have a dynamic quality in order to capture student interest. What gets student interest and involvement is the human element: What happened to these people? Why did they do what they did? What kinds of people and what kinds of lives are we talking about? Can we connect with life situations such as these?

Providing Verbal Emphasis Part of your task as a teacher is to help students to focus on individual units of meaning, to appreciate significances, and to sort the important from the less important. You can emphasize particular points you want to make through voice modulation, verbal highlighting, and probing for below-surface meanings. Through deliberate voice adjustments, such as periodically raising or lowering, slowing or speeding up your voice, you can vary the speed of your delivery in order to provide emphasis. Pausing over or purposely giving vocal stress to a particular point can be a way of telling students that something here is worth special attention.

You can use *verbal highlighting* to tell students directly, "This is important," or "This is a key point," or "I'd like you to think for a moment about what this means." When you have occasion to add information that is less important or tangential to the explanation, it is helpful for you to advise students, "This is just an aside," "These remarks are parenthetical," or "This is unrelated to what we've just been talking about."

Taking the opportunity to dwell momentarily on particular ideas allows you to emphasize meanings and implications; for example, "Now, we've been told that the upper-class Athenians did not want the fighting to turn into a revolution. What did they stand to lose if a full-scale revolution were to happen? Before we answer that, maybe we ought to consider some of the typical happenings in a country during a revolution."

◆◆◆ APPLICATION EXERCISES ◆◆◆

1. Organize brief interpretive, descriptive, and reason-giving explanations in subjects you will be teaching. Try to figure out how to anchor these explanations in what you think may be the frames of reference of a particular group of students. Keep formal or abstract terminology to a minimum. Concentrate on communicating your ideas as conversationally and nontechnically as possible.

2. Examine the explanations you have just put together to determine which make clear the purpose of the new learning. If one or more don't, add whatever you need to achieve clarity.

3. Looking at the explanations you have developed in Exercise 1, decide what visual aids or other materials you would want to use to make these explanations as graphic as possible. Would any of your explanations call for demonstrations? Which would be enhanced the least by physical props?

4. Analyze the explanations you have constructed in Exercise 1 to determine key points or understandings that need verbal highlighting. Underline these key ideas.

5. Examine a textbook currently being used in an area you are qualified to teach to determine the way it sets out ideas in a typical paragraph. Do the paragraphs generally represent single units of meaning or do they present meaning units in multiples? (Reminder: A meaning unit is ordinarily represented by a single proposition, e.g., "The early government of the United States was formed by men with an aversion to monarchies.")

6. Think of analogies you might use in your teaching to offer insights into concepts or realms of understanding that would otherwise be difficult to explain without using highly abstract terms and definitions (e.g., in introducing the list of atomic elements in a chemistry class, a teacher might show their functional similarity to the letters of the alphabet in the English language).

7. Develop a diagram or flowchart to assist students in understanding a concept, a series of events, or a chemical or biological change.

A SUMMARY OF GUIDELINES FOR EFFECTIVE EXPLANATIONS

The following list of do's and don'ts constitutes a summary of guidelines for developing sound, meaningful, and effective classroom explanations:

Do

1. Know what a sound explanation entails and be sure of your purpose before starting to explain something.
2. Take what you know about the level of the learners' knowledge and perspective into consideration in formulating and giving an explanation.
3. Be as conversational and informal as possible when explaining new ideas or skills.
4. Be as clear and simple as you can when describing processes, procedures, and structures.
5. Make explanations as graphic as possible through the use of visuals and other teaching aids.
6. Cultivate your capacity to give vivid descriptions and make effective emphases during explanations.
7. Use analogies to help students understand abstract ideas and processes.
8. Focus on one unit of meaning at a time.
9. Check continually that students are understanding the explanation.

Don't

1. Load students with more information than they can or will accept at any one time.
2. Rely exclusively or even mainly on formal or abstract language to assist students to grasp complex ideas.
3. Use a textbook form of organization as a model for your explanations.
4. Allow synonyms and examples to substitute for understanding when giving interpretive explanations.

5. Make use of circular definitions or circular reasoning.
6. Provide incomplete reason-giving explanations.

◆◆◆ SUGGESTED ACTIVITIES AND QUESTIONS ◆◆◆

1. It could be argued that a major part of a teacher's job is to function as a professional explainer. Discuss the basis for and some of the implications of this claim.
2. Define explaining behavior and the underlying purpose it serves as a teaching skill.
3. Summarize your understanding of this chapter by enumerating eight to ten considerations you would want to keep in mind when formulating explanations for your students.
4. In reflecting on your career as a student, can you recall teachers you would regard as highly proficient explainers? Were they some of your favorite teachers? What particular techniques did they employ to make their explanations effective? Would you or would you not ordinarily expect school counselors to be good explainers? Why so?
5. Pay special attention to the explanations you encounter in your everyday life. Do you find many people who take pains to ensure they are being properly understood when they explain things to others? Do you? Can you think of particular areas outside of school where it is especially important for people to be able to deliver clear and concise explanations? Would you favor a course in explaining behavior, for example, for doctors? For salespeople? For parents?
6. What are the most common violations of good explaining technique you find in your encounters with other people? What do you think leads to the development of these bad habits? One of the premises of this chapter has been that good explanation technique is unaccustomed behavior for most people in our fast-paced society. Discuss reasons why this is true. What are the implications for teacher education? For *you?*
7. Make an effort to attend to how teachers explain things to their students. Do the teachers you observe place a high priority on being able to provide students with good explanations? Take the opportunity to study the techniques of teachers you consider competent explainers. Ask them to share their strategies. Compare their ideas with the explanation strategies developed in this chapter.
8. Take deliberate steps to improve your powers of explaining as a developing teacher. Practice formulating good explanations, and giving good explanations both in and out of school (e.g., in giving someone directions, or in describing events, ideas, or processes). Learn to monitor and assess your own explanatory skills as you progress through teacher training, for example, during student teaching. Arrange to get periodic tape-recorded or videotaped samples of your explaining tech-

nique in formal teaching situations. Ask students to give you their assessment of your ability to give them clear and intelligible explanations. Use this information to check your own development as a professional explainer.

NOTES

1. David Perkins, "Teaching for Understanding." *American Educator* (Fall 1993): 6, 28–34. Gardner points to the fact that explanation, *by itself,* does not guarantee understanding. In an interview, he said that he viewed the findings of cognitive research over the past 20 to 30 years as "quite compelling" and as demonstrating that "students do not *understand* in the most basic sense of that term. That is, they lack the capacity to take knowledge learned in one setting and apply it appropriately in a different setting. Study after study has found that, by and large, even the best students in the best schools can't do that." Ron Brandt, "On Teaching for Understanding: A Conversation with Howard Gardner." *Educational Leadership* (April 1993): 4.
2. The discussion in this section is adapted from Robert H. Ennis, *Logic in Teaching.* Englewood Cliffs, N.J.: Prentice-Hall, 1969, Chap. 14.
3. Jonas F. Soltis, *An Introduction to the Analysis of Educational Concepts,* 2nd ed. Reading, Mass.: Addison-Wesley, 1972, pp. 59–62.
4. Anne Westcott Dodd, "Engaging Students: What I Learned Along the Way." *Educational Leadership* (September 1995): 66. Perkins, "Teaching for Understanding," p. 31.
5. Adapted from Morris L. Bigge and Maurice P. Hunt, *Psychological Foundations of Education,* 3rd ed. New York: Harper and Row, 1980, pp. 454–456.
6. Frank Smith, *Comprehension and Learning.* New York: Holt, Rinehart and Winston, 1975, p. 159.
7. Richard Mayer, "Models for Understanding." *Review of Educational Research 59* (1989): 43–64. D. Gentner and A. L. Stevens (Eds.), *Mental Models.* Hillsdale, N.J.: Lawrence Erlbaum Associates, 1983.
8. From John R. Hall, *Biology.* New York: David McKay, 1974, pp. 13–14.
9. William Cox, Arthur Greenblatt, and John Seaberg, *Human Heritage: A World History.* Columbus, Ohio: Charles E. Merrill, 1981, p. 147.
10. Jere Brophy, "Probing the Subtleties of Subject-Matter Teaching." *Educational Leadership* (April 1992): 5.
11. Thomas L. Good and Jere Brophy, *Looking in Classrooms,* 7th ed. New York: Longman, 1997, p. 366.
12. Perkins, "Teaching for Understanding," p. 31.

CHAPTER 8

Developing the Art of Interactive Teaching

Teaching involves conceptual changes in students,
not infusing knowledge into a vacuum.

Jere Brophy

Directive and Interactive Teaching Styles

An important key to consistently good teaching is the ability to talk *with* rather than *at* students or even *to* students in the classroom. Skilled teachers are able to get away from a predominantly teacher-centered, or directive style of teaching and to move to an interactive style in their classrooms in a manner that is learner-paced, conversational, and personally engaging. Interactive teaching not only promotes far more active student participation in the learning process, but it also gives teachers a chance to be more spontaneous and natural when working with student groups.[1]

Teachers are often inclined to regard teaching as simply a matter of telling, of imparting information, of *instructing*. The previous chapter, and what is said about *direct* teaching in Chapter 4, will already have indicated that teachers often need to give students instructions, provided that they are aimed at helping students learn, and in particular to learn how to organize and pursue their own learning. Information is, today, readily available in overwhelming amounts, more than ever since the development of the Internet and World Wide Web. What students need most crucially these days is assistance in assembling material into meaningful wholes, suggestions about ways of sifting out the trivial from the significant, ways of making sense out of the dizzying mass of facts, and the experience of learning to work productively with each other. That is where the teacher comes, or should come, in.

There is little doubt that students learn more and develop more positive attitudes toward learning when you are able to employ a less direct, more personal, interactive mode of instruction.[2] You will also find that, when you cease to rely on the direct approach as your primary means of communicating with students on sensitive issues, they become far less reluctant to discuss matters involving feelings and emotions. To be able to provide instruction that actively engages students in their own learning and to share thoughts, feelings, and personal concerns with students, you will have to develop a capacity for dialogue rather than depending largely on monologue.

Interactive teaching ability requires considerable interpersonal skill, but in return it relieves you of the burden of continual presentation and involvement in direct control. Proficiency in interactive teaching means that you have the ability to generate and promote discussion, as well as talk to and with students about feelings and problems. Not infrequently in the midst of this process, and arising out of some question that has come up during it, you may feel you need to do some direct teaching, but you will do it with more relaxation, focus, and creativity because there is clearly a real need for it. This kind of teaching enables you to explore new areas of learning with students, and to function without worrying about always knowing all the answers. Interactive teaching emphasizes the shared communication process in learning and should reduce, if not entirely eliminate reliance on prepackaged materials and tightly structured programs. As you develop the art, you will become increasingly able to take a more relaxed and subtle approach to the demands of classroom instruction.

This chapter introduces you to the basic elements of interactive teaching and spells out some specific maneuvers you can adopt to increase your classroom effectiveness.

The Essence of Interactive Teaching

A competent teacher's ability to manage communications within a group becomes evident when he or she is able to in a sense *orchestrate* productive interaction rather than dominate the proceedings. Exemplary discussion leaders have developed a series of skillful maneuvers that allow them to preside over lively and stimulating flows of exchanges with and between students, while keeping the discussion organized, focused, and respectful of individual needs and sensitivities. This is a complex process that you should not expect to acquire fast or with ease, but it is of the highest value in assisting the learning process. As you struggle with it, you should bear in mind that participating in the process is eventually one of the most exciting and rewarding parts of being a teacher since it brings you into real contact with young people in ways that continually stimulate your own ideas and keep you alive as a teacher.

In practical terms, there are a number of verbal and nonverbal tactics that help promote positive and productive classroom interaction. They fall within four general categories[3]:

- *Structuring* techniques
- *Questioning* techniques
- *Attending* behaviors
- *Responding* behaviors

Structuring Teacher-Student Interaction

Structuring techniques are useful in setting up a class discussion, establishing the nature and context of the interaction, regulating student participation, providing continuity and emphasis, and helping foster a functional group atmosphere. They include focusing, gatekeeping, climate-setting, redirecting, transitioning, informing, and summarizing.

Focusing

Your first task is to draw student attention to the problem, issue, or inquiry being discussed. To get students into an appropriate mental frame for discussion, you should ordinarily begin by providing a context for learning, which simply means getting students to switch their thoughts from whatever they are when they come into your room to whatever they need to be if they are going to learn something there. This process is commonly referred to as building a *set*, and its importance is quite often completely ignored by teachers. You might develop a learning set by citing a recent newspaper article, by reading a passage of poetry, or by giving a brief history of a social problem. Pictures, posters, physical objects, and short films or videotapes can also make good starting points for discussion. You will want to establish a well-defined focus before launching into discussion. This initial focus becomes the point of reference for keeping the discussion on track.

Gatekeeping

Gatekeeping entails acting as a sort of chairperson, keeping tabs on who has or has not yet spoken, recognizing students who are next in line to contribute, and making sure only one person speaks at a time. You may find it necessary to call on high frequency participants less often than they would like in order to give less vocal students an opportunity—and it might be a good idea in some groups to explain that you will be doing this, and why. You should vary your techniques for bringing students into a discussion. On one occasion you may give a student the green light by simply saying, "Yes, Chandra," in another instance it could be "Let's hear Enrico's opinion on this," and in some situations you may use a simple nod or hand gesture in the direction of the student.

Climate-Setting

Climate-setting strategies are usually not-too-obvious verbal or nonverbal ways that teachers employ to create good feeling and direction in group interaction. In showing genuine interest and enthusiasm, for example, you are setting a constructive tone for discussion. By demonstrating a balanced, carefully reasoned approach to human problems, you are setting a precedent for students themselves to be moderate and reasonable in expressing opinions on sensitive issues. Saying, or possibly even doing, something that makes people laugh good-humoredly can sometimes help reduce tension in the group.

Redirecting and Transitioning

To keep a discussion moving and help students avoid belaboring irrelevant or sufficiently established points, you may need deliberately, but tactfully, to redirect student thought to the original focus or turn it in a new direction. You might say, for example, "I think we've had an opportunity to hear a number of different views on that idea. I'd like to raise a somewhat different question?" or "I believe we're beginning to stray from the main issue. Let's remind ourselves what the original disagreement was."

You should ensure that new focuses are accompanied by clear and smooth transitions. Transitioning moves all students' attention to changes in the direction of a discussion, for example, "Now that we're clear on what happened, it looks like time to consider the cause" or "We've been discussing the role of primaries in a presidential election; let's shift gears now and talk about the campaigns that follow."

Informing

Skilled discussion leaders are able to provide information that has a structuring effect on group interaction without becoming directly involved in the discussion. You may give reminders of the time limits of the discussion: "Please keep in mind we have 20 minutes left. You may want to keep your comments short." You might also offer information that has to do with principles of sound reasoning: "Remember the rule of logic that says you can't go directly from factual statements to value conclusions in your reasoning." A teacher may also give factual information that moves a discussion beyond impasse: "For the record, I did notice in this morning's paper that the new landfill project you're debating about does not include environmental impact provisions."

When entering a class discussion as an information-giver, you should avoid telling all you know about a subject. Otherwise, you may needlessly turn the discussion into a lecture, and thereby defeat its purpose.

Summarizing

Resourceful discussion leaders will use internal summaries at main junctures in a discussion to pull loose ends together or to remind students of what has transpired to that point, for example, "O.K., before we go on, let's summarize the arguments pro and con that we've heard so far," or "We've talked about many things that contribute to poor driving records. Let's see if we can reduce all of these to several main causes."

It is also important to provide a final summing up at the close of a discussion. It's a good idea to ask students to do this, or at least to get them to assist in providing internal and/or final summaries.

◆◆◆ **A P P L I C A T I O N   E X E R C I S E S** ◆◆◆

1. Label the particular structuring move represented by each of the following teacher statements:
   a. You've all been doing a good job of researching these topics. I'm anxious to see what you've found."
   b. "O.K., now that you understand the idea, let's look at a few practical examples."
   c. Remember, as chairperson, I'm asking for hands when you have something to say. I believe Bill had his hand up first, then Nancy is next."
   d. "All right, it's important for us to recognize the point that's being made here. What I'm hearing many of you say is . . ."
   e. Now for openers, I'd like to ask this question: What do you think you'd do if faced with a situation where . . . ?"
   f. "This is a topic we've discussed before in some detail. I'm going to ask that we table it for now and consider a more basic issue."
   g. Let me give you a hint. There's one piece of information that you seem to be overlooking. Will you look at the word in italics in the first paragraph of this chapter."
   h. "O.K., let's stop for a moment and see if we can retrace the steps we've taken to solve this problem."

2. Compose a verbal structuring move for each of the following teaching situations, identifying each tactic with an appropriate label:
   a. You wish to tighten the ground rules for turning in late homework and have decided to initiate a class discussion of the problem as a means of getting student input and cooperation.
   b. You feel a need to call a group's attention to the fact that people are repeating comments that have previously been made, perhaps indicating insufficient attention to one another's contributions.
   c. A number of students are wanting to join a discussion. Two, in particular, have kept their hands waving while others have had the floor.
   d. A class of capable students has been taking a somewhat matter-of-fact approach to group interaction. You want to set a more spirited tone for today's classwork with a few well-chosen comments at the beginning of class.
   e. You have been working with a class on the basic procedure for multiplying fractions. You want to reiterate the essential steps they should be mindful of before beginning to work problems.
   f. A class discussion has moved from a consideration of why South Americans experience summer during our winter months to an argument over who produces the better soccer players, North or South America. You wish to reestablish the original focus.

Questioning Techniques

A teacher's questioning strategies and techniques play a central role in interactive teaching. Skillful questioners set the stage for discussion, draw students into the dialogue, and evoke higher-order thinking.[4]

Some guidelines for the use of teacher questions are to: (1) have a thought-out strategy, one that will ensure that you use a variety of questions to promote different levels of thought, (2) ask questions in clear and succinct language, only one question at a time, (3) give students ample time to answer, and (4) use follow-up questions when needed to elicit more information.

Using Questions to Promote Thought

Different types of question foster different thinking processes, and it would be useful for you at this point to review Bloom's taxonomy as described in Chapter 3. This provides a handy framework for asking questions as well as for considering objectives.

1. *Memory-recall.* The most commonly used type of teacher question requiring students to recollect names, dates, events, and other factual items: for example, "When did Columbus arrive in what came to be called the 'New World'?"; "Who was the author of *Great Expectations*?"; or "What does *effervescent* mean?"
2. *Comprehension.* Comprehension questions aim at checking understanding rather than just the ability to recall facts. They call for relational thinking because they require students to demonstrate understanding of information by generalizing, comparing, contrasting, or relating it to some larger principle or process: for example, "Why do you think the leaves have shriveled on this plant?"; "What is the main idea of this story?"; or "How do today's lifestyles contrast with those of your grandparents?"
3. *Reflection.* Reflection questions call for higher-order thinking skills and invites students to go on from recalling and understanding information to making projections that require reflective thought. They ask students to make educated guesses, to form hypotheses, to create new forms, or to evaluate situations: for example, "How can we get the community to support our beautification project?"; "Can you suggest a new way to heat your home"; or "Do you agree that honesty is the best policy?"

Whether discussing a short story in English, a famous battle in history, or a laboratory experiment in science, a teacher needs to have worked out and to have ready to use a questioning scheme that entails a progression from lower to higher levels of thought.[5] With this in mind, an English teacher might decide to open a discussion of a short story by focusing on factual-level questions about the story: "Where did the story take place? Who were the main characters? What did they do for a living? What problem did they encounter at the beginning of the story?" Having developed a factual base to work from, the stage is set for comprehension-level questions. These questions serve to advance beyond factual detail and engage the understanding of the student: "During what time of year did the story take place?" (a question requiring the student to make an inference—assuming the story did not give this information directly). "Would you consider the people in the story to be a close-knit family? Why? How would you describe the standard of living of this family?" (calling for another inference). "How would you compare the personalities of the two main characters in the story?" At this point the teacher might move to some questions requiring reflective and evaluative thinking. These call on students to do divergent thinking, going a step beyond understanding the story: "Could you see a family like this adapting to life in the United States today? Would you consider the father in the story to be a good parent? What might be a way to reorganize the welfare system to alleviate problems such as this family encountered? If you could change one thing about this story, what would it be?"

Clarity in Questions

Clarity in questioning is essential because students have little time during a discussion to contemplate the meaning of a question. Questions should be clear and brief. You should ask the exact question in explicit and unambiguous language, avoiding unnecessary words, parenthetical expressions, and multiple questions.

The following are examples of questions that should be rephrased for greater simplicity and clarity:

"Tell us, if you can, what contribution police officers make to our society. (Better: "Why do we need police officers?")

"Explain, in as much detail as possible, how rising temperatures can affect the humidity of a particular area of the country." (Better: "Explain the effect of rising temperatures on humidity.")

"How do the basketball, football, and baseball players you see on TV keep themselves in good condition day after day?" (Better: "How do professional athletes stay in shape?")

"Considering the amount of traffic on our freeways, the lack of effective devices for controlling pollution, and the apathy of the average person, is there any answer to the smog problem in our metropolitan areas?" (Better: "What can we do about smog in our large cities?")

Pausing to Allow "Think-Time"

When you pause to allow students sufficient time to formulate answers, you can expect more adequate responses, involving more complex thinking.[6] Students will be more confident in their responses and more inclined to participate in discussions. You should make a habit of asking the question first before calling on a student to answer. After asking the question, you should pause for approximately three seconds before calling on a student. You should allow another pause of three to five seconds after calling on the student to give time for an answer, then another three- to five-second pause after the student answers before commenting or asking for additional input.

Probing for More Information

Your students will give more serious thought to questions when you encourage them to think beyond their first answers.[7] You can use follow-up questions or *probes* to elicit further thought when you feel students' ideas could be more complete or imaginative. These probing questions may come from any of the three questioning modes: "Do you remember anything else about it?" (memory-recall); "Can you explain in more detail?" (comprehension); "Can you think of any other way to accomplish that?" (reflection).

Probing questions are always to be used for the purpose of stimulating more comprehensive and creative thought, never to grill students or to punish them for lack of preparation.

◆◆◆ APPLICATION EXERCISES ◆◆◆

1. Design a 12- to 15-minute interactive teaching segment in an area you are qualified to teach, using teacher questions to determine the direction of the lesson. Attempt first to establish a factual base with descriptive questions, then work to encourage higher conceptual thought through a series of comprehension questions and, finally, introduce several reflection questions as a means of stimulating divergent thinking.
2. Prepare yourself to practice the previous lesson on a group of your peers in a simulated teaching situation. Using the questioning guidelines presented in this chapter, take the opportunity to practice clarity, proper wait-time, and probing skills as main emphases in your questioning techniques.

Attending Behaviors

Teachers who listen thoughtfully and attentively to students are conveying their respect for them and what they have to say. By clearly showing interest and attention, you are also encouraging students to take group discussion seriously and to use their best listening skills when others are speaking. Active, attentive listening is demonstrated primarily through body language and involves such things as eye contact, leaning slightly toward the speaker, showing evidence of contemplation, and offering subtle encouragement.

Eye Contact

In our culture, one of the first essentials of showing authentic listening is direct eye contact.[8] Failing to look directly at a speaker may reflect nervousness or a lack of interest. Similarly, darting eyes may indicate that the listener's thoughts are not with the speaker. On the other hand, compulsive eye contact on the part of a listener, if not broken periodically with pensive glances away from a speaker, can also be disconcerting. This form of communication is sometimes difficult for people and may require deliberate cultivation. You should bear it in mind that students from other cultures, particularly Eastern ones, may find such eye contact embarrassing or threatening, *experienced* as a stare or a glare.

Leaning

When you lean away from a speaker this tends to be interpreted as showing less interest and attention than when you lean slightly in that person's direction. Leaning toward students when they are talking communicates a concern to hear what is being said. Your posture, however, must appear natural and unexaggerated to be effective.

Contemplating

Good listeners usually show they are thinking about what is being said. Face and eyes directed upward with a thoughtful expression generally signal listener involvement; eyes looking down at the floor or out the window tend to convey preoccupation with other thoughts. A furrowed brow, on the other hand, or eyes intently fixed on the speaker can usually be seen as signs of concentrated attention. As with other attending behaviors, indicators of contemplation should not be allowed to become mere tokens. When you really are an attentive listener, these nonverbal manifestations will neither be, nor appear, artificial. For this skill to be effective, what you say and the appearance you give must correspond.

Encouraging

It is important as a teacher to be able to offer tactful encouragement to students who speak in class. This is especially beneficial when students are shy or lacking in confidence. One of the most effective "encouragers" is the empathetic listener who nods appreciatively as a speaker offers ideas. Sometimes a soft verbal nudge such as "keep going, you're doing fine!" can be invaluable support. More than anything else, such actions convey your sincere involvement in students' efforts.

◆◆◆ APPLICATION EXERCISES ◆◆◆

1. Working in groups of three (triads) on a designated discussion topic, practice effective attending behavior when other group members are

talking. Design a pattern for providing one another with constructive feedback on the nature and effectiveness of demonstrated attending skills.

2. Practice attending behavior in your interpersonal encounters, formal and informal, both in and out of school. Make an effort to get to the point at which good attending skills are second nature to you, where they become an integral part of your interpersonal style.

Responding Behaviors

The manner in which you respond to student contributions is critical to a free and harmonious interchange of ideas in your classes. It will usually have an important bearing on the confidence and enthusiasm students show toward class discussions.[9]

Your repertoire of responding behaviors should include techniques for: (1) acknowledging and reinforcing students for their contributions, (2) clarifying, to ensure messages are being properly understood, (3) evaluating both right and wrong answers, and (4) mediating between individual contributors and the group at large.

Acknowledging and Encouraging

Classroom participation should be a positive experience for students. Class members who feel ignored or put down when they contribute will be reluctant participants or entirely withdraw. You can avoid some potential negative experiences by insisting that students show respect and sensitivity toward one another as they attempt to communicate their ideas to the class.

Realizing how easy it is for some comments to be lost in the course of a lively discussion, it is important to try to acknowledge all student contributions, regardless of quality or length. Recognizing contributions does not require that you evaluate them, but simply that you allow students to know they have been heard and what they have said (and that they said it) did not go unnoticed. Comments such as ; "O.K. Thank you," "Alex agrees with the minority on this," "I hear you," or "That's one way of looking at it," can be quite enough. With some students, a nod or other nonverbal gesture may be adequate to convey recognition and appreciation for their efforts. A teacher's use of student ideas to make a point or to compare points of view is always gratifying[10]: for example, "Mary also took that position a few minutes ago," or "Jules had a good answer to the question you're asking." You may have noticed that none of these comments are couched in terms of *praise* even though they may be experienced as such. Students need to know that what they do or say matters to the teacher—even if it is not always correct, and even if the teacher does not always agree with it—and that it is attended to by other students. Praise is in general not necessary, may be resented as patronizing, or in fact may be unhelpful if the student becomes, or continues to be, dependent on the teacher's opinion and good graces and thus is concerned to do or say only what the teacher, as authority figure, will approve, a dysfunctional habit for citizens of a democratic society.

Clarifying

In addition to the encouragement you provide students by acknowledging what they have said, you should also make sure that these messages are properly understood. By playing back to students what you take to be the substance and import of their messages, you demonstrate interest and a concern to understand. This can be accomplished by a simple paraphrase of the idea or feeling just communicated: for example, "So you believe we'd be better off with fewer automobiles on the road", or "You think the war was unnecessary."

A *paraphrase* should be a brief restatement of the message (not a question *about* it) delivered in as neutral a manner as possible, and implying no obligation for the student to respond. It should avoid repeating the student's message word for word. It is important that the clarifying paraphrase merely reflect, not question or confront. Simply letting the student know you have heard correctly may be all that is needed to encourage further dialogue.

Evaluating

In discussion situations, in which evaluation of student knowledge or thought is appropriate, a major part of your response to student contributions will be your reply to correct and incorrect answers. As a general rule, it is good practice to confirm correct answers. Short answers should ordinarily receive brief confirmation: for example, "Good," "Good point," Right," "Fine," "Exactly," "That's correct," or "You've got the idea." You should try to vary these responses so that they do not become monotonous and obviously mere knee-jerk reactions. For them to have any worthwhile effect they must be, and be seen by the student to be, genuine. With longer answers, your response may need to be lengthier, in order to inform the student of just what it is that you are commenting on: for example, "Yes, you've done a good job of separating the main cause of the war from the contributing causes," "Very good, I think you've managed to identify each step of the process," "Yes, that's an interesting point," or "O.K., I hadn't thought of that before."

In responding to incorrect answers, it is generally advisable to avoid giving a direct "No, that's not right."[11] Instead, your first effort should be to remain noncommittal, to avoid making a ruling until other students have had an opportunity to be involved, possibly to have the student in this way see his or her answer as mistaken. When you place a high priority on student thought processes you should in any case be less inclined to feature right answers as the focal point of evaluation. Rather than immediately passing judgment on an answer, you will be more interested in working with students on the process for arriving at answers. This may entail giving hints, probing to locate "sticking-points" and confusions, and so forth.

During value-based discussions, you will at times find yourself in disagreement with a student's opinion. It may be difficult for you to resist the temptation to jump in with an "I disagree" or a "Yes . . . but." It may help you to avoid doing this if you bear it in mind that responses that begin this way have a tendency to put students on the defensive. Learning then becomes less important than defending oneself by remaining silent. To maintain your supporting role in a discussion, you should learn ways of disagreeing with finesse, without being confrontational. This is best accomplished when you can present your differing view in language that downplays the disagreement while acknowledging the student's right to an opinion: for example, "Those are some good arguments against a curfew. I'm inclined to favor the curfew because studies indicate that students in towns with curfews get better grades"; or "A lot of people feel as you do in opposing gun control. On the other hand, I'm aware that law enforcement officers feel helpless without it."

Mediating

Another of your main functions during discussion is to ensure that individual contributions are being properly understood and noted by the group. You are in effect a mediator between individual students and the larger group, which means that, besides leaving as much of the talking to the students as they can handle, you must alternate between talking to individual contributors and addressing the group as a whole. It will sometimes be necessary to rephrase or amplify particular ideas so they are usable in the discussion: "Have we heard Marna's point? She thinks that. . . ." On other occasions you will need to play advocate for the group at large to prevent individuals from monopolizing or diverting the discussion: "We may need to put that idea aside for the time being. I'm afraid it's going to get us sidetracked."

You may need to intervene in the discussion periodically to ask for definitions or to inquire where a particular line of thought is leading. As an illustration, in a discussion on teenage crime it may become apparent that some students are using the term "juvenile delinquent" uncritically. Rather than allow key arguments to be built on ambiguous language, you as discussion moderator have a responsibility to call attention to the need for definition. Later in the same discussion a student may be succeeding in advancing an argument based on a premise that you know lacks factual support: for example, the notion that jailing juvenile delinquents would teach them not to break the law. By requesting evidence for this assumption, you are not only teaching principles of sound reasoning, but are protecting the group from a potentially mistaken conclusion.

We refer in the title of this chapter to the *art* of interactive teaching, and there is no other aspect of the process that requires more delicacy of judgment and discernment than considerations of when, whether, and how to intervene in a discussion, which, while it is flourishing may, nonetheless, have gone far off-track in terms of what is actually known, or in respect to values that are at loggerheads with what parents, administrators, and the general public can accept. The degree to which the teacher can affect the discussion without being seen as dictating its course—and thereby losing his or her credibility as a moderator—is a function of the relationship of trust that has been built up over the weeks. That trust is always fragile, in the school context, and art lies in sensing correctly how it can be maintained without betraying the trust placed in the teacher by the students, school authorities, parents, and community as a whole.

◆◆◆ **A P P L I C A T I O N   E X E R C I S E S** ◆◆◆

1. Working in groups of three (triads) on a designated discussion topic, practice reflecting back (paraphrasing) the message of the previous speaker each time you offer a brief comment of your own. The ground rules for this exercise are (1) each speaker provides a brief paraphrase of the preceding speaker's message, as a precondition for entering the discussion, (2) the previous speaker must verify the accuracy of the paraphrase before the discussion is allowed to proceed, and (3) the third person in the group plays the role of monitor when not the paraphraser or the person receiving it.
2. Make an effort to practice your reflective listening skills in your day-to-day conversations, both in and out of school. Attempt to make this an integral part of your communication style. In the degree that you succeed, it will become a more natural behavior for you in the classroom.
3. Being mindful of the desirability of varying teacher response patterns, write out a list of phrases you will use to convey acceptance and approval of what students say or do in your classes. Commit the list to memory.

Dealing with Common Problems in Class Interaction

When you encourage high levels of interaction and involvement in your classes, you should anticipate and be prepared to deal with some of the possible problems student-centered activities engender. Classroom discussions, in particular, can be a special challenge to your managerial skills. The following are some of the potential difficulties you should be aware of, along with suggestions for dealing with them.

Nonparticipation

There may be times during a planned discussion when you have trouble getting students to say anything. It is important that you not convey immediate displeasure with the students for their apparent reluctance to become involved. Periods of silence in the classroom should not cause you to become nervous. Patience is usually the answer here. Don't be afraid to ask students what the silence means. Sometimes lack of response means reflection rather than apathy. It could also mean that students did not understand the question posed. You may need to regroup and come at the topic or issue from a different direction. If you sense that the silence simply reflects difficulties getting started, let students know you are able to empathize with shyness or reluctance to be the first one to talk. One good way to prime students for class discussion is to allow them to work in small groups of three or four as a warm-up (an idea-generating session) for large-group discussion. Another useful tactic is to play a short video clip of someone making a provocative statement on the issue, or of two people offering sharply different opinions in adrenaline-raising terms. One or more students will likely be incited into reacting—and the discussion is on.

Overexcitement

It is also possible to have to cope with the other extreme, namely, discussions that get out of hand. Group discussion should afford students opportunities to express thoughts and opinions on subjects of particular interest to them. As such, the best discussions are often those in which students demonstrate the most exuberance and animation. However, interest and excitement can turn out to be counterproductive when it leads to shouting matches or displays of uncontrolled emotion. It can also be disturbing to adjoining classes or disconcerting to more reserved students. Skillful interaction leaders usually have a knack for bringing discussions to the boiling point without allowing them to boil over. Here are several things you can do to avoid the problem of overstimulation during class discussions:

1. Select topics that are appropriate to the maturity levels of students.
2. Attempt to keep the discussion on-track by maintaining an appropriate balance between opposing points of view. This discourages students from vociferously celebrating one-sided victories in debate.
3. Avoid emotionally charged language when providing your own contributions. Show students how to control their own behavior by tempering your own enthusiasm with reason and self-control.
4. Attempt to redirect discussions that seem to be heading toward verbal confrontations or strong emotional displays.
5. Help your students to recognize that productive discussion is possible only when participants agree to be rational.
6. Call a halt, if nothing else works, and turn the discussion to a discussion of the discussion process itself.

Conformity

One of your main concerns in group interaction should be to encourage the interplay of differing ideas and personal styles. Class discussions should be opportunities for students to express minority opinions as well as occasions for students representing the majority view to express themselves. Peer influence in a typical classroom often militates against this objective. Conformity is an especially prevalent phenomenon among groups of school-age young people. It takes a particularly self-confident and strong-willed youngster to avoid acquiescing in the wishes and opinions of the majority or the most popular students in the group.

One of the things you can do to discourage majority attitudes and patterns from holding sway over the entire class is to make determined (but unobtrusive) efforts to elicit diverse viewpoints and to ensure they are allowed thoughtful consideration. Another is to foster alliances among those who hold minority opinions. Students who feel they are supported by at least one other member of the group are less likely to yield to the views of the majority.[12]

Teacher Influence

The honest exchange of thoughts and opinions can equally well be hampered by students feeling they need to conform to the teacher's views. You should therefore be careful to avoid letting your own opinions and personal agendas influence the direction of students' thinking during a discussion. Unless you are conducting a recitation session, open discussion should not be allowed to degenerate into a situation where students are feeding you the ideas they believe you want to hear. There are several things you can do to ensure that your presence does not affect the authenticity of student contributions:

1. Tell students directly that what matters in discussion is *their* thinking, not simply a reflection of your own.
2. Keep students in the dark about your views on questions that allow for more than one conclusion. Frequently play the devil's advocate to show the range of possibilities.
3. Do not take your own opinions so seriously that students are afraid to have different views. Take opportunities to poke fun at your own lack of certainty in some areas: "I'm still not sure what I believe about this. One of these days I'll figure it out."
4. Support students who express honestly held views different from your own. Show that you are supportive of their attempts to think for themselves: "I'll have to admit, you may have something there. I hadn't thought of it that way."

Controversial Issues

Teachers are sometimes reluctant to engage students in discussions of controversial topics for fear they will be entering forbidden territory.[13] At the other extreme, some teachers have no reluctance to lead students into sensitive areas, often giving little thought to the biases they encourage through one-sided approaches to disputable issues.

Generally it is possible to involve students in fruitful discussions of controversial issues without stepping on toes or prejudicing students' thinking. This will require that you have an appropriate objective as you lead students into a discussion of a controversial subject. Perhaps the most educationally justifiable purpose is to have students appreciate the basis for controversy, usually involving the clash of significant human values. Your ultimate objective here should be to get students to understand what makes an issue an issue rather than simply a problem (i.e., issues persist because they represent strong tension between competing social values). One good way to foster a balanced approach to controversial topics is to have students role-play arguments for both sides of difficult issues. When one of your goals is to encourage social empathy and understanding rather than simply the taking of sides, you have a sound basis for approaching the discussion of controversial issues in your classes.

Simulated Dialogue

This is a more indirect and conversational way of promoting learning and it brings a quasi-interactive quality to classroom communication. It is a way teachers who want to go along at the pace of the learner can engage students' interests, imaginations, values, and experiences. Although you and the students are not engaged in live discussion, you are anticipating and appealing to their frames of reference and you make liberal use of rhetorical questions, personalized references, and significant pauses. Simulated dialogue is a great deal more involving than impersonal teacher monologue. In opening a unit on the colonizing period in U.S. history a teacher using simulated dialogue could begin,

> NOT BY SAYING: "Today we start reading about the colonies, first Jamestown, then Plymouth, and so on. You will want to get the dates fixed first and then find out about which people colonized which section and why."
>
> BUT BY SAYING: "Let's go back about 300 years and think about who was around here and what the countryside must have looked like. Were your ancestors around here then or did they come later? What brought them here? If we could talk about the questions for a while maybe we could get some ideas about what a colony was."

Although the teacher in the second case is still doing all of the talking, this simulated dialogue would be more likely to give students the feeling this teacher was discussing the topic with them rather than simply talking at or past them.

In another teaching example, a woodshop teacher in a brief, relatively teacher-dominated portion of instruction uses the interactive mode, with some simulated dialogue, to provide a short introduction to the final stages of a student project:

- Let's all gather around this bench right here. That's right, bring your projects over with you. . . . Let's hold up our projects so we can see how the sanding work is coming. . . . All right, fine. I'm seeing some good efforts here on this one. . . . What grade of sandpaper are you going to be using next, Sarah? . . . O.K., that's a good choice. . . . Will you all pull in a little closer so we can see one another's work. . . . How many of you are getting ready for the next step? What is the next step? . . . The finish coat . . . That's right. . . . What are some things we'll want to do to prepare for this? . . . Evan do you have an idea . . . Yes, you've apparently been thinking ahead. . . . Where will we want to look for the keys to the finish cabinets? Who remembers? . . . Now most of you were probably planning to use the same approach with this one as you did the last. . . . I want to suggest a minor change.

The use of questions and second-person references gives this teaching episode an interactive character that might easily have been missing had the teacher decided to take the simpler and shorter route and merely tell students what he wanted them to know. In examining this dialogue we recognize the skillful weaving of elements of structuring, questioning, attending, and responding into one concise sequence of interactive teaching.

◆◆◆ A P P L I C A T I O N   E X E R C I S E ◆◆◆

1. Design (on paper) a segment of simulated dialogue that you might use to introduce a lesson, to present a concept, or to provide instructions of one sort or another to students in a subject area you are qualified to teach.
2. Write out the beginning of a simulated dialogue that you could use to stimulate the interest and imagination of a class.

Promoting Interaction Among Students

Cooperative Learning

Another even more indirect approach to instructing is what is called *cooperative learning*, or CL, a process which the teacher initiates and structures but that becomes largely student-centered and conducted. It is a way of teaching built on some fairly evident facts about how students, and people in general, learn most effectively, facts that many teachers spend a lot of time and energy ignoring or even opposing. Young people[14]

- *Want* to talk
- Want some choice in how and what they learn
- Want to help others learn and themselves receive help in learning
- Want success in learning

Fortunately, numerous studies have shown that what students want is what they actually *need* and benefit from in terms of academic progress.[15] There are, besides, numerous other gains, as Slavin, one of the pioneers, points out:

> [T]he attraction of Cooperative Learning for many humanistic educators probably lies not so much in accelerating student achievement as in the consistently found positive effects of cooperative learning on such variables as race relations, attitudes toward main-streamed classmates, self-esteem, and other non-academic outcomes.[16]

There are a number of ways in which a teacher can set a class up for cooperative learning, but certain elements are common to, and essential for, all of them:

1. Students are divided up into small groups (three or four often work best).
2. Each group is presented with a task or problem that requires the involvement of all group members for it to be done, or solved.
3. Each group must eventually be able to demonstrate in some way—orally, in writing, visually, or in action (prescribed by the teacher or decided by the group)—that they have mastered the assigned task.
4. Each individual in each group must be able to show that he or she has personally understood, and participated in, the undertaking.

For CL to work, it is essential that students develop the capacity to use a range of social skills. As the Johnson brothers, who pioneered the approach remarked, "Good group members are made, not born." Students must, for example, learn how to encourage others to join in discussion, to listen to others' ideas without making judgmental statements, to offer constructive and supportive feedback, to share materials, and to use a range of what are sometimes referred to as "helping" skills. You as teacher have a vital role to play in modeling these skills, giving direct instruction in them, providing opportunities for practice, and giving plenty of useful, informative, and encouraging feedback. In the words of one classroom teacher,

> Persevere in practicing the skill[s]. Teachers of reading know that it takes a long time—many years, in fact—for students to master such higher order skills as inference and interpretation. Likewise, it takes time to learn cooperative skills; yet many teachers drop group activities in their classrooms at the first hint of a problem.[17]

As with any innovation, learn as much as you can before you embark on it, start slowly and gradually, maybe just starting off having the students meet in pairs in one class, or one segment of the day, and work with other teachers as much as possible (cooperative learning works fine with teachers, too).[18]

At some stage—maybe at the very beginning—you will need to decide whether you see cooperative learning as one method among many for promoting academic and social growth, or whether you perceive it as a part of a move toward a generally cooperative classroom.[19] Two proponents of this more extensive view argue that

> within a cooperative classroom, democracy is not something that is studied about, but something that is lived. . . . Cooperative classrooms create communities of caring in which students see themselves as having specific responsibilities to one another, regardless of race, age, class, gender, or disability.[20]

Videotapes on CL are available, demonstrating a complete lesson taught by this method.[21]

Computers

A natural focus for cooperative work is increasingly available in classrooms—the computer. As the authors of a recent work on the value and effects of technology in schools remark:

> Interaction among and between students is also [promoted] when students use computers. Cooperative learning centered around a computer activity, for example, leads to increased content-related student talk and an increase in the number of ideas presented for consideration. These structured groups also permitted students with different academic abilities to interact in a more positive and helpful manner.[22]

Software programs such as the Decisions, Decisions series, provide material expressly designed to stimulate small group discussion and problem solving. Topics range widely—the environment, ancient history, immigration, prejudice, and balancing the budget, for example. Simulations like "The Oregon Trail" and "The Great Ocean Rescue" are also highly involving and encourage close teamwork. As always with technology (see Chapter 4), the teacher has to consider how available materials can be used to the best advantage by a particular class in relation to a particular curriculum, but of their general effectiveness in engaging students in active learning and genuine cooperation there can be little if any question.

On a more advanced level, the creation of interactive video projects such as those described by Knapp and Glenn can provide the stimulus for valuable cooperative and individual research.

> Student groups [in a high school English class] were asked to select the piece of literature they thought best depicts the conditions of the Industrial Revolution. . . . they first had to propose and discuss members' individual suggestions . . . make a democratic decision, and then begin planning the presentation. . . . Members began working independently or in pairs . . . and the group continued to meet daily to and to help one another solve problems.[23]

Eventually each group presented their work, and discussed its effectiveness, and whether they had had their opinion changed by what they had seen.

◆◆◆   **SUGGESTED ACTIVITIES AND QUESTIONS**   ◆◆◆

1. Identify teaching tasks that you believe can be accomplished most effectively through interactive teaching. What do you see to be the main advantages of interactive teaching? Does it have any significant limitations? What are the main shortcomings of a directive style of teaching?

2. Summarize your understanding of this chapter by identifying what you take to be the main components of an interactive teaching pattern. Describe in your own words what each of these elements requires of the teacher.

3. Discuss the theory of learning that supports an interactive approach to teaching. Compare this with the conception of learning that underlies a directive style of teaching. Which, in your experience as a student, is more effective in promoting significant learning?

4. How would you rate your present abilities as interactive communicator? What would you consider to be your main strengths and weaknesses when it comes to engaging in genuine dialogue with young people? Will you have to make substantial changes in how you deal with students in order for you to teach this way?

5. Find occasions to observe the interactive techniques of teachers in schools where you are involved. Make note of the specific *interactive maneuvers* used by these teachers. As you observe classroom interaction, make an effort to identify points in these lessons where you might employ specific interactive maneuvers were you the teacher, for example, places in the lesson where you would use a teacher paraphrase, where you would insert an internal summary, a probing question, and so forth.

6. Make it a point to focus on the *questioning techniques* being used in the classrooms you are able to observe. Do an informal survey of (1) the frequency and types of teacher questions you encounter, (2) how clear the teacher's questions are, and (3) the amount of think-time teachers are allowing when asking questions.

7. Study the attending and responding patterns of teachers you have occasion to observe. Do you find many teachers using highly effective skills in these areas? Do you encounter teachers who demonstrate poor attending and responding behaviors in their interactions with students?

8. To what extent are the attending and responding behaviors of teachers a reflection of teacher attitudes as well as skills? How high a priority are you presently willing to place on this kind of skill development, and for what reasons?

9. Some teacher educators recommend that teachers adapt their response patterns to the self-concepts and ability levels of their students. Does this seem like a reasonable idea to you? For example, what would you think of using a different—perhaps briefer and more direct technique—

when responding to the contributions of more confident, intellectually mature students than the approach you employ with less assertive, less academically talented students?

NOTES

1. Mary Lynn Crow, "Teaching as an Interactive Process." In Kenneth E. Eble (Ed.), *New Directions for Teaching and Learning*. San Francisco: Jossey-Bass, 1980, p. 42. Merrill Harmin's *Inspiring Active Learning: A Handbook for Teachers* (Alexandria, Va., Association for Supervision and Curriculum Development, 1997) describes an extensive range of practical ideas for promoting what its title claims.
2. Ned A. Flanders, *Analyzing Teaching Behavior*. Reading, Mass.: Addison-Wesley, 1970, p. 401.
3. Arno A. Bellack and Joel R. Davitz, "The Language of the Classroom." In Ronald T. Hyman (Ed.), *Teaching: Vantage Points for Study*, 2nd ed. Philadelphia: J.B. Lippincott, 1974, p. 168.
4. Deborah B. Strother, "Developing Thinking Skills Through Questioning." *Phi Delta Kappan* (December 1989): 324.
5. Ibid., p. 325.
6. Francis Hunkins, *Teaching Thinking Through Effective Questioning*. Needham Heights, Mass.: Christopher-Gordon, 1989, p. 64.
7. N. L. Gage and David C. Berliner, *Educational Psychology*, 4th ed. Boston: Houghton Mifflin, 1988, p. 551.
8. Sandra Sololove Garrett, Myra Sadker, and David Sadker, "Interpersonal Communication Skills." In James M. Cooper (Ed.), *Classroom Teaching Skills*, 2nd ed. Lexington, Mass.: D.C. Heath, 1982, p. 240.
9. Flanders, *Analyzing Teacher Behavior*, p. 415.
10. Gage and Berliner, *Educational Psychology*, p. 555.
11. Ibid., p. 556.
12. Ibid., p.445.
13. Ibid., p.435.
14. For introducing CL to early childhood classes, see Jonathan Trudge and Dawn Caruso, "Cooperative Problem Solving in the Classroom: Enhancing Young Children's Cognitive Development." *Young Children* (November 1988): 46–52.
15. Richard Strong, Harvey F. Silver, and Amy Robinson, "What Do Students Want (And What Really Motivates Them)?" *Educational Leadership* (September 1995): 8–12.
16. Robert E. Slavin, "Cooperative Learning and Group Contingencies." *Journal of Behavioral Education* 1, No. 1 (1991): 113.
17. Strong et al., "What Do Students Want?" (p. 9). The authors use the acronym SCORE as a practical way of remembering the human needs involved in learning: *Success* (the need for mastery), *Curiosity* (the need for understanding), *Originality* (the need for self-expression), and *Relationships* (the need for involvement with others). The *E* stands for "the energy . . . that is essential for a complete and productive life."
18. Roy A. Smith, "A Teacher's View on Cooperative Learning." *Phi Delta Kappan* (May 1987): 663–667.

19. Claudia Edwards and Judy Stout, "Cooperative Learning: The First Year." *Educational Leadership* (December 1989): 39. This issue was entirely given over to cooperative learning.

20. Mara Sapon-Shevin and Nancy Schniedewind, "If Cooperative Learning's the Answer, What are the Questions?" *The Journal of Education* 174, No. 2 (1992): 21–24.

21. In consultation with Robert Slavin and David J. Johnson, ASCD has produced a comprehensive series of five videotapes on cooperative learning, the last of which shows a complete lesson being taught by CL.

22. Linda Knapp and Allen Glenn, *Restructuring Schools with Technology*. Boston: Allyn and Bacon, 1996, p. 26.

23. Ibid., pp. 87–88.

CHAPTER 9

Staying on Top of Classroom Management

*For workers, including students, to do quality work,
they must be managed in a way that convinces them
that the work they are asked to do satisfies their
needs. The more it does, the harder they work.*

William Glasser

*Discipline problems are minimized when students
are regularly engaged in meaningful activities
geared to their interests and aptitudes.*

Brophy and Good

Making the Necessary Investments

The task of teaching in today's schools become considerably less burdensome when you are able to manage a classroom firmly, smoothly, and humanely. Competent classroom management is essentially a human relations skill. It will reflect your ability to purposefully organize group learning activities with a minimum of confusion and distraction. You will need to possess the leadership skills to draw students into orderly encounters with activities toward which they may initially be indifferent or resistant. This usually requires a firm presence and a strong sense of purpose, qualities that need to be balanced with considerable patience and good humor.

There are no simple formulas for developing and maintaining an appropriate learning atmosphere in a school classroom. You should avoid thinking of classroom management as a set of prescriptions to be applied when behavior *problems* arise, that is, as synonymous with "discipline." Instead, your ability to keep students constructively involved in learning will be the result of an environment you manage to create, a group climate you have a major role in establishing, which makes possible and supports the learning you are seeking to bring about. To become a skillful director of group learning, you will have to *plan* class management, that is, collect ideas and methods for setting up procedures—organized ways of doing things—as an integral part of your teaching. Class management is the essential complement to your capacity to teach interesting material in ways that engage the interest and effort of students.

This chapter provides management strategies and disciplinary approaches that will help you develop a smooth flow of classroom activity. It emphasizes behavior control and the preservation of teaching energy through saving your voice, artful response tactics, and preventive maintenance measures.

Three Main Requirements

Effective classroom management depends on three factors.

First, that you approach it with *commitment*. Class control is made easier if you are sure you have something of importance and of worth for the students you are teaching, and the determination to maintain a supportive environment in which they can learn it.

Second, that you possess *perceptual sensitivity*. Effective group management involves an ability to recognize when the classroom climate is appropriate to a developing activity and to sense immediately when some adjustment is needed.

Third, that you have an appropriate set of *management strategies*. To maintain a productive class atmosphere you will need to have at your disposal a repertoire of behavioral management tactics that you can skillfully apply to a variety of classroom situations.

The Psychology of Classroom Management

Above all, effective classroom management absolutely requires that there be something personally and educationally important that you want to achieve with the class, something that is at the same time maximally involving for the students.[1] When you come to class feeling confident because you have done your homework and know that you have a lesson worth your students' attention and cooperation, you will be more mentally prepared to insist on a favorable learning climate than when your primary concern is merely to get through a class period. You will be conscious of having a personal stake in the outcome of the lesson. The management task will not loom in your mind as something extraneous to the act of teaching, as something you do out of self-defense or because it is expected of you. This is a discovery that conscientious teachers often make at some early point in their careers:

> I guess I should have figured this out before, but I know I teach differently when I have a lesson I feel real confident about, one that I have a special interest in teaching. I think I'm more focused and in a way I'm more demanding. I expect students' attention when I'm well-prepared myself. And I think

they can sense when I've done the job with my own homework. It's almost as though they feel they owe me something in return.

We were told in methods classes that we would have less discipline problems if we planned well for our classes. Although I admit it didn't mean much to me at the time, I'm finding it to be true now that I'm teaching everyday. I seem to teach more naturally when I have a definite objective and a lesson that I've thought a lot about. And my students seem to have less trouble staying with me.

Conversely, when you allow yourself to approach a class with little or no personal commitment to a clear and worthwhile learning goal, you lack a strong motive for promoting student involvement. You are less able to generate the kind of teaching momentum that will, at its best, allow classroom management to become an integral part of the lesson itself. In other words, you put yourself at a psychological disadvantage when you fail to think of the control function as simply a means to help students accomplish a goal to which *you* are educationally committed. Unless you see it in this light, your endeavors to keep the class quiet and orderly are bound to appear artificial. In the students' minds, your attempts to control them will tend to be perceived as a coercive or manipulative game. Students have become used to teachers insisting on their paying attention and cooperating without getting any significant learning out of the deal, and they can be expected to respond with anything from apathy to overt compliance, to outright resistance, thus creating the potential for control problems of one sort or another.

It does of course take continued hard work, and in particular hard *thinking* to keep coming up with lessons that will help to have "management" arise out of the nature of the task itself, so that it is what the students are doing, and their interest in doing it that, in a sense, manage their behavior. Yet, teachers who are consistently good classroom managers do by and large succeed in keeping themselves mentally prepared to meet their students mainly because their *teaching* also emerges out of what *they* are concerned about, in their case the learning and personal development of their students. Although at times they may feel weighed down by the long hours they spend with student groups, and the heavy pressures involved in working within a system (see Chapter 2), they nonetheless find ways to maintain, and when necessary to renew, their enthusiasm and to avoid becoming stale (see Chapters 1, 2, and 12). Your own endeavors to stay vital as a teacher will heavily depend on whether you really want students to learn, for purposes that you have fairly clearly in mind.

◆◆◆ A P P L I C A T I O N   E X E R C I S E S ◆◆◆

1. What is your own tolerance for inattention or distraction when you are attempting to communicate important thoughts to others in either formal or informal situations? Do you generally keep talking, even when

there are indications others are not listening? Why is that? How insistent on attention are you likely to be when talking to groups of students in a classroom?

2. It has been maintained that a teacher's frame of mind has an important bearing on his or her effectiveness as a classroom manager. Speculate on the kinds of class management patterns that are likely to be associated with each of the following teacher attitudes: (1) feelings of need to get through a series of activities; (2) feelings of minor irritation over student inattention or poor effort; (3) feelings of quiet confidence and determination; (4) feelings of basic insecurity and indecision; and (5) feelings of passivity or boredom—a "let's see what happens" attitude. Which of these mental sets would you consider most functional for a competent classroom manager? Which least functional? Why?

Sensitivity to the Learning Environment

To be an effective class manager you have to become a skillful orchestrator of group activity, not exclusively or even largely a soloist. You will need to recognize when students are in sync with you and with one another, to have a feel for the type of classroom atmosphere that supports productive group communication. This is in large part a perceptual and observational skill. It entails an ability to sense when environmental conditions are right for the kind of learning activity you want to promote. Teachers who are awake to the situation are quick to notice when students' attention is elsewhere, when they are fidgeting, glancing at one another, or working on an assignment for another subject.[2] They immediately sense when a group is slow to settle down or when they just aren't ready or willing.

One major impediment to classroom communication is unrestrained chatter, the inclination of some students to talk compulsively, often to no one in particular. This sort of talking has become an increasingly difficult management challenge for teachers in today's schools.[3] Otherwise competent teachers sometimes allow themselves to become used to accepting a certain amount of classroom noise as though it were normal conduct. These teachers' perceptual faculties seemingly become desensitized to behavior that so obviously interferes with teaching, learning, and genuine discussion.

So why do teachers put up with classroom conditions that get in the way of group learning? Knowing the answer to this question can be the first step to dealing constructively with the problem. One reason, and the primary emphasis of this section, is the lack of finely tuned classroom sensitivities.[4] This usually involves a failure to work from a clear notion, a mental picture as it were, of just what constitutes appropriate classroom conditions, and thus a failure to recognize when these conditions are or are not being met.

Another possible factor (the main focus of the preceding section), is the absence of an abiding resolve to develop and maintain a classroom atmosphere that contributes to a meaningful teaching goal. This lack of resolve can of course contribute to class inattention. Teachers who feel disorganized or uncertain may ignore inattention and minor forms of misbehavior because they are not clear about *why* they are teaching *what* they are teaching, or they may ignore it out of the inability to see the connection between student behavior and a well-defined teaching goal.

Probably the most common reason why some teachers appear insensitive to inattentive and distracting behavior in their classes is a lack of confidence in their management skills. This lack of confidence usually stems from not having a knowledge of the skills needed for class management.[5] The remaining sections of this chapter concentrate on basic techniques that will help you maintain good order in a modern classroom with finesse and self-assurance.

◆◆◆ A P P L I C A T I O N   E X E R C I S E ◆◆◆

As you observe classrooms in schools where you are involved, practice sizing up whether, as a whole, the classroom is working. Make an effort to notice not only what the teacher says and does, but what the students are doing, that is, where their attention is, how they are responding, their attitude toward the class, and so forth. Are there things you are seeing and hearing to which the regular teacher is failing to attend? If so, do they seem to be behaviors that the teacher is aware of but is choosing to ignore for one reason or another? Decide whether these would be appropriate learning environments for your own purposes as a teacher.

Low-Profile Management Tactics[6]

The most obvious requirement for competent classroom management is an appropriate set of techniques for structuring group activity and dealing with any behavioral problems that may arise. The former have been labeled "procedural rules" (or just "procedures") and the latter "behavioral rules" ("rules"). Both serve to regulate activities such as giving out materials, using the pencil sharpener, leaving and entering the classroom, which happen frequently. Procedures are also needed for academic matters such as making up of work missed, checking on work in progress, and so on. Rules, on the other hand, apply to how students should act *in general*, and they are considered in the next section.

The best classroom managers possess an assortment of low-key tactics for gaining student attention, maintaining a smooth and productive flow of activities, and responding to inappropriate behavior.[7] Once they have been mastered, many of these maneuvers can be performed almost automatically and effortlessly, becoming subtle ingredients of your classroom style. Others require a greater degree of calculation and planning to implement. Some of these are essentially verbal moves, whereas others involve nonverbal skills. These can be categorized as: (1) getting attention; (2) correcting misbehavior; and (3) preventing misbehavior.

Getting Attention	*Correcting Misbehavior*	*Preventing Misbehavior*
1. Cueing	5. Eye contact	14. Scanning
2. Tuning	6. Gesturing	15. I-messages
3. Pausing	7. Moving in	16. Synchronizing
4. Restarting	8. Relocating	17. Prepping
	9. Insisting	18. Renewing
	10. Defusing	19. Positive framing
	11. Time-out	
	12. Conferencing	
	13. Referral	

Attention-Getting and Beginning Class

One of the first requirements for effective class control is to be able to obtain student attention with a minimum of effort. The moves you undertake to get a class period underway, to change the direction of class activities, or to reconvene a class after a break are crucial. You will need reliable techniques for bringing the focus of attention to where you happen to be. It is a common mistake for teachers to attempt to begin lessons before they have everyone's attention or for them to move prematurely into activities before students are tuned in.

Ways of getting attention and of beginning class are indispensable for getting a class ready for what is to follow in the lesson. The ability to perform these tasks skillfully can make the succeeding job of managing the class much less difficult. As such, they will deserve your concentrated attention as you seek to develop workable management strategies.

Cueing

Resourceful teachers sometimes rely on nonverbal cues to let students know that class is about to begin. This may involve positioning oneself on the edge of the desk in front of the class, placing the attendance slip in the door, or raising one's hand as a signal for quiet. You will probably need to let students know that this nonverbal sign is a call for everyone to pay attention.

Skillful cueing can also be used as an initiatory device for other purposes: for example, holding a book in the air to accompany a request that the class take it out. The essence of good classroom management is getting students to work cooperatively and productively in a group setting, so a large share of the task amounts to having students respond appropriately to signs that certain behaviors are in order. You will be able to save yourself considerable stress as soon as you can get groups of students to do what is needed with a minimum of commotion or resistance.[8]

Tuning

Although you may use cueing as a nonverbal signal for student attention, actually starting a class activity will normally call for some sort of verbal opener. It is important that you give serious thought to getting students in tune with you before any kind of group-centered activity begins to unfold. Teachers who ignore this requirement, allowing class proceedings to evolve in a haphazard manner, find it increasingly difficult to keep students on task for the remainder of the lesson.

If it is necessary to call for student attention, you should face the class and do so directly and emphatically; for example, "I'd like everyone's attention, please." If students are relatively settled at the beginning, you may start off with a message or an announcement, for example, "Just a reminder that we'll be meeting in the library tomorrow." Another way to begin is by asking the class for information of some kind, for example, "I'd like to take just a few minutes to get an idea of how you are getting on with your special projects."

When students appear ready to get down to work without special prompting, one of the best ways to begin is to move directly into the lesson set (also known as the "set induction," the "grabber," or the "hook"): for example, "Did any of you have occasion to watch the evening news on television last night?"; "I have a question I've been thinking about . . ."; or, "There were several comments made during our discussion yesterday that I'd like to follow up on."

Whatever the means for initiating class proceedings, you should make a special effort to get students in sync with you at the beginning of a class period as well as at transition times when it may be necessary to refocus student attention. The investments made here, however, will usually make the subsequent management considerably less strenuous.

Pausing

Deliberate pauses can generally be used to good advantage when seeking group attention. You should use pauses to wait students out when they are slow to pay attention. When the competition is relatively mild, pausing for attention should be a first move. It is a low-key maneuver designed to provide a slight jar to the awareness of inattentive students. The tactic will normally be effective once you have established that you mean business. Teachers who have not yet succeeded in doing this will find it less effective and need to be more insistent.

To get the desired result, teacher pauses should be accompanied by a look or a stance that helps to convey the message, "I'm waiting" or " Let me have your attention, *now*." You should be prepared to wait several seconds or longer for *all* students to focus their attention on you. If pauses are ignored by students, you should make it quite clear that you expect future calls for attention to bring more immediate compliance. If you get into the habit of pausing for attention, and allow students to ignore the stimulus, you need to change management strategy.

Restarting

In keeping with the principle that teachers should insist on concentrated attention when addressing groups of students, another effective low-key move is for you to stop talking in the middle of a sentence and to restart as a sign of refusal to endure inattention, for example, "I'd like to read a short . . . I'd like to . . . I'd like . . ."

As with pausing, restarting is another wait-them-out maneuver that will normally bring positive results when skillfully applied. If several attempts to restart should fail to gain attention, this is likely an indication that a brief time-out (to be discussed in a later section) is in order.

◆◆◆ A P P L I C A T I O N   E X E R C I S E S ◆◆◆

1. Think up several nonverbal cues you might employ as a classroom teacher to signal the need for student attention at the beginning of a class period.
2. As you observe teachers in the schools where you are involved, notice the techniques they use to start classes and to gain student attention. Do the majority of these teachers get students in tune with them before they attempt to teach? What attention-getting and initiatory maneuvers do the effective teachers employ most frequently? What do the less successful classroom managers fail to do or do ineffectively when they attempt to initiate classroom activities? Think about what specific initiatory moves you would use in some of these situations.

Corrective Maintenance Moves

To be an effective classroom manager you will need to have a range of ways of responding to and correcting minor or major instances of misconduct in your classes. You should learn to apply these techniques quietly and efficiently, yet firmly and persistently, while calling as little attention to the problem as possible. By working to implement good low-profile corrective strategies, you can begin to ensure that you do not inadvertently become a serious distracting influence in your own classroom.[9]

Eye Contact

With a reasonably well-established classroom presence you can usually eliminate minor forms of inappropriate behavior—inattention, for example, or private conversation—by focusing your attention on the misbehavior.[10] In many instances the simplest and most effective corrective move is for you to be able to make solid eye contact with these students. Proficient classroom managers often rely heavily on their eyes as basic tools for keeping a class orderly and attentive. This avoids the unnecessary use of the voice to deal with localized and relatively routine problems, thereby averting a potential distraction for students who are busy working. Once you have organized a systematic management policy that includes predictable consequences for chronic misbehavior, a fixating stare is frequently all that is necessary to say "I want your attention" or "Please don't do that again."

Eye contact as a corrective measure needs to be penetrating. A fleeting glance in the student's direction is usually of no consequence. The eye contact needs to last long enough to communicate some of the emotion that accompanies it. As a beginning teacher, you would do well to rehearse your piercing stares as one of the first and most important management behaviors you will need to perfect.

Gesturing

Like sharp eye contact, well-placed teacher gestures can be useful low-profile maneuvers for effecting minor behavioral adjustments during a busy class session. By pointing emphatically to a student's seat, you may effectively signal "Sit down, please." By extending an open hand toward one section of the room, you can use sign language to say, "Please hold your comment for a moment until we've had a chance to deal with the one that we're working on at the moment." On a different occasion, and with a younger class, a deft finger to the lips serves as a reminder to students that the present activity requires silence. Most good classroom managers have cultivated their sign language to the point where they are able to save themselves and their students a lot of unnecessary verbalization, at the same time maintaining orderly and productive classrooms.

Moving In

When for one reason or another eye contact or gesturing fails to remedy minor forms of inattention or distraction, you can often get positive results by moving calmly and deliberately in the direction of the misbehaving student or students. In these instances, your physical presence will generally serve as a corrective without the need for verbal intervention. It may be appropriate at times to cap the moving-in maneuver by leaning over a student and whispering a quiet message; for example, "We need your attention, too," or "I'd like you to put that other book under your seat."

Teachers who make it a practice to move toward and among their students during the course of a lesson tend to fill more psychological space in a classroom than those who remain planted in the front of the room for entire class periods. Among the many possible conditions found to contribute to successful classroom management, a teacher's ability to know what is going on in the classroom, or "*withitness*," has turned out to be a major factor.[11] Other things being equal, students are generally more inclined to respect and cooperate with teachers whom they regard as highly perceptive or "with it." They tend to create fewer and less serious management problems for teachers who demonstrate a moment-to-moment awareness of what is happening everywhere in the classroom.

Moving in is a low-profile strategy, then, that can help to curb localized, minor types of misbehavior and to increase the degree of withitness you are seen to possess.

Relocating

When you are aware of the ongoing social dynamics within your classroom, you may on occasion find it appropriate to make certain unplanned changes in seating arrangements. Relocating certain people can be an effective maneuver when you wish to impress on students the need for consistent attention and work. When you have decided on a change, make the move as expeditiously and good-naturedly as possible, with a minimum of on-the-spot discussion.

Although seat changing is not a cure-all for classroom behavioral problems, if you can accomplish it without bruising a student's self-esteem or triggering more serious management difficulties, you may find it a useful strategy for breaking up unworkable student combinations or bringing inattentive students closer to the teacher's desk, where you can keep a closer eye on them.

Insisting

In order to maintain credibility with student groups, there are occasions when you will need to insist on prompt student compliance with your directives. For example, when you ask a student to make a seat change or to refrain from sharpening a pencil in the middle of class, you have a stake in seeing to it that the behavior be carried out as quickly and smoothly as possible. Be calm, but allow no argument. If necessary, repeat your directive once or twice and most students will yield. If insistence does not cause the student to yield, this ordinarily means you have a more serious discipline problem on your hands, one that needs to be dealt with through other measures.

Defusing

Alert class managers have an eye for emerging situations that could put them in an awkward position or that might threaten the order and productivity of the class. You can usually divert or defuse a potentially distracting incident, for example, a student comment you think may stir up trouble, by ignoring it, by tactfully changing the subject, or by countering it with sharp wit. For example, when confronted by comments like, "Hey, let's have class outside today," or "Mrs. Smith, do you want to come to our party after school?", you may, if you prefer not to deal with the remark, deliberately ignore it in the expectation that it will simply go away.

In other instances, you can effectively counter an objectionable turn of events by meeting it head-on and refusing to allow the class focus to be moved in that direction. For example, veterans of the classroom are normally able to spot looming gripe sessions, and they learn to avoid no-win situations in which a few students may attempt to play on the sympathies of the rest of the group to initiate grievances over matters such as the grading system, homework policies, or class activities. A good tactic for heading off a developing "get the teacher" maneuver is to say firmly and forthrightly to the class, "I'm quite willing to listen to your thoughts about the homework assignments. However, I don't want to take class time to involve the whole group in what may be the complaints of just a few people. If you're interested in talking to me personally about this, see me after class and we'll arrange a time."

Time-Out

Eye contact, gesturing, moving in, relocating, insisting, and defusing are low-profile strategies for dealing primarily with individual cases of minor misconduct. Their usefulness is limited, however, when it comes to more serious or more pervasive management problems. You must be able to recognize when classroom noise or misbehavior is becoming too widespread to justify continued efforts to combat individual "brushfires." To attempt to deal with problems on an individual basis when new ones are emerging in other parts of the room can be an exercise in futility and frustration for a teacher. Under these circumstances the best course may be to stop and to discuss with the whole group what is going wrong.

Particularly during the early stages of working with a new group of students, it may be appropriate to call periodic time-outs to review ground rules with the class. When a time-out becomes necessary, it should be regarded as a vital step in the process of getting students to operate within the class rules. It should not be treated as an occasion to harangue the group, but rather as an opportunity to remind students of certain behavioral expectations and to review what you will have to do if the expectations are not met. You should try to make these brief critique sessions quite matter-of-fact. The message should be as positive as possible, with perhaps you yourself accepting some responsibility for what has gone wrong: for example, you could say something to the effect that "some of you have apparently misunderstood what's expected. Perhaps I haven't made myself clear. Let's review matters once again."

Conferencing

Private conferences for discussing a behavior problem can be thought of as time-outs with individual students. This should be the next move when students fail to respond constructively to low-profile strategies or time-outs from the lesson. As with group time-outs, you should be prepared to arrange an early private conference with any student who is misbehaving. Depending on the severity of the problem, these private conferences may range from short, spontaneously arranged talks with individuals during, or as they are leaving, class, to more formal after-school meetings with student and parents (see Chapter 11). Whatever their degree of formality, they are investments that can serve to correct minor misunderstandings or personality conflicts before they become serious.

Referral

In the interests of your personal relationship with the class, you should handle your own discipline problems as far as possible. However, if an occasion arises when you can't (and this happens even to veteran teachers), refer the student to the administrator in charge of discipline firmly and unceremoniously. Needless to say, don't insult, or argue with students, and avoid creating an embarrassing scene in front of the class. Make sure you are well aware of any schoolwide discipline policies that might apply, the person to whom you are sending students, and the kind of support you can expect to receive from the school administration.

◆◆◆   **A P P L I C A T I O N   E X E R C I S E S**   ◆◆◆

1. Based on the strategies for correcting misbehavior presented earlier, indicate which tactics you would consider appropriate for dealing with the following kinds of student behavior:
   a. Students slow to settle down when it is time to start class.
   b. Students argue with me when I ask them to do something or refrain from doing something.
   c. Students frequently out of their seats when they should not be.
   d. Students chattering when they should be listening.
   e. Some students not following directions very well.
   f. Students saying insensitive or off-the-wall things.
   g. Some students consistently failing to pay attention.
   h. Some students constantly wanting to talk to their neighbors.
   i. Some students being discourteous or openly hostile toward others.
   j. Some students working on assignments for other classes.
   k. A student who is usually well-behaved talking to a friend at the wrong time.
   l. A student using foul language to protest an assignment.
2. Imagine that as a classroom teacher you are confronted with the following situation: Jesse and Allison, two of your seventh-grade students, have interrupted class with a loud argument over ownership of a pen. Both are adamant in insisting it belongs to them. It has taken you

longer to quell this disturbance than you would have wished, leaving you with a feeling of irritation that something like this could happen in the middle of an otherwise productive lesson. You have arranged a short private conference with Jesse and Allison to express your concern and to ensure this kind of disruption does not happen again. Describe in detail what you would say to them.

Preventive Maintenance Strategies

Most of your potential discipline problems can be prevented if you take steps to avoid the conditions that foster them. Generally speaking, students are most likely to become restless and disorderly when they are unsure of what is expected of them, when teachers are neglectful of group dynamics, when teachers fail to model a positive and constructive approach to classroom activities,[12] and above all when the teacher and/or the curriculum is boring.[13] Recognizing this, you can anticipate situations that lead to management problems and take actions to prevent these situations from arising. There are certain identifiable strategies that will not only enhance your instructional effectiveness, but will serve as preventive measures to minimize instances of student misbehavior.

Scanning

As mentioned earlier, one of the main attributes of effective classroom managers is their ability to remain acutely aware of what is going on in their classrooms. Such teachers are able to use their eyes (in concert with their ears) to scan the classroom and rapidly size up behavior, while at the same time attending to other teaching tasks, for example, attendance taking, helping individuals with seatwork, or presiding over a discussion.[14] It is crucial that you develop the ability to glance over a class and immediately assess students' state of attention and activity. Teachers' thought patterns sometimes make it difficult for them to have an overall awareness of classroom conditions. However, once one has an appreciation of its importance as a preventive maintenance skill, the ability to use one's eyes effectively in the classroom can be developed through concentrated practice.

I-Messages

It is important to be firm and direct in letting students know what they are to do, or not to do. It is not a matter of what you want or would like them to do, or to refrain from doing. It is a matter of what needs to be done in order for learning to take place. By using a confidently delivered I-message ("do this"), you convey to students your commitment to a classroom where learning is first priority. Some examples:

"Drew, please stop talking to Kipp and get back to work." (As opposed to, "You two are being too noisy back there.")

"Shannon, will you please take this first seat in the second row, and Antonio, you move two seats forward." (As opposed to: "Class, we're going to need to move some seats because you can't stop talking. Shannon and Antonio, can you both move away from Kipp?")

"These interruptions are irritating everyone. I'm glad you want to say something, but everyone has to take a number!

Synchronizing

As you work to develop an effective class management system, you should take steps to ensure that student groups learn to function in harmony with you. This is crucial when beginning to work with a new class (see Chapter 5). It is important that when you ask students to pass their homework forward, they are able to do this without a lot of unnecessary movement or conversation. Similarly, when you call for students to locate a particular passage in a textbook, they ought to be able to do so relatively quickly with a minimum of noise and confusion.

During the first several days with a new group you should find occasions to walk through certain precisely structured activities (procedures) with the class as a whole. You might, for example, request initial information from students on a three-by-five card. This is an opportunity to give students practice in following simple teacher directions. You should attempt to be as focused and deliberate as possible, using this as an appropriate time to check whether everyone has followed your instructions. By moving briskly among the group and telling them as you do so that they are to complete the procedure quickly and quietly, you set important precedents for future group behavior.

Prepping

When you depart from the conventional teacher-centered format, it is important that students be adequately briefed on relevant procedures and responsibilities before they are expected to perform effectively in more learner-centered activities. With certain kinds of these it is especially necessary that you do a thorough job of "prepping" before releasing students to their own devices. Some examples:

1. Students are required to give formal speeches before groups of peers in an English class. This can turn out to be a negative experience for teacher and students if the teacher fails to take prior measures to ensure that the audience know their proper roles, that students know the ground rules for evaluating their peers, that individual performers have some guidelines to cling to when necessary, and some reasonable escape hatches in cases of extreme anxiety, and so forth.
2. Classes are divided into a number of individual teams to play half-court basketball on separate outdoor courts during physical education class.

Problems can be anticipated if students fail to receive a sufficient briefing on specific objectives and ground rules for these particular games, expectations for etiquette and fair play, rules for settling disputes, and so forth.

3. Students are broken into groups to discuss a current-events issue in history. Teachers can expect disorganized, nonfocused discussions if this activity is initiated without a clear framework within which to organize discussion or without provisions for keeping the groups on task during the allotted time, and so forth.

Renewing

Proficient classroom managers are inclined to begin and end class sessions with brief attempts to identify where the class is, where it has been, and where it is going in relation to its learning activities.[15] It is important to renew learning perspectives with your students on a regular basis so that class activity does not become stale routine. Losing your grip on the direction of student learning can serve to weaken your effectiveness in behavior control.

Particularly in classes in which students become accustomed to working in subgroups or on independent projects, it will take extra effort to maintain a strong sense of class goals and teacher leadership (see Chapter 8). In activity-based subjects where classes tend to become disjointed, it is advisable to bring students together at the beginning and end of the class period to provide group feedback and reorientation to learning objectives. Besides the educational value of such continued renewal of direction, it is good for you to regularly establish your managerial presence so as to maintain a close working relationship with your students.

Positive Framing

As a teacher, you are a central influence on the prevailing atmosphere in your classroom. The attitudes you demonstrate toward day-to-day activities will have a large bearing on the nature and frequency of the management problems you encounter. As long as you think of teaching and learning in positive and constructive terms, you stand to avoid much of the negativism and ill-feeling that often characterize today's crowded classrooms.[16]

There are several ways in which a positive approach can make a valuable contribution to avoiding misbehavior:

1. Ensure that rules and procedures are phrased as do's rather than as don'ts. "Remember to walk," rather than "Don't run"; "One at a time at the pencil sharpener," instead of "Don't all try to sharpen your pencils at the same time."

2. Make a point of noticing and commenting on the good things students do, for instance:
"I appreciate the efforts you people have been making to get to class on time. I know that the short interval between classes makes it difficult for you."

"I thought most of you gave some really effective demonstration speeches today. I also felt you evaluators had some excellent comments to offer and I'm sure they will help those who found making a speech difficult."

3. Be as consistently good-humored, cheerful, and reasonable as you can in your dealings with students. Irritation and frustration, displays of ill-temper, snapping at people, standing on your dignity, and in general being heavy-handed and oppressive, all contribute to classroom management problems because negativity is infectious. Bear in mind William Glasser's notion that school should be a "good place."[17] Happy and interested students have no reason to be misbehaved (as distinct from the quite different natural tendency among the young to be mischievous).

◆◆◆ APPLICATION EXERCISES ◆◆◆

1. Discuss the advantages of natural authority as opposed to role-based authority when implementing preventive maintenance as a classroom management strategy. What are some of the key indicators of natural authority in teacher-student relationships? What are the main signs that teachers are depending primarily on role-based authority in managing a classroom? Describe the relationship with students that teachers must establish if they are to work from natural authority in a classroom.

2. Using "positive framing," specify the kinds of behavior you would want to communicate to your students. Which would have the highest priority?

3. Select a learning activity in your teaching area that would ordinarily call for some teacher "prepping" before students are allowed to begin. Plan a short presentation, indicating as precisely as possible what instructions you would give to a group of students who were about to engage in this activity.

 ## A SUMMARY OF CLASSROOM MANAGEMENT GUIDELINES

A summary of basic guidelines and strategies for effective classroom management in today's schools includes the following:

1. Always make sure that you are teaching something for which you are satisfied there is good reason and that you anticipate will have meaning to your students. Have confidence that, *if* you set the class up appropri-

ately, your teaching will be effective. The sense of purposefulness that this brings will do much to give you the confidence that makes the chance of success a good deal likelier.

2. Be aware of the attitude with which you are teaching. Does it manifest confidence, enthusiasm, and purpose, or uncertainty, indifference, and a lack of conviction? Learn to take inventory of your moods and to get yourself mentally ready to face a class. If you are constantly negative, get advice about what you should do.

3. Be aware of the danger of falling into routine teaching. If you find what you are doing boring, so will your students, with predictable behavioral results.

4. Come to grips with the question of what is and is not desirable and tolerable behavior in your classroom. As a teacher of groups of young learners you need to make up your mind about what is reasonable and acceptable group behavior and to work at establishing it.

5. Learn to keep your fingers on the pulse of the class. Move swiftly and purposefully to curb behavior that threatens to distract from the lesson. Do not get in the habit of ignoring minor behavior problems in the hope they will simply go away. In most cases they won't.

6. Get students in tune with you before you start teaching. Be careful not to allow slippage here. Do not attempt to talk above the competition. Use pauses, restarts, or lowering of the voice to cause students to attend to your teaching. Walk through exercises periodically with your students to keep them used to working harmoniously with you.

7. Learn to use silence to advantage and learn to cultivate your sign language. Your eyes and your gestures are critically important to you here.

8. Anticipate likely consequences of what you ask students to do. Try to avoid always being in a reactive (corrective) position with your classes. Learn to use preventive maintenance to keep yourself out of the corrective mode as much as possible.

9. When it becomes necessary, use corrective maintenance calmly and confidently, but make it stick. Do not interrupt the whole class to deal with one offender whenever it is possible to avoid doing so.

10. Tell the class, or come to an agreement with the class in clear terms, about what is and what is not acceptable behavior. Learn to recognize signs that adjustments in strategy are necessary.

11. Do not put up with chatter in your classes.

12. Do not get in the habit of doing classroom management on the run. Take time and care to plan it as a key aspect of your teaching.

◆◆◆   SUGGESTED ACTIVITIES AND QUESTIONS   ◆◆◆

1. Attempt to describe ideas about classroom management that you have brought with you into teaching. How did you acquire them? How has the approach presented here supported, changed, or extended your ideas on classroom management?

2. Based on your own experiences with education, take a position on each of the following statements:
   a. Students in today's schools need more discipline than they are presently getting.
   b. Young people should be allowed a maximum of self-expression in the classroom. When students are required to spend most of their time listening to the teacher, they cannot be expected to learn much of importance.
   c. Lack of effective discipline is a major reason for low achievement in our schools.
   d. One of the teacher's main responsibilities is to keep the classroom quiet and orderly for those who want to learn. Students who disrupt the learning atmosphere should be removed from the school.
   e. Teachers need to be more sympathetic toward the predicament of students in today's schools. Most school discipline problems result from the difficult conditions young people have to endure in our crowded, boxlike classrooms.

3. Have you had experience in situations where you were responsible for structuring the behavior of other people, either individuals or groups (e.g., previous teaching, recreation programs, youth camps, babysitting)? How well did you handle this kind of responsibility? Were you able to give directions, and let those you were responsible for know what you expected, when you were dissatisfied, and so forth, with firmness and confidence? Were you able to use your voice, eyes, and gestures to good advantage in these situations? What has been your experience when it comes to criticizing and correcting the behavior of other people? What particular feelings, anxieties, or reservations do you have about being in a position of authority like this?

4. What do you anticipate will be your most difficult challenge in terms of classroom management? What steps are you taking to prepare to deal with it? Based on your present experience, what do you consider to be the kinds of behavior problems that constitute the most serious challenges to teachers who are working to have orderly classrooms in today's schools?

5. It has been emphasized that one of the key roles of teachers is to be an effective climate-setter in their own classroom. Discuss some of the things a classroom teacher can do to help develop an appropriate environment for learning. What will *you* do?

6. Take the position that classroom management approaches are to a large extent an expression of a teacher's personality. What kinds of personality traits are most functional for carrying out the classroom management system presented here? What sorts of personality characteristics would be least appropriate for implementing the behavioral management strategies outlined in this chapter? Where do you stand?

Notes

1. C. M. Evertson and E. T. Emmer, "Preventive Classroom Management." In D. L. Duke (Ed.), *Helping Teachers Manage Classrooms*. Alexandria, Va.: Association for Supervision and Curriculum Development, 1982, pp. 22–30.
2. Jacob Kounin, *Discipline and Group Management in Classrooms*. New York: Holt, Rinehart and Winston, 1977, pp. 79–83.
3. Neil Postman, *Teaching as a Conserving Activity*. New York: Delacorte Press, 1979, see Chap. 4.
4. For an in-depth treatment of this subject see Thomas L. Good and Jere E. Brophy, *Looking in Classrooms*, 7th ed. New York: Harper and Row, 1997, Chap. 2.
5. E. T. Emmer, C. M. Evertson B. S. Clements, and M. E. Worsham, *Classroom Management for Elementary Teachers*. 4th ed. Boston: Allyn and Bacon, 1997.
6. The expression "low-profile classroom controls" has been used by Carl Rinne to contrast this approach to classroom management with more conventional high-profile control measures that distract students' attention first before focusing on lesson content. See Carl H. Rinne, "Low-Profile Classroom Controls." *Phi Delta Kappan* (September 1982): 52–54.
7. Frederic Jones, *Positive Classroom Discipline*. New York: McGraw-Hill, 1987, see Chap. 1; and Kounin, *Discipline and Group Management in Classrooms*, see Chap. 4.
8. Good and Brophy, *Looking in Classrooms*.
9. Rinne, "Low-Profile Classroom Controls," p. 52.
10. Jones, *Positive Classroom Discipline*, p. 26.
11. Kounin, *Discipline and Group Management in Classrooms*, pp. 80–81.
12. Kounin, *Discipline and Group Management in Classrooms*, see Chap 6.
13. Seymour B. Sarason, "Classrooms as Uninteresting Places." In *Schooling in America*. New York: Free Press, 1983. Jules Henry earlier commented on this connection: "Lessons in subjects in which children are not interested are lessons in disjunction, for the child cannot be detached from the classroom, and in an effort to escape from boredom may cast around for some way of escaping from the situation." Cited in Seán Desmond Healy, *Boredom, Self, and Culture*. London: Associated University Presses, 1984, p.122.
14. Kounin, *Discipline and Group Management in Classrooms*, Chap. 6.
15. Kounin, *Discipline and Group Management in Classrooms*, pp. 109–115.
16. Jere E. Brophy, *Child Development and Socialization*. Chicago: Science Research Associates, 1977, p. 435.
17. William Glasser, *Quality School: Managing Students Without Coercion*. New York: Harper and Row, 1990, especially Chap. 9, "Building a Friendly Workplace."

CHAPTER 10

Evaluating and Grading Students

"Evaluation" refers to two very different activities:
measurement (or grading and ranking), and
commentary (or feedback).

Peter Elbow

An Integral Part of Effective Teaching

You will want to develop effective procedures for finding out whether or not your teaching is succeeding. This requires that, along with planning and conducting lessons, you regard evaluation of what students are able to do, and have learnt, as an integral part of teaching, as an ongoing aspect of instruction.

Even though evaluation is directly related to the quality of teaching, it seldom gets the concentrated attention it deserves. Too often it is viewed by teachers as a burdensome chore that is peripheral to the instructional process, and a task that requires very little theoretical or practical knowledge. Because teachers often feel themselves under pressures to emphasize measurable results of learning rather than the learning process itself, they are apt to reduce evaluation of student learning to postinstructional testing. Evaluation thus becomes an activity performed ad hoc in order to assign grades.

There are a number of good reasons for avoiding this narrow approach and employing a broader concept of evaluation in your own teaching. First, students learn more effectively when evaluational processes are used not just to assess ultimate learning outcomes, but play a part in their learning activity in all of its stages. In addition, teaching becomes a great deal more efficient and less hit-or-miss when teachers make it a practice to assess what students already know before beginning instruction and monitor their progress throughout the learning cycle.

Moreover, in adopting a broadly based concept of educational evaluation, you become less apt to place undue reliance on tests and testing because you are able to see evaluational processes in larger, fuller perspective, that is, as a means to appropriate educational goals. Besides this, a balanced, well-designed, and comprehensive approach to the assessment of student learning can have a decidedly positive effect on student attitudes toward test taking. Finally, and perhaps most important, is the fact that what and how you intend to evaluate determines to a large extent what and how you teach, and that, in turn, plays a major role in what students learn, how they go about learning, and how they come to regard the whole learning process.[1]

This becomes easier to understand if you are aware that evaluation can occur for two quite different purposes: on the one hand, to find out and to measure what students have learnt, and on the other to assist, to support and to encourage students in the process of learning.[1]

The former type of evaluation is referred to as *summative*.[2] Standardized tests are used on the local, state, and national level to establish what is called accountability, that is, the results are passed on to inform various groups—parents, state and federal authorities, and the general public—often by way of such devices as "report cards" on a particular school or school system, of how well (or poorly) they are doing. In relation to individual students, the outcome of such tests is a judgment, recorded in the form of a grade. There is a tendency for school people to treat evaluation as primarily, if not exclusively, a matter of *testing*, and to regard it as something teachers do at the end of courses or units to measure what students have learned, for purposes of assigning grades. Paper-and-pencil tests are generally used for this purpose, but because of rising dissatisfaction with these, other methods, generically referred to as "alternative assessment" are increasingly being brought into service. More will be said about them in a later section of the chapter.

The other important function of teacher evaluation, referred to as *formative*,[3] is to obtain initial, and subsequently ongoing, information to help you assist students to learn better and possibly faster. These assessments of student aptitudes and abilities before instruction, and while learning is in its developing stages, allow you to make good strategic decisions as you proceed with a lesson or unit. You may have noticed, as Wolf and her fellow writers pointed out, that there is a tension between these two functions of assessment. As these researchers remarked,

> There is no question that schools owe their constituencies (legislators, families, and the businesses who hire their students), honest accounts of what they have, and have not, achieved. Even so, assessment has been driven too exclusively by concerns for measuring and reporting achievements for outside audiences. Often forgotten is the equally important work of *internal accountability*—that is, encouraging students, teachers, and families to think hard about what is worth knowing and making sure students know it.[4]

One instance of assessment that succeeds in being all three, is *pretesting*, the term applied to assessing student knowledge and abilities as a means of establishing particular strengths or skill weaknesses that need to be taken into consideration when planning a particular lesson or unit. Information from such tests, or from processes such as brainstorming that help a teacher assess what a student already knows, can be used to place students in appropriate groups, to assign them suitable tasks, or to review prerequisite lessons with those who lack what is needed to go on.

The advantages of a properly thought-out system of classroom evaluation will become increasingly apparent to you as you find out more about the subject. This chapter should assist you in developing a functional theory of evaluation by exposing you to some ideas and terms that are fundamental to the topic. It also provides you with practical suggestions for constructing, administering, and scoring classroom tests, and guidelines for grading student performance.

Measurement and Evaluation

Evaluation can be done in a variety of ways, but before examining some of these in detail, it is essential for you to be clear about the difference between *measuring*, on the one hand, and *evaluating* student performances, on the other. A measuring instrument such as a formal test can provide you with quantitative data, numbers, that you may wish to take into consideration when making evaluative judgments about student achievement. A particular measurement, however, has no meaning until you assign a value to it. A score of 65 on an exam says very little about the quality of the student's performance. It could be a high mark on a hard test, or a low mark on an easy test. It must first be interpreted, or compared with a *standard*, before it becomes an evaluation. In short, measurement is a *descriptive* activity, whereas evaluation involves a *judgment* based on values and standards. As Gage and Berliner summarize the distinction, "Measurement gives us numbers. Human judgment, concern, and interpretation turn those numbers into evaluations."[5]

This distinction has some important implications for the evaluative decisions you will make in teaching. For one thing, it cautions against the tendency to equate evaluation with testing, to regard testing as evaluation, period. In recognizing evaluation to be the larger concept and the end toward which testing is a potential vehicle, we are reminded that a test is not the only means, nor in many cases the best means, of sampling learning progress. Depending on the subject, the grade level, and the kind of learning being promoted, teachers' informal observations, student projects and written assignments, together with other kinds of learning, may provide more useful information for evaluative decisions than a written test. Learning objectives in the affective domain, for example, normally required qualitative rather than quantitative means of evaluation. Test scores and other measurement data have no inherent meaning until we as teachers give them meaning, so the responsibility lies with us to determine their relevance to our professional purposes, and to know what other types of evaluation can be used to provide a balanced view of a student's position.

The information you receive from both types of assessment can help you decide whether you need to change part or all of your approach in light of specific learning errors that students are making or in areas in which they have not yet firmly grasped a new concept.

Organizing Your Efforts

As you plan each unit of instruction you should give some concentrated attention to the various means you will employ to assess student learning. There are ordinarily a number of sources of information available to you in your efforts to gain information on student progress and development, some formal and some less so.

Observations and Interchanges

Your system of *informal assessment* normally entails day-to-day observations, at the time or soon after, recorded in a notebook or on a clipboard of student behavior (what Yetta Goodman calls "kid watching"):[6] together with interactions with individual students that enable you to get an idea of such things as:

1. How much and how effectively they take part in class activities.
2. The kinds of questions they ask both during and after class.
3. The cooperative learning skills they demonstrate while working on group projects.
4. The way they respond to teacher questions.
5. Their ability to follow tasks through to completion.
6. The kind of initiative they demonstrate in seeking information and attacking problems.
7. The kinds of verbal skills they demonstrate in expressing thoughts and explaining ideas.
8. Their ability to manage time and to complete assignments on time.

This type of informal evaluation requires observation skills that often take time to develop, and call on the teacher to be able to monitor the behavior of individual students, while performing other classroom activities. You can take steps to make your classroom observations as objective and reliable as possible by (1) determining in advance what to look for, and (2) by setting up a checklist, rating scale, or some other written guide to help organize them. Using a clipboard or notebook to make very brief notes at the time, or soon after, can provide you with a very valuable running record of student progress. It is important for you to bear in mind that what one might call "interactive observation," collecting information from a student that shows whether he or she is familiar with and understands the matter in hand, can also be a powerful form of teaching, as it enables you to intervene with more information, another question, or a word of encouragement just when one or more of these is needed to give a student an indication that what they have done, or an answer they have given, is valid, thoughtful, or well expressed.

Formal Sources of Evaluation

Since the most widely used means of *formal evaluation* are written tests, some of which you will almost certainly be called on to construct, test construction and test utilization are treated in considerable depth in succeeding sections of this chapter. The question "what makes a good test?" needs to be considered before we go on to deal with the various types of test item.

What Constitutes a Good Test?

Validity

First, the test must be *valid*—it must measure what it is supposed to. Although this may sound self-evident, it turns out that without careful attention to this requirement a test can easily be unrelated to the learning you are or should be attempting to promote. For example, in an English class unit on public speaking, written tests of knowledge will be largely invalid if your purpose is to make judgments about speaking ability.

A valid test should also sample the various elements of knowledge that were taught, in proportion to the emphasis that was placed on them. If a group of students had spent the bulk of their class time learning grammar with very little time devoted to application, it would not be valid to follow up with a test that stressed the ability to use these rules rather than just know about them. This points up the need to have clearly stated instructional objectives so both you and your students know precisely what knowledge is going to be evaluated.

Reliability

Another major consideration in judging the adequacy of tests is the consistency with which a particular test can be expected to produce useful data. If you give a student a test on Monday and a similar test on Friday, and the resulting scores prove the same or close, you could judge the test to be *reliable*. If the scores differ significantly, you would have some legitimate doubts about the test's reliability. To do the job for which it is intended, a test must provide consistent and dependable measurement. When a test is reliable, inconsistencies have been largely eliminated. The reliability of tests can also be affected by factors external to the test itself, such as the test environment or the state of mind of the test taker. The physical condition or anxiety level of the student, or a student's preferences for oral, written, or activity tests, can each affect the ability of a test to deliver accurate and consistent results. There are a number of things you can do to enhance the reliability of the tests you use.

Objectivity

A good test should also be *objective*. A test can be considered objective to the extent that the personality of the examiner does not affect the way it is scored. In other words, there should be precautions taken to ensure that the biases, prejudgments, or personal feelings of the scorer have no bearing on the results. A truly objective test would have to be scored in exactly the same way by every scorer. The category of measurement devices commonly referred to as *objective tests* attempts to build in objectivity by allowing one clearly established right answer per item, and by a scoring system that allows for no ambiguity or examiner bias in marking the exam. One of the reputed shortcomings of essay examinations is their subjectivity, or their vulnerability to reader biases and changing dispositions while scoring.[7]

As we begin to apply the criteria of validity, reliability, and objectivity to various types of tests, we become aware of the difficulty in locating or constructing an instrument that adequately satisfies all three criteria. A test that is long on objectivity, may turn out to be short on validity. For example, while pointing to the inherent objectivity of true-false or multiple-choice tests, we must also recognize the relatively narrow range of knowledge they can adequately test. When we attempt to use them to sample other than memory-level knowledge, their validity immediately becomes suspect. In other words, objective-type tests are not a reliable way of evaluating higher-order thinking. Similarly, although reliability is an important property for measuring instruments to have, it does not guarantee a good test.

The indispensable quality that all good tests must have is validity. "As long as validity is not sacrificed, the more objective the instrument the better. However, a valid instrument may be a good instrument even though it is not objective, while an objective instrument that is not valid is always worthless."[8] In this respect, you should realize that, unless you require students to justify the item they choose, you can never be sure that they know the right answer, or have given the "right" answer for the right reason, hence such tests without a requirement of this sort are always somewhat deficient in validity.

Concrete suggestions for making classroom tests of this sort as valid, reliable, and objective as possible are treated in more detail in the following sections on test construction.

Constructing Classroom Tests

General Guidelines for Test Construction

The following are some general guidelines to keep in mind as you approach the work of test construction:

1. Have some questions that are easy enough for every student in the class to answer correctly. Begin with the least difficult question so all students will get a good start and will be encouraged to go on to the questions that follow.

2. Make test items reflect instructional aims and the content taught. Test teaching objectives in proportion to their importance. If the test overemphasizes, underemphasizes, or omits representative portions of learned content, it will lose validity.

3. Watch the vocabulary level of test items. To be valid your test should measure the content students have learned, not reading ability (unless previously stated).

4. Make it easy for students to demonstrate what they have learned. Do not allow writing ability, or speed in test taking to be a factor in student success. Everyone should have a chance to do well on the test.

5. Make sure test directions are entirely clear to students. Ensure that students don't miss an item because they misunderstood the details for answering it.

6. Place all items of the same type together so students are not confused.

7. Include several test items for each objective. This will give students ample opportunity to demonstrate competence, thus avoiding the possibility that a chance error could give a false assessment of ability.

8. Include all the information and material students need to complete each item. When you have to provide missing information or when students find it necessary to stop working to seek clarifications, the reliability of the test is affected.

9. When one of your purposes is to determine differences in students' achievement, do not allow choices in the questions to be answered. You must use exactly the same measuring instrument for everyone, otherwise you jeopardize validity.

10. Make more items than you will use. Select only the best items, then rework them as necessary to make the test reflect your best professional effort. The final product off the duplicating or copy machine should be neat, grammatically perfect, and clear.

Choosing and Preparing Objective Test Items

The preceding guidelines for constructing tests in general apply specifically to the development of objective tests. Among the most common varieties of objective test items are true-false, completion, multiple-choice, and matching questions.

True-False Questions In this familiar type of objective test item, students are given statements they are to judge for accuracy. This kind of test can be useful for finding out if students can discriminate fact from opinion and valid from invalid generalizations. To rule out guessing (which would affect the reliability of the test item), students need to be called on to justify their answers with a sentence telling why they answered one way rather than another. On the surface, a true-false test seems simple to construct, but to produce true-false items that are free from ambiguity or false leads is usually a challenge. By taking the following precautions, however, you can avoid some of the main snags in making good true-false tests:

1. Avoid broad generalizations. Words like *always* and *never* can serve as clues that statements are false.
2. Attempt to keep a balance between true (T) and false (F) statements.
3. Avoid using negative statements as items when possible. If you do use a negative construction, be sure the key word is underlined or capitalized to call attention to it (e.g., NOT, NEVER).
4. Use clear language for questions. Textbook wording is likely to test memory rather than understanding.

True-false tests have the following major advantages:

1. Items can be scored easily.
2. Directions to true-false items are easy for students to understand.
3. A good number of items can be answered in a short time.
4. They are good for initiating discussions and for pretesting.
5. They are a quick way to test for simple factual knowledge.

These are their main weaknesses:

1. It is difficult to avoid ambiguous items because a statement is seldom entirely true or entirely false.
2. Unless students are required to give reasons for their answers, student performance is subject to guessing and chance effects, thus affecting test validity.
3. True-false tests tend to encourage memorization and guessing.

Completion Questions ("Gap-Fillers") These are statements with important words or phrases left out that are to be written in by the test taker. These items are useful in testing whether students actually know anything because they require the student to supply information that is not visible in the test. The following ideas should be helpful to you in developing completion questions:

1. Be sure students know what is expected in terms of length and detail in their answers.
2. Word the item so only one correct answer is possible. "Michelangelo was a famous _____" would be a poor question of this type because there are a number of answers that would be equally correct (among them "Italian," "male," "painter")
3. Supply enough context in the statement to give the item meaning. The following is an example of an item with an inadequate ratio of words provided to words omitted: "The _____ protects _____, liberty, and _____."
4. Avoid grammatical clues such as a blank following the letter *a*, which indicates that the missing word(s) would begin with a consonant.
5. Design questions so only significant words are omitted. A poor example would be, "Washington _____ the Delaware to defeat the Hessians."
6. Use a direct question if possible, and avoid textbook language.

The main advantages of completion items:

1. They are easy to construct and relatively easy to mark.
2. They allow a rapid survey of information over a large area of content.
3. Students find it difficult to guess right answers.
4. They are useful when recall is all that is required.

Their central weaknesses are:

1. It is difficult to construct items for which there is only one correct answer.
2. When used exclusively, or excessively, completion items tend to encourage memorized learning of isolated facts rather than understanding.

Multiple-Choice Questions These are the most commonly used form of objective test items, and they can be used in all subject areas. A multiple-choice item contains two major components, its stem and its alternative answers. The *stem* may be phrased as a question or a simple statement: "Most automobiles are propelled by." Of the alternative responses, one is the correct answer and the others are the *distractors*, so-called because they are intended to mislead students who are not certain of the correct answer. In this case, the alternative responses might be:

a. A steam engine
b. An electric storage battery
c. An internal combustion engine
d. A solar cell

Multiple-choice questions are relatively versatile types of test items because, depending on the complexity of the item, they can assess recognition of information that has been memorized as well as some kinds of higher-level thinking. To produce good items requires considerable skill and attention to detail. The following guidelines apply to the development of multiple-choice tests:

1. The stem of the question should be clear and contained separately from the possible answers. If the stem is in the form of an incomplete statement, it should provide enough meaning so students will not have to read the answers to understand the question.
2. At least four responses should be provided. This will decrease the likelihood of guessing correctly and increase the validity of the item by requiring students to be more discriminating.
3. Questions that call for "best answers" are more useful for measuring higher thought processes than those that call for correct answers.
4. Make all the responses plausible, and when testing at higher levels, increase the similarity in the choices under each item in order to better test the powers of discrimination.
5. If you can, avoid the use of negatively stated items. These tend to be somewhat more ambiguous than positively stated items.

6. Distribute the order of correct answers randomly and equally, avoiding any discernible pattern, such as favoring first or last choices.
7. Each item should test individual information that gives no clues to other items in the test.
8. Make the wording simple and clear. The language should be easy enough for even the poorest readers.

These are the primary virtues of multiple-choice items:

1. A wide range of subject matter can be tested in a short time.
2. They can be administered and scored quite rapidly.
3. Items can be written to test for relatively fine discriminations in students' knowledge in a number of subject areas.
4. They can be used to test both simple memory and higher mental processes.

The most significant disadvantages of multiple-choice tests are:

1. Good items are difficult and time-consuming to write.
2. Like all structured response items, they do not require students to provide information in their own words.
3. They normally require a level of concentration and discrimination on the part of the test taker that may make them inappropriate for use with younger learners.
4. Mechanical scoring of items requiring complex thinking provides no basis for checking the thought processes of students.
5. It is never possible to be sure that the student identified the "right" answer for the right reason, that is, knows the right answer (as distinct from getting it by guesswork, or for the wrong reason).
6. They encourage a view of learning that plays down thinking and rewards recognizing or guessing.
7. They encourage a process of learning in which students read by "bitting," concentrating on identifying discrete pieces of information of the kind that turn up in tests, rather than on "texting," reading for meaning.[9]
8. The use of "distractors" to mislead students puts the teacher in the position of being seen by his or her students as trying to trick them into making a mistake.

Matching Questions Matching items are a convenient means of testing for correct associations between related classes of information, such as names and dates, people and events, authors and books, terms and definitions, laws and illustrations, and the like. They are well suited to testing who, what, where, and when but not to measuring understanding as distinct from mere memory. In constructing these items, two lists are drawn up and the test taker must match an item in the first list with the one in the second list to which the relationship is closest. The following are suggestions for constructing good matching items:

1. Include no more than 10 to 12 items to be identified or matched.
2. There should be more items in the "answers" column than in the "questions" column. If the numbers are equal, students will be helped to make correct choices at the end through a process of elimination.
3. All items in each column should be in the same general category. For example, events and their dates should not be mixed with events and the names of historical characters.
4. Directions should clearly state what the basis for matching is. The directions should specify if choices may be used more than once.

The main advantages of matching questions are:

1. Their compactness allows you to test a good deal of factual information in a short period of time.
2. They are particularly appropriate for surveying knowledge of definitions, events, personalities, and so forth.
3. They are easy to score.

The most prominent weaknesses of matching items are:

1. They cannot check the understanding of concepts or the ability to organize and apply knowledge.
2. It is difficult to avoid giving clues that tend to reduce validity.
3. The format requires the use of single words or very brief phrases.

Essay Questions Essay tests require the learner to supply an unprompted, extended written response to a stated question or problem. They are appropriate for measuring ability to select and organize ideas, writing abilities, and problem-solving skills requiring originality. The student must create an answer from memory or imagination, so these items are capable of testing a higher level of knowledge than most objective tests. Essay tests are widely used, particularly by high school teachers, although they are often criticized for their subjective nature. The following are guidelines to be used in writing essay questions:

1. Make the wording of the question as clear and explicit as possible. It should precisely define the direction and limits of the desired response. It is important that all students interpret each question in the same way.
2. Include some items that expressly call for a paragraph response requiring shorter answers rather than a very few questions requiring long answers. This allows a better sampling of subject-matter knowledge and encourages more precise responses.
3. Decide whether or not to include grammar and sentence structure in your evaluation of answers. You may wish to give two marks, one for the substance of the answers and the other, less crucial grade, for form

and writing style. Be sure to announce to the class the basis on which you will be grading their answers before they begin the exam, and leave time to answer their questions.

4. Provide students with guidance on how to use their time in answering the items. Suggest approximate time limits and answer lengths for each question, so students will distribute their time appropriately.

5. Write the question while planning the unit of instruction rather than near the conclusion of the unit. This will help you to focus more clearly on the objectives of the unit as you are constructing the test.

6. In general, do not allow students a choice on essay items unless there are different objectives for different students in the course. All students must take the same test if you are to have a sound basis for comparing scores.

7. In general, do not ask questions that only sample a student's opinion or attitude without having the student justify the answer in terms of the cognitive content of the course.

8. Have a colleague critique the test as a means of eliminating ambiguity and possible misinterpretations.

Essay questions have the following main strengths as evaluative instruments:

1. They can measure more than the ability to remember information.
2. They encourage students to learn how to organize their own ideas and express them effectively.
3. Students tend to use better study habits when preparing for essay tests.
4. They permit teachers to comment directly on the reasoning processes of individual students.
5. A teacher need only write a few items for a test.
6. Guesswork is largely ruled out.

Essay tests are subject to these drawbacks:

1. Answers may be scored differently by different teachers or by the same teacher at different times.
2. They are usually very time-consuming to grade.
3. Only a relatively few questions on limited areas of knowledge can be responded to in a given period of time.
4. Students who write slowly may not be able to complete the test even though they may possess adequate knowledge.

◆◆◆   **A P P L I C A T I O N   E X E R C I S E S**   ◆◆◆

1. Read each of the following test questions to determine whether they qualify as good items. If you identify deficiencies in a particular item, rewrite it to make it a better test question.

A. Multiple-Choice Questions:
   1. Good multiple-choice items (a) are easy to write; (b) can only test memorized content; (c) are better than essay items; (d) there is no such thing; (e) can test a wide range of content.
   2. Which of the following characteristics is not true of completion test items, but is an important distinguishing attribute of matching tests, multiple-choice questions, and true-false items?
      a. They are objective test items.
      b. They require knowledge recognition but not production.
      c. Much more difficult to construct.

B. Matching Questions:
   1. Completion items   a. Depend on good distractors
   2. Multiple-choice items   b. Most susceptible to guessing
   3. Matching items   c. Best for testing associations
   4. Objective tests   d. Usually simple to score
   5. True-false items   e. Tend to resist one correct answer

C. True-False Questions:
   1. The advantages of true-false tests include the ease with which they can be constructed and scored, the simplicity of their directions, their ability to test the discriminatory powers of students, and the relative number of items that can be answered in a short time.
   2. Because of the ever-present potential for guessing, true-false tests should always contain at least 25 items.

D. Essay Question:
   Discuss essay tests compared with objective tests.

2. Construct an essay question to test knowledge of some section of this chapter. Write a model answer for that question. Share your question with at least two of your peers and ask them to answer it. Compare their answers with your model answer, and then respond to the following questions:
   a. Was the question clearly stated? Did you get comparable answers from each of the other people?
   b. Did any of the responses include ideas other than those in your model answer?
   c. Did this exercise provide any insights into the writing and scoring of essay questions that might be helpful to you as a teacher?

3. Produce 8 to 12 objective test items taken from material covered in this chapter. Include items from each of the four formats: true-false, completion, multiple-choice, and matching. Ask one of your peers to answer these test items. After providing this person with the correct answers, give them an opportunity to critique your test.

Administering and Scoring Tests

Guidelines for Administering a Test

To administer formal tests in a systematic and controlled manner requires some careful preplanning on your part. You also need to use your best classroom management skills to ensure that test security and proper testing atmosphere are maintained throughout the exam. Your first effort should be to incorporate a proper routine for test taking in your classes. This will entail establishing certain "test-day" expectations, then accustoming students to act according to the procedures you have set up. The following are steps you can take to make the testing process as smooth and efficient as possible:

1. Once the test has been prepared, do a careful job of proofreading to be sure it contains no errors. The test should be neat and highly legible with no typos or spelling errors. You should also be certain that all directions are clear and make special note of any items that need to be further explained before students begin the test.
2. Decide on an appropriate seating arrangement. Plan to have students spread out as much as possible to remove any possible temptations toward cheating. Have students place books, notebooks, and other extraneous material under seats or away from the test area before starting the exam.
3. Make sure the physical condition of the room is conducive to test taking. Improper heat, light, or ventilation, as well as distracting noises or interruptions, can affect student concentration and thereby reduce the reliability of the test.
4. Be sure students have everything they need before the test begins. Check to see that each student has a good copy of the complete test. Any other materials, such as maps, extra paper, or special pencils, should be supplied before beginning the test.
5. Have a controlled procedure for distributing test materials and beginning the exam. To allow all students to start at the same time, you may want to have them keep tests face down on their desks until everyone is ready to begin.
6. If it is necessary to explain last-minute corrections, do this before the test begins and also write the explanation or correction on the chalkboard so students can be reminded after the test begins. Try to avoid interrupting with announcements once the test is underway.
7. Ask students to look carefully at the test and ask questions *before* the test begins so they will have less need to ask questions once they have begun.
8. Make a conscientious effort to monitor test-taking behavior throughout the exam. Be sure all students are occupied with the test and that everyone's eyes remain on their own work. Regardless of the maturity level and trustworthiness of the group, it is not good practice to ignore

the class once the test begins. By standing strategically at the back of the room, then quietly roaming among the rows from time to time, you help to ensure proper test-taking behavior on the part of your students.

9. Have students raise their hands to receive assistance if a question arises once the test has begun. Avoid discussing questions aloud with a student while other students are working. If a student genuinely needs help, go and talk quietly with them individually.

10. Be sure students know what they are to do with their tests and their time if they finish early. Insist that early finishers respect the needs of those who are still working.

Procedures for Scoring Tests

The procedures you use to score students' tests should be thought out in advance. It is usually advisable to prepare an answer key, indicating the acceptable answers, as you are constructing the test. This is when you are highly focused on the specific objectives you are testing and the most appropriate responses. One of the easiest ways to make a key for an objective test is to fill in the proper responses on a blank test, which can then be placed against the answer column of the tests you are scoring.

Essay exams require a more strategic approach. As indicated earlier, objectivity in scoring is a major concern with essay questions. However, there are some basic measures you can take to make your scoring of essay items as objective as possible, including:

1. Be sure you have appropriate responses firmly established before you begin scoring the exams. Write these out as though you were taking the exam yourself. Determine the number of points each answer is worth and show on your model answer how these points will be distributed. Use this material as your key.

2. Score only one question at a time for all papers. This increases the likelihood that you will use the same standard for every student. If you decide to give credit for points not included in your answer key, be sure to reread papers already scored to ensure everyone is given credit for the additional point.

3. Attempt to read all papers without knowledge of the "author." One way of keeping papers anonymous is by asking students to write their names on the back rather than the front of the test. Another is to number the tests, then provide a separate sheet of paper on which the student signs his name and test number. Whatever you can do to counteract potential biases or preconceptions as you read essay exams will help to make them more objective and reliable measures of student learning.

4. If there are a large number of papers, do not attempt to score them all at one sitting. If possible, take several sessions to read all of the questions. This helps you to prevent reader fatigue and a resultant lack of consistency in your scoring pattern.

Alternative Assessment

Many if not most of the kinds of test items previously described give you a very restricted view of the extent to which students really know (and then quite possibly only fleetingly) what you consider important enough to include in the test. If, as suggested earlier, you make it necessary (possibly for full credit) for students to explain their choice in each case, you add significantly to the validity of the test. If, further, you discuss answers after a test or quiz of this sort, there is evidence, as you might expect, that student learning is significantly increased.[10] Discussion of this sort may in fact be one of the most educationally valuable outcomes of this sort of testing.

However, all of the above ways of assessing and grading students suffer in some measure from similar flaws:

1. They only indicate a student's knowledge at one point in time.
2. With the partial exception of essays, they do not require the student to show whether he or she understands what it is they "know."
3. The student is not called on to apply what he or she knows.
4. Apart from essay questions, students do not have to produce and organize material, or to apply it in any way; they merely remember and recognize it.
5. Objective-type questions do not require students to be able to express connected thoughts.
6. The validity of the test result is brought into doubt by the number of students who suffer from test anxiety.
7. Overall they tend to produce a view of education as an extended game of Jeopardy or Trivial Pursuit, in which the prize goes to the student who gathers and is able to identify, suitably prompted, the maximum number of items of information.
8. There is little or nothing in them to stimulate students to show their real capacities, to demonstrate their creativity and originality, or to show how they have progressed and developed.
9. As presently constituted, they can test only a limited range of student intelligences (see Chapter 3), those involved in working with words and numbers.

Partly in consequence of these limitations, teachers are increasingly using other sources of information to assess student understanding and achievement. Teachers have, of course, always done this to some extent in the course of assigning and reading, listening to, or observing a variety of written and oral work, among which the most common have been:

1. Written work—essays, lab reports, workbook exercises, book reports, math exercises, poems, research papers, and journals
2. Oral work—individual reports, class discussions, panels, debates, simulation games, and oral recitations

3. Performances and exhibitions—athletic activities, speech, drama, and music performances, shop projects, art and craft exhibits

There has recently been a significant shift toward using a number of these, and in particular those in the third category, for what has come to be called *alternative assessment.*

> Classrooms are moving from a *testing* culture—where teachers are the sole authority, and students work alone, and learning is done for the test—to an *assessment* culture—where teachers and learners collaborate about learning, assessment takes many forms for multiple audiences and distinctions between learning are blurred.[11]

These alternative kinds of assessment have found favor because they can be used both for formative and summative purposes, and because they can provide a truer, more rounded picture of students. They enable teachers to see whether students are simply familiar with facts and routines or really understand what they are doing. Although the categories overlap, alternative assessment can be usefully considered under two headings.

Authentic Assessment These activities require a student to apply and extend what they know or can do in relation to a significant and engaging problem or question that occurs in real life, outside as well as inside school. A simple example of this in a language arts, social studies, or art class (or, better, running across all three as a theme), might be devising and carrying out an advertising campaign for some product or service. Writing, illustrating, graphic work using one or more computer programs, formulating questionnaires, deciding on target populations, devising mailing lists, and so on, would all approximate the knowledge, skill, imagination, and resourcefulness needed in adult life.

Unlike conventional forms of evaluation, in which the teacher judges the product, the teacher can here be involved in the process—as commentator, asker of probing and proleptic (those that lead a student on to further thoughts or insights) questions, as resource person, as supporter and encourager—since the object of the whole maneuver is to have students display the fullest range of their abilities at the highest level. Again, contrary to custom, students can and should be involved at various stages in evaluating the worth of what they have done, being thus provoked into thinking about and describing their own thinking, an activity called *metacognition.*

Performance Assessment This type of assessment involves anything students produce (as distinct from respond to) and is in some sense a "performance," but in this context the term can be reserved for student activities that culminate in some form of public performance or public exhibit: drama productions, spoken recitals, music recitals, athletic displays, art shows, craft displays, science fairs, and technological contests such as the Olympics of the Mind. Here again, the teacher is not separated from the process but acts as coach and encourager rather than as director, as advisor when consulted rather than as unbidden imposer and judge. Performance-based examinations and exhibitions, as Howard Gardner pointed out, "are tailor-made for the foregrounding of a student's multiple intelligences."[12]

Portfolios

During a semester, or over a longer period, the student may be engaged in a variety of forms of work subject to alternative assessment, produce various pieces of written and oral work, and take one or more tests or quizzes. In order to bring these together, and to provide teachers, students, and parents with an overall view of these activities, more and more use is being made of portfolios, a device that was first developed by artists and performers, and others who wanted to have available for examination some of the best of what they had done together with others' comments on their work. As a group of educators usefully defined the term in its educational application,

> [A] portfolio is a purposeful collection of student work that exhibits the student's efforts, progress, and achievements in one or more areas. The collection must include student participation in selecting contents, the criteria for selection, the criteria for judging merit, and evidence of student self-reflection.[13]

It is important to understand that portfolios are not just work folders, random collections of "work" a student has done. "A portfolio," as one of the authors of the definition just cited wrote,

> is a portfolio when it provides a complex and comprehensive view of student performance in context. It is a portfolio when the student is a participant in, rather than the object of, assessment. Above all, a portfolio is a portfolio when it provides a forum that encourages students to develop the abilities needed to become independent, self-directed learners.[14]

Methods of Grading

Whatever form of assessment you use, you have the problem of consolidating the results into one letter or number grade at the end of the marking period or semester. In a sense this is an impossible task since, among test results, the outcome of homework assignments, classwork, and, now, work to be evaluated through some form of alternative assessment, you are called on to lump together educational apples and oranges, chalk and cheese. Somehow or another, however, you will have to do just that! And you will therefore have to decide for yourself, and let the students and parents know in advance, the basis on which you will be giving final grades; specifically, what weight will be given in that grade to tests and quizzes, homework assignments, alternative assessment projects, and the like.

You are caught in something of an educational dilemma. Should you grade a student on the basis of his or her progress and development in your class (in which case a particular student may have done very well, and deserve an "A")? This would be called *self-referenced evaluation*. Should you, on the other hand, grade the student on the basis of his or her standing in the class, that is, grade his or her achievement in comparison to, or in competition with, his or her classmates (in which case the student in question might only get a grade of B if his classmates were moderately able, or a grade of C if they were unusually gifted)? This is known as *norm-referenced evaluation*. Finally, is it your responsibility to grade the student in relation to some absolute standard, a standard that is statewide, or even national as many are now urging (in which case the student with the B or C grade might get no more than a grade of D)? This would be using a *criterion-referenced evaluation*—such as the SAT. Each of these three evaluation standards used in our schools has its distinct advantages and disadvantages. It will be important for you to have a general understanding of these different approaches to grading and to be acquainted with some practical methods for arriving at student grades.

Norm-Referenced Evaluation

The traditional way of assigning grades has been to divide students into categories based on what was conceived to be a natural distribution of abilities in any normal population. According to this bell-shaped classification system, approximately one-sixth of the students receive grades of A and B, the middle two-thirds are assigned a grade of C, and the bottom one-sixth either fail or barely pass. In recognition of its shortcomings, the bell-shaped curve is seldom used in our present schools, although most teachers still adhere to a modified and generally more liberal grading curve that judges student learning performance in terms of comparisons and competitions with peers.

Norm-referenced evaluation continues to be popular because it reflects the entrenched expectations of educators, employers, and society at large that academic learning will be a competitive endeavor. Also, the system of letter grades it produces is one that has come to be well-understood by students and parents and is useful in keeping school records. Some good examples of norm-referenced evaluation instruments are the standardized achievement tests prepared by test publishers and national assessment agencies. These tests compare academic performances of individual students, classes, or schools with what are considered normal or typical performance levels for students throughout the country.

In the final analysis, scores made by a student on a norm-referenced test can tell us something about that student's performance compared with the average student, but they give little insight into the student's learning strengths and weaknesses. Unfortunately, these scores and grades do not have a universal meaning to the educators and others who are called on to interpret them. The meaning of letter grades often vary greatly from teacher to teacher and from one school or school system to another.

Criterion-Referenced Evaluation

Criterion-referenced evaluation systems rate student performance against an absolute standard. The emphasis here is on mastery of prespecified skills or information rather than on meeting or exceeding group norms. Thus, it is conceivable that everyone could pass or, by the same token, everyone could fail. Some advocates of mastery learning have proposed strategies whereby all students in a class could achieve close to 100 percent success in satisfying stipulated learning criteria.[15] However, because criterion-referenced evaluation seldom produces the spread in scores that is obtainable with norm-referenced systems, many educators would consider it less appropriate for assigning grades.[16]

Others have argued for more criterion-referenced evaluation in our schools, claiming it has these merits:

1. It enables students to tell at a glance how they have progressed in a given area of learning.
2. It can be used in ways that are more individual-student–centered than norm-referenced tests (e.g., standards can be adapted to ability levels of students).
3. It makes it more possible for educational administrators to control what students learn and the rate at which it is learned.
4. The goals of mastery learning can be stated in behavioral terms, thus making it easier for agencies outside the school to monitor accountability.[17]

Self-Referenced Evaluation

There have long been serious criticisms of both norm-referenced and criterion-referenced evaluation systems in terms of their appropriateness for assigning grades. Some educators have considered both approaches to be based on arbitrary standards, and thus to be unfair to students. Many critics, teachers and nonteachers alike, have maintained that the only educationally justifiable form of evaluation is one that allows learners to be in competition with themselves.[18] From this point of view, a teacher's evaluative judgments should be based largely, if not entirely, on the progress or improvement students have made in their learning performances since the beginning of instruction. Many might agree that there is a great deal of room and need for more self-referenced evaluation in our schools, particularly in areas where external standards of achievement are less pronounced. However, teachers feel under pressure to meet group norms or preset standards. Many would in any case maintain that the fairest, and also the most informative system, would be one that some school districts have already begun to move toward, namely, giving each student *three* grades: one for achievement (criterion-referenced), one to show where he or she stands in relation to the other members of the class (norm-referenced), and a third indicating the extent to which the student has grown in certain defined areas. This would do much to ensure that each student could succeed on their own terms and yet be aware of their position at that time in relation to others around them or across the nation.[19]

Finding Your Own Method

After examining some of the underlying theory together with advantages and disadvantages of different standards of evaluation, you will have to make some important practical decisions regarding an evaluation and grading system for your classes. To a significant degree you will be required to follow the policy of the school or school system in which you are teaching; moreover, the pressing need to have an effective method of deciding on grades will become apparent to you as you prepare to mark your first set of papers, and see the results of the first test you construct and set.

At that point it would be a good idea to consult those "supra-system perspectives" that you may remember reading about in Chapter 2, the educational principles that a teacher with a creative orientation uses to guide his or her actions and decisions. We all need to bear in mind that students have to live and make their way in and through several worlds: the "real" world, in which they will have to deal with the hard facts of competition for entry and the often rigorous demands of work (i.e., the criterion-referenced world); the world of the school, in which students are presently concerned to make their mark, find respect and liking from others, and gain self-respect (i.e., the norm-referenced world); and the self-world, in which young persons seek to know who and what they are, and to explore and demonstrate what they can do. You as teacher have a responsibility to help your students make their way in *all three* worlds, and your evaluative and grading procedures need to encompass and give due weight to all three.

◆◆◆   **A P P L I C A T I O N   E X E R C I S E S**   ◆◆◆

1. Consider each of the following test attributes listed and determine whether they are characteristic of norm-referenced or criterion-referenced measures:
   a. Students are compared to a set standard.
   b. Most appropriate when performing formative evaluations.
   c. Results in a more or less equal distribution of letter grades.
   d. Determines whether a student is in the top or the bottom of the group.
   e. Most suited for teaching mastery of knowledge or skills.
   f. Puts students in competition with one another.
   g. Makes it possible for all students to receive a grade of A.
   h. Allows students to know their standing within the group.
   i. Represents the more traditional way of assigning grades.
   j. Is clearly established before testing occurs.

◆◆◆ SUGGESTED ACTIVITIES AND QUESTIONS ◆◆◆

1. It is sometimes claimed that tests encourage an elitist attitude on the part of academically able students while discouraging low-achieving students from trying. As a teacher, how would you attempt to minimize these unfavorable potentials of testing and grading? What do you see to be the principal purpose of tests and grades? Which grading model best realizes that purpose?

2. Have you had any particularly unpleasant experiences with testing and grading during your years in school? How have grades affected your performance as a student? Can you think of testing or grading practices that you believe unfair or irresponsible? What basic principles of evaluation or test construction did they violate?

3. Are you able to cite important objectives of high school or elementary school education that tend to be overlooked by the types of tests that are commonly used in our schools? What kinds of evaluation strategies would you use to measure these objectives?

4. Could universal criterion-referenced evaluation (national standards) ever become a reality in U.S. education? What are the most persuasive arguments in favor of a criterion-referenced approach to measuring learning achievement? Does it have significant disadvantages? Elaborate.

5. Identify teaching situations where you believe self-referenced evaluation would be most appropriate. What are some of the main advantages and disadvantages of this approach to evaluating student learning?

6. What are some of the main arguments in favor of a pass-fail approach to evaluation in contrast to the grading system currently being used in our schools? Can you think of any serious disadvantages to a pass-fail system of reporting student progress?

7. What are some basic steps a teacher can take to enhance the validity of teacher-made tests?

8. Evaluation experts have maintained that the decision to use essay questions on a test implies a trade-off between the inherent advantages and disadvantages of this testing format. If so, what kinds of measurement values are you exchanging when you choose to use essay items to sample learning achievement? Could it also be argued that a decision to use objective test items involves similar trade-offs? Elaborate.

9. Would you be inclined to assign more weight to tests or to homework assignments when it comes to grading learning achievement in your classes? What factors would you take into consideration in making this decision?

NOTES

1. Lorrie Shepard reports that "researchers found ample evidence that testing shapes instruction." She cites studies that found instructional time taken from un-tested subjects (such as social studies) and given to tested ones (such as

math). Other studies found that "even within the bounds of test-driven content there was 'dumbing down' of instruction. Teachers taught the precise content of the tests rather than underlying concepts; and skills were taught in the same format as the test rather than as they would be used in the real world. For example, teachers reported giving up essay tests because they are inefficient in preparing students for multiple-choice tests." (p. 5) As Shepard goes on to say, "In today's political climate, tests are inadequate and misleading as measures of achievement. Assessment tasks should be redesigned, indeed are being redesigned, to more closely resemble real learning tasks." (p. 6) Lorrie A. Shepard, "Why We Need Better Assessments." *Educational Leadership* (April 1989).

2. Benjamin S. Bloom, J. Thomas Hastings, and George F. Madaus, *Formative and Summative Evaluation of Student Learning*. New York: McGraw-Hill, 1971, p. 20.
3. Ibid.
4. Dennie Palmer Wolf, Paul G. LeMahieu, and JoAnne Eresh, "Good Measure: Assessment as a Tool for Educational Reform." *Educational Leadership* (May 1992): 10.
5. N. L. Gage and David C. Berliner, *Educational Psychology*, 4th ed. Boston: Houghton Mifflin, 1988, p. 572.
6. Cited in Regie Routman, *Invitations: Changing Teachers and Learners K–12*. Portsmouth, N.H.: Heineman, 1994. Routman's work has an excellent section on evaluation, and especially its alternative forms, pp. 295–373.
7. Henry C. Lindgren and W. Newton Suter, *Educational Psychology in the Classroom*, 7th ed. Monterey, Calif.: Brooks/Cole, 1985, p. 383.
8. Leonard H. Clark and Irving S. Starr, *Secondary and Middle School Teaching Methods*, 4th ed. New York: Macmillan, 1981, p. 291.
9. Richard C. Richardson, Jr., Elizabeth C. Fisk, and Morris Okun, *Literacy in the Open-Access College*. San Francisco: Jossey-Bass, 1983. For "bitting," or "learning of discrete pieces of information," see p. 71.
10. Lindgren and Suter, *Educational Psychology in the Classroom*, p. 379.
11. Marcia M. Seeley, "The Mismatch Between Assessment and Grading." *Educational Leadership* (October 1994): 4–6. Diane Hart writes of "the assessment revolution" in pointing out that "by 1991 at least forty states had plans underway to implement some form of authentic assessment." See Diane Hart, *Authentic Assessment: A Handbook for Teachers*. Menlo Park, Calif.: Addison-Wesley, 1994, pp. vi–vii. Hart's book is a clearly written and highly practical survey of all forms of authentic assessment, and is replete with examples based on students' work.
12. Howard Gardner, "Reflections on Multiple Intelligences: Myth and Messages." *Phi Delta Kappan* (November 1995): 208.
13. F. Leon Paulson, Paul R. Paulson, and Carol A. Meyer, "What Makes a Portfolio a Portfolio?" *Educational Leadership* (February 1991): 60.
14. Ibid., p. 63.
15. Bloom, Hastings, and Madaus, *Formative and Summative Evaluation*, pp. 44–53.
16. Clark and Starr, *Secondary and Middle School Teaching Methods*, 297.
17. Lindgren and Suter, *Educational Psychology in the Classroom*, p. 404.
18. See Carl R. Rogers, *Freedom to Learn*. Columbus, Ohio: Charles E. Merrill, 1969, pp. 91–93; and John Holt, "I Oppose Testing, Marking, and Grading." *Today's Education* 60 (1971): 76–82.

19. Grant Wiggins, "Toward Better Report Cards." *Educational Leadership* (October 1994): 28–37. The same issue contains a number of valuable articles on traditional and alternative forms of assessment. A recent study distinguishes between "ability goals" (norm- and criterion-referenced) and "learning goals," which define "success in terms of developing skills, expanding knowledge, and gaining understanding." Success, the study maintains, "means being able to do something you couldn't do before." Rachel Buck Collopy and Theresa Green, "Using Motivational Theory with At-Risk Children." *Educational Leadership* 53 (September 1995): 37–40.

CHAPTER 11

Communicating with Students and Parents

Many teachers are acutely aware that their interactions with parents are far from simple, frequently unsatisfactory both to teachers and to parents and often approached on both sides with a mixture of suspicion, mistrust, and resignation.

Sarason, Davidson, and Blatt

A Helping Relationship

In your role as a teacher you will have many occasions to interact with students on a one-to-one basis in relation to subjects ranging from common interests to personal problems. You will also be called on to meet with parents from time to time to discuss mutual concerns relating to students' school life. The communication skills that will allow you to be effective in these personal encounters are likely to be considerably different from those you use to teach your classes. They will involve the ability to relate sensitively and authentically on a nonacademic level. The capability to enter into genuine two-way conversation over matters of feeling as well as matters of fact is one of the things exemplary teachers have in common with good counselors. For most of us, the skills and attitudes necessary to perform well in a helping relationship do not come naturally. They need to be deliberately cultivated.[1]

Many teachers never acquire the aptitudes to conduct productive meetings with students and parents over delicate issues.[2] For them, serious parent conferences and emotion-generating interactions with students are sometimes a dreaded part of the job. Yet, in a service profession such as teaching, a willingness to take the lead in arranging and directing personal meetings is essential to maintain positive working relationships with those you are serving. The ability to establish authentic communication with students and their parents on a personal level will greatly enhance your success in teaching.

This chapter discusses fundamental principles of one-to-one communication in a helping relationship. It also provides specific strategies and techniques for effective interaction with students and parents on a personal level.

Some Underlying Principles

There are some fundamental principles of human interaction that will have a direct bearing on the quality of your personal communication with students and parents. They are:

1. *People tend to withdraw from close interaction when fear, uncertainty, or suspicion is present.*[3] This is an important consideration to keep in mind when it comes to arranging conferences with parents, particularly when the purpose is to discuss a problem or to give an evaluation. It is natural for people to feel anxious and apprehensive about a situation that poses a possible threat to their security or self-esteem. When placed in that situation, most of us tend to play it close to the vest until we are able to feel more confident and comfortable.

2. *People are much more likely to share their true selves when they feel they are being understood and accepted.* There is much evidence to confirm that individuals are more inclined to be honest and self-revealing in the presence of those who accept and appreciate them for what they are.[4] This points to the need for unconditional acceptance and positive regard as preconditions for getting people to be open and trusting in their interactions with us. Unconditional positive regard means a willingness to respect and value the personhood of the other individual with no strings attached, in spite of behavior that may be difficult to tolerate. It is also important to exhibit a caring, nonjudgmental attitude when people attempt to share their deepest feelings and concerns. Other individuals are more likely to be self-revealing when they sense we are attempting to see things from their point of view.[5] Carl Rogers stresses the importance of nonevaluative listening when he asserts that "the major barrier to mutual interpersonal communication is our very natural tendency to judge, to evaluate, to approve (or disapprove) the statements of the other person."[6]

3. *Feelings and emotions are generally more powerful than facts and reason in human interaction.* Someone who is experiencing physical or emotional pain, or affection, fear, or disappointment is unlikely to be receptive to appeals to rationality, particularly if they involve an unsympathetic effort to discount the emotion. The feeling is often a more dominant reality to that person than the competing consideration someone would attempt to impose. "Denying or ignoring the existence of feelings in communication is like building a house without a foundation or framework."[7] To undertake to judge or talk someone out of an emotion is folly. The best way to gain entry to the psychic space of someone who has just expressed a strong feeling (e.g., an attraction, a distaste, a wish) is to enter at the feeling level.[8] That is to say, expressions of feeling should receive feeling-level responses (e.g., an understanding gesture, an expression of empathy).

4. *Your body language communicates a great deal more than what you say.* Experiments have shown that people generally consider nonverbal, bodily

messages to be a great deal more reliable than verbal messages. It has been claimed that as much as 90 percent of the feeling conveyed by verbal messages comes from the vocal tone and facial expression of the speaker.[9] "A student is much more likely to attend to a teacher's face than to his or her words for indications of approval or acceptance."[10] Unfortunately, in human interaction our body language very often contradicts what we are able to verbalize. We are telling people one thing, but our physical being is conveying something quite different. Rogers discusses the need for congruence in the messages we communicate to another person. To Rogers, congruence means being "genuine and without 'front' or façade, openly being the feelings and attitudes which at that moment are flowing in you." Although no one ever achieves total congruence, we can begin to approach it by being attuned to what is going on inside us, by being able "to *be* the complexity of our feelings without fear."[11]

5. *Words do not carry meaning, people do.* This is a reminder that words symbolize thoughts and images that people have inside them. In and of themselves they have no meaning. Particular words may have significance to some people and mean nothing to others. The same words may be meaningful to a number of people, but in very different ways (e.g., love, education). To be effective communicators we must be able to place ourselves in the situation of the listener, to be able to imagine the perspective and feelings of the person receiving our message. Ambiguous terms like "good student" or "quality education" leave room for many possible interpretations. They can lead to serious misunderstandings when we use them as though they carried the same meaning for everyone. The best assurance we can have that the other person is receiving the meaning we intend is to be as descriptive as possible in the messages we send. Rather than characterize someone as a "good student," we communicate much more effectively when we describe that person as someone who, among other things, listens attentively in class, asks intelligent questions, shows initiative, works well with other students, completes assignments on time, and scores well on comprehension exams. The realization that words themselves carry no meaning should caution us against using specialized terminology (jargon) when talking with people who are not teachers themselves.

6. *Telling someone something does not ensure they hear what you actually say.* This may appear to be an obvious truth about communication. The fact is, however, that educators are especially apt to ignore this fact. It is easy for teachers who, especially at the high school level, make such extensive use of lecture or other forms of "presentation," to imagine that a message well sent is one well received. However, effective communication requires attention to how the other person is attuned to our messages. One of the main determinants of whether your idea gets into the mind of the listener is the degree to which he or she is concentrating on and trying to understand the message.[12] One of the best

ways to stimulate another person to think about what you are saying is by asking certain well-placed questions to encourage him or her to talk about your ideas:

"What do you think would be the consequences if we were to try this?"

"Do you know of any examples of this?"

"Where do you suppose I got this idea?"

When one person voices an idea and the other person does not have a chance to discuss it, or does not even reflect upon it internally), there's a strong chance that it will not stick.[13]

Personal Interaction with Students

Knowing Your Goals

Keeping in Touch with Students It is important to be aware of what you can accomplish in talking with students. Many of your one-to-one encounters with these young people will be of the informal variety. They will occur spontaneously without any particular objective. However, they can be very helpful in establishing or maintaining a certain kind of relationship with an individual student. These "maintenance encounters" as they might be called are essential to a constructive helping relationship. They let students know you are interested in them and that you are a person with whom they can share personal thoughts and feelings. Some of your best teaching may be done during brief one-to-one exchanges with students during which you help them to clarify thoughts and feelings, to deal with contradictory emotions, or to examine points of view other than their own. There is a body of evidence suggesting that healthy emotional development in young people (i.e., depth of feelings and meanings) is dependent to a large extent on the quality of the interaction they have with significant adults in their lives (e.g., parents, teachers)."[14] Studies have also demonstrated the importance of personal relationships in assisting a youngster's intellectual achievement.[15]

Problem-Based Meetings The other main type of personal interaction you will have with students will be prompted by the need to discuss a problem or concern that is troubling either you or the student. It is especially important for you to develop effective ways of handling *problem-based encounters* of various kinds in your professional life. You may want to discuss some difficulty a student is causing by their classroom behavior, or is experiencing in their academic performance, or in their relations with other students. A student (or parent) may ask to talk about a criticism they have of some aspect of what you do (e.g., one of your teaching techniques). Whatever your feelings may be, as a professional you have a responsibility to deal with the problem calmly, reasonably, and in a way that respects the feelings, needs, and agendas of the other person.

This takes considerable patience and interpersonal sophistication, because there are often strong emotions and tensions involved, sometimes initial tendencies toward suspicion, defensiveness, or withdrawal. Problem-centered discussions generally require a more strategic approach than maintenance encounters. From a practical standpoint, your concern must be not only to solve the problem to your own satisfaction, but to sustain a positive helping relationship for the future. This requires that your methods be consistent with the goals you hope to achieve. By having a firm sense of what you, the helper, are trying to accomplish in the encounter, you are less likely to sabotage your own purposes.

Tuning in to the Student's Agenda

Free and honest communication between two people generally involves some risk for these individuals. In personal interactions with students in which strong feelings are involved, you can normally expect some reluctance on their part to share themselves openly until they are made to feel they are in the presence of an interested and understanding listener. It is important that you not move too quickly to present your own thoughts and agendas. Your initial effort should not be to impose your ideas or to resolve a problem, but to open the channels of communication.

Questions as Conversation Enhancers You can begin to accomplish this by showing a genuine interest in students' situations, including important thoughts and feelings they may be holding. Simple, nonthreatening questions are usually very helpful at the beginning of such discussions. You can help to relax students by asking questions that are easy to answer. These may be simple factual questions that can be answered with little elaboration (e.g., "Are you still working after school?"), or they may be open-ended questions that allow students to warm up to the discussion by talking about something they know well and would have little reluctance to share (e.g., "How does the school year seem to be going for you so far?"). Be prepared to tolerate some initial wandering into areas that have no direct bearing on the point of the meeting. Although your time is important, so is the need to establish the groundwork for a fruitful discussion.

Reflective Listening You show genuine interest and respect by listening attentively and empathetically to the other person's messages. One effective indicator of active listening is the ability to reflect back to the speaker through a simple *paraphrase* the essence of the message as you understood it:

"You're saying school is becoming hard to cope with these days."
"You believe students should have more elective classes to choose from."
"So you and Jessica have become good friends."

Paraphrasing as a reflective listening technique is intended to convey one's effort to hear and understand. To have its proper effect as a conversation "lubricant" it should be offered in a low-key and neutral (not inquiring) tone that does not suggest disagreement or disbelief.

Nonjudgmental Responding Teachers who can listen without jumping in with judgments as students express feelings and personal concerns will have more success in talking with students at this level than teachers who are quick to offer advice and criticism.[16] Some of the nonverbal accompaniments to empathetic listening are a comfortable posture, looking sympathetic, and affirmative nods that signal "Yes, I'm hearing you." The ability to resist the temptation to interrupt is also very important.

Responding analytically to student expressions of feeling is generally counterproductive. Appeals to rationality when the other person is in a nonrational mood may only serve to intensify the feeling and create defensiveness. When students say privately, "I dread this test. I'm just not ready for it," your first impulse may be to respond with rational statements like "You did have plenty of notice," or "Don't worry about it, you'll do all right." A better reply would match the feeling level of the student. A nonevaluative paraphrase is often the best response: "You don't feel prepared for this one," or "You're especially nervous about this test." In a case where a student remarks sincerely to a teacher, "I really wish we could get out of school earlier for the summer vacation," an appropriate feeling-level response would be, "You'd like to have a longer summer," or "You're ready for a break."

Nonjudgmental paraphrasing is especially appropriate in one-to-one situations in which personal problems or interpersonal tensions exist. If a student is willing to share the feeling that "Nothing is going right for me lately," teachers do well to respond at that level rather than to react with information or advice. By simply reflecting, "You've had some bad days lately," or "This just isn't your week," teachers indicate a willingness to begin the conversation on the student's wavelength rather than their own. Although you may feel a desire to get to the heart of the problem and to move more quickly to impose your own solution (e.g., a student has been violating an important class ground rule), if one of your purposes is to establish two-way communication with the student, your agenda should temporarily remain in the background. It is imperative that you avoid criticizing at this point in the conversation if your concern is to stimulate open, trusting interaction with the student.

By initially resisting judgment or advice, teachers do not give up their right to an opinion, nor do they abdicate their position of influence. Instead, these nondirective responses will usually turn out to be communication enhancers. By allowing their initial responses to match students' level of concern, teachers let students know that they are in the presence of teachers who are able to suspend their own ideas and objectives long enough to entertain those of the students. Under these circumstances, students will not only be more willing to confide in such teachers, but will be more receptive to their teachers' influence.

Providing Feedback and Support

Accepting and Encouraging. Once you have made progress in engaging the other person in open and trusting conversation, it is important for you to offer something of your own in the way of a substantive response. You help to sustain the momentum of the conversation when you are able to provide positive, nonevaluative reactions. Students who have begun to share a part of themselves—their thoughts, their feelings, their intentions—should have that willingness reinforced by your acceptance and encouragement. Sometimes it is a matter of directly conveying your appreciation and support for their efforts:

> "I appreciate your willingness to be honest with me about that."
> "I imagine it's difficult for you to talk about that—I'm glad you made the effort."
> "I've never been in that situation before—I'll bet it was quite an experience."
> "It sounds like something that's worth pursuing—I'd like to be of some help to you if I could."

By taking opportunities to offer supportive statements, "ego boosters," that show that you respect and think well of a student, you can do a great deal to promote the person's confidence and good feelings toward self, prerequisites for the authentic sharing of that self with others[17]:

> "That's an interesting point. You seem to have some good insights."
> "I can see why you have so many friends in this group. Many of the others in the class seem to respect you and look to you for leadership."
> "As I listen to you talk, I can't help but think how well you express yourself."

A word of caution, however. Your comments need to be based on a genuine regard for the other person. Otherwise, they can very rapidly become, and be seen to be, manipulative, intended to flatter the student, and to win the student over for the *teacher's* benefit. In what you say during a conference or discussion, you need to bear it in mind that your main role is to be of assistance to others rather than use this as an opportunity to promote your own needs and interests. You should be aware of any tendencies you may have to introduce irrelevancies, to moralize, to use unnecessary jargon, or to talk too much about yourself. Here are some suggestions for making what you say relevant and understandable:

1. Stick to the point. Offer only ideas that contribute to the idea-pattern you are trying to convey.
2. Space your ideas by speaking briefly. This gives your listener time to think about each idea as it is presented.
3. Do not tell the other person what he or she already knows. Repeat your meaning but not your words, and avoid saying the obvious.

4. Use concrete words whenever possible. Whenever you use abstract words illuminate them through use of concrete ones.

5. After presenting ideas, encourage the other person to think by asking questions.

If your encounter with a particular student is essentially maintenance-based (i.e., generally informal, aimed at promoting openness, trust, or self-disclosure), you may have no need to move to a problem-solving stage in the conversation.[18] The communication enhancers embodied in these first two interactive phases of tuning in and providing feedback and support to the student will have been instrumental in making the relationship one of mutual trust and respect. Students are likely to feel comfortable in your presence and regard you as a person who is generally interested in them as people.

Addressing Problems

When the central purpose of the conference is to address a problem or concern you have identified, the time should now be ripe for you to bring the discussion to a head by making your reason for the meeting clear. Essentially what you want to communicate at this point is, "I respect and value you as a person with purposes and agendas of your own. However, I have a concern I want to call to your attention." Your positive support and willingness to consider the other's thoughts and feelings should have earned you the opportunity to bring attention to the problem without giving rise to troublesome defensiveness. If it is a problem of behavior you are attempting to resolve, you should now be able to get the student's attention and cooperation without having to invoke your authority.

Of course, you need to be prepared for the fact that the student may have things to say that conflict with your own values or the way you see the situation, which is quite possibly the basis of the problem or disagreement that made the meeting necessary. However, it is important that you not allow these differences and accompanying feelings to jeopardize the positive flow of the discussion. There are ways you can respectfully disagree without being confrontational or authoritarian. Your effort should be to show that you support the other's right to a particular feeling or opinion, without necessarily agreeing with it:

"Yes, I hear what you're saying. . . . On the other hand, this is how I see it."

"I can understand how you might feel that way. . . . My own experience has been rather different. . . ."

"I respect your position on this . . . I also think there's something else we need to understand about the situation. . . ."

Low-key, nonconfrontational disagreement is best achieved when the tone of your voice reflects a concern to understand rather than to be right, and when you are able to leave expressions like "Yes . . . but . . ." and "I disagree" out of your conversation. Such language tends to carry adversarial overtones, usually causing the other person to dig in and defend a chosen position rather than listen to your point of view.

Problem-Solving Tactics By promoting in-depth dialogue during the early stages of the discussion, you hope to set the stage for a reasoned, cooperative approach to the problem that made the meeting necessary. Having arrived at the point at which both parties are aware of some difficulty that needs to be resolved, there are at least three kinds of approaches you can use to produce action. One is to invite an *action proposal* by asking directly, "What do you think we should do about this?" or "Would you like to think some more about what we've discussed and let me know tomorrow what you propose to do?" This approach attempts to place the responsibility on the student to come up with a solution. It conveys the message that "I think of you as a basically reasonable and responsible person and I'd like to give you first opportunity to suggest a way of dealing with this." This method is not suitable if the student has broken a clearly defined rule for which there is a preestablished penalty.

A second approach is to offer a possible solution that involves *shared responsibility for action on the problem*. It contains a provision that you would be willing to contribute something to help students resolve the difficulty, if they will do the main part. For example:

> "If I remove these last two tardies, will you make it a point to show
>   up on time for the rest of the semester?"
> "If you would get that assignment to me by 8:00 tomorrow morning,
>   I'd be willing to give you credit for it."
> "I'll allow you to keep that seat if you can show me you won't talk
>   while I'm teaching."

This strategy is particularly appropriate in the case of a student who would benefit from a slight nudge to action or a second opportunity to demonstrate proper behavior. It represents a show of good faith on your part, saying in effect, "I'm willing to contribute something to help you resolve this because I believe you will follow through with your part of the bargain." It is less appropriate a second time, after your first expression of good faith has not borne fruit.

The third approach to problem resolution is a straightforward *teacher directive* that describes in precise terms the expected behavior:

> "The rule about throwing food in the lunchroom is quite clear,
>   Emilio. You'll eat lunch in the classroom for the rest of the week."
> "Jennifer, you know what my standard is for neatness in your written
>   work. Please redo this assignment."
> "Trevor, it wouldn't be fair to the other players for you to miss prac-
>   tice to attend to this other business. You'll need to make all of our
>   practices this week if you want to play in the game on Friday."

A teacher directive is most appropriate when you decide there is no room for negotiation. This may be the case when a clearly defined rule or standard has been violated, or when you feel the student's behavior does not merit further discussion or a second chance. When using this direct and unilateral approach to problem resolution, it is important that you be as objective as possible in defining proper behavior and reasons for a particular decision. Be as descriptive as possible when discussing appropriate and inappropriate behavior, and avoid labeling students as nasty, inconsiderate, sloppy, or other characterizations that can be damaging to the person and to the teacher-student relationship.

◆◆◆ A P P L I C A T I O N   E X E R C I S E S ◆◆◆

1. For each of the following student comments, provide brief responses that would serve to accomplish the specified purpose (assume in each case that you are alone with the student):
   a. "I'm afraid I won't make the team. There are so many people trying out this time." (Realizing the student probably is not talented enough to make the team, you want to be sympathetic, but also positive.)
   b. "Wow! I got the shaft today. Two failure notices—one in math and the other in English." (You want to find out more about the problem without being judgmental.)
   c. "This is the best score I've had so far. I'm really feeling good about this one." (You want to share in the student's good feeling.)
   d. "What's so wrong about missing a day of school once in a while? My dad is able to take days off from his job; you teachers can take personal leave days. Students shouldn't be treated any different." (You want to offer a different point of view without seeming unpleasant or defensive.)
   e. "For a while I was doing O.K., but now I'm worse than ever. Nothing I do seems to help. What's the use of trying?" (You want to show empathy and a desire to be helpful.)
   f. "I'm sick of school. I need a vacation." (You want to accept the expressed feeling without being judgmental or moralistic.)
2. Imagine yourself as a teacher in each of the following personal encounters with students. Say what you might be trying to achieve and the main communication strategies and techniques you would employ in each instance:
   a. As a junior high school teacher, one of your students approaches you to discuss a problem he is having with test taking in your class. This boy, a cooperative and seemingly average student, manages to perform satisfactorily on homework assignments and in-class recitations, but has had little success with the first several written tests. He is preoccupied with the thought he might fail the class.
   b. As a fifth-grade teacher, you have decided to talk privately with a girl in your class who has recently been disrupting other student's games

during recess. This student, a relatively well-behaved participant in regular in-class activities, has been teasing other girls and kicking their game-balls on the playground. She has on one other occasion confided to you her feeling that girls in the class have been slow to warm up to her because of her outsider status as a recent transfer student.

c. As a popular high school teacher, you have been invited to join a small group of students with whom you have very positive relationships for an upcoming Saturday afternoon picnic. You are reluctant to accept the invitation for two main reasons. First, because you would like to spend a quiet weekend at home after a hectic week at school. Second, because you do not really think that it is professional to extend the relationship to this level of informality in spite of the fact that these are especially enjoyable and loyal students. One of the students has cornered you during lunch for the purpose of trying to talk you into accompanying them in this weekend outing.

Conducting Productive Parent Meetings

Setting the Stage

There are several things you should do in preparation for a parent conference, but before you embark on those, William Ayers' comments on the fathers and mothers of the children in your class are worth remembering:

> Parents are a powerful, usually underutilized source of knowledge about youngsters. Parents are often made to feel unwelcome in schools, and we too often dismiss their insights as subjective and overly involved. In fact, the insights of parents—urgent, invested, passionate, immediate—are exactly what we need.[19]

First, of course, you will need to come to an agreement on a mutually convenient time and place for the meeting. If you are initiating the conference, the best method is a phone call to make the first contact personal. However, some parents may be difficult to reach during the times you might call. A second choice is to send a written request home with the student. If all else fails, send a note through the mails. Try to find a time that is convenient for both you and the parent. After school may be your best time. For parents who work, early morning, lunch hour, or evening meetings may be necessary.

The setting in which you hold the conference is very important. Unless you are sharing a classroom with other teachers, the most natural place for the meeting will be your own classroom. If so, make an effort to ensure privacy. Students taking tests or moving in and out of the room can be a bothersome distraction, as can calls from the office, street noises, and so forth. If an empty classroom or teacher's office is not available, frequently an administrative office or nurse's room will afford the necessary privacy. Make sure the time and place for the meeting are well understood by the parent and that you have these firmly set in your schedule. Mix-ups or missed meetings can be especially embarrassing for both parties when you are trying to establish a good working relationship. If it is the parent who asks to meet with you, make sure you have a clear idea of the problem he or she wants to discuss so that you can prepare yourself to deal with it. If it has something to do with school policy, check the exact terms of the policy, and its rationale, and if you think it necessary, ask a colleague or the principal to advise you how best to deal with the parent.

Wherever you hold the conference, set the chairs up so that the parents feel as comfortable and at ease as possible. If the classroom only has attached chairs and desks for students, make sure that you get other chairs for the parents so that you eliminate or reduce to a minimum any feeling that you are lording it over them.

Overcoming Initial Barriers

As your meeting with a parent, or parents, begins (and try to avoid thinking of it as a "parent conference," i.e., a sort of ritual performance), you should be aware of some of the possible psychological barriers that could work to make free and open discussion difficult.

Parent Anxiety Bear it in mind that parents bring with them memories of when they were students, not always very enthusiastic ones, and continually subject to the authority of the teacher (which role *you* now occupy). This means that parents sometimes feel apprehensive and defensive about meeting teachers (some of whom they may not remember with any great fondness) within the school environment (which they may not have much enjoyed) to discuss matters about which they generally suppose the teacher has greater knowledge and authority. In addition, within the larger society, teachers are generally thought of as relatively well-educated people with above-average language skills. In contrast, some of the parents with whom you meet may have less formal education and less verbal facility in formal conversation. In many instances, the parents' home language will not be English, and some may even have difficulty in understanding what you are saying, especially as they may also come from cultures in which teachers are relatively remote and intimidating figures. As a result, you may very well notice some initial anxiety and reluctance on the part of the parent to enter into easy conversation at the beginning of a meeting.

Stereotypes and Preconceptions Based on their own school experiences, parents may be harboring stereotypes of teachers—the kinds of behavior to be expected from them, and preconceptions about what and how their children should be learning—that affect a parent's ability to relate to a teacher on a personal level. They may expect teachers to dominate the conference with their explanations and prescriptions, and come prepared to simply listen and endure. Some parents may regard teachers as primarily academic in their orientations and interests, with little inclination to be interested in them and what they might contribute to the meeting. In these times of rapid change, parents may feel uneasy about, or even hostile to, new ways of teaching and curriculums that are different from those they experienced in their own school days. You will need to be able to give them clear, straightforward, and convincing explanations of whatever you are doing that is relatively innovative—problem-based math, whole language, calculators, computers, cooperative learning, and so on. As one teacher described his experience,

> We had some parents who were successful in their professional life who learned with paper and pencil. They felt that what was good enough for them was good enough for their children. People are real comfortable with spelling books and lists of words. We tried to tell them that what was good enough for them wouldn't suit their children well twenty years from now.[20]

Adversarial Feelings For a variety of reasons, therefore, parents (or even teachers) have a tendency to see the relationship as adversarial rather than cooperative. In the eyes of the parent, teachers are authority figures who function primarily as critics and evaluators. Teachers themselves may unintentionally contribute to this feeling. Being highly sensitive to the need to maintain system and control in their work, teachers are liable to construe conferences with students or parents over school problems as encounters with those who would disrupt that system. They need to remember that "parents," as Fiske points out, "are becoming increasingly sophisticated about the differing needs of their children.[21] Teachers need to keep it in mind that parents are more and more informed about what goes on in school and deserve and will, if they see it as necessary, demand to be treated as adult clients, not ignorant nuisances or irritating intruders.

When the occasion for a meeting is a difficulty with student behavior or achievement, or dissatisfaction with the teacher's methods, each party may approach the interaction with blinders, with a tendency to see only their side of the problem, and to blame the other party for what is going wrong.

When confronted with behavior in these conferences that suggests resentment, prejudgment, or distrust, it is critical that you not respond in kind or allow yourself to be drawn into a battle of egos. As the professional in a helping relationship, it is your responsibility to provide a positive and constructive tone to the meeting and not let matters deteriorate as one teacher at a gathering of elementary school teachers described his experience:

> Some parents approach me with a chip on their shoulders, unrespectful of what I know, what I do, or why. Before I know it, we are talking past each other.[22]

Providing Direction and Focus to the Meeting

Once you have completed the process of greeting parents and expressing your appreciation for their willingness to meet, you should make an effort to size up their readiness to enter into a productive dialogue. Being mindful of some of the potential obstacles to open and trustful communication, allow sufficient time at the beginning to set a positive tone for the meeting and to give the parent an opportunity to warm up to the discussion. Your ability to be a good listener is critical here, effective listening being the single most important skill you can bring to a parent conference.

Conversation Lubricants It is often helpful to begin the meeting with a little small talk to stimulate conversation. Unless the parent shows an interest in moving directly to the main agenda, you should work up to any sensitive issues by employing the same sorts of communication enhancers that were discussed in connection with teacher-student interaction (i.e., nonthreatening questions, careful listening, supportive statements, positive feedback). In the case of self-confident, highly social people, the dialogue may be relatively free-flowing from the beginning.

Taking the Lead Considerations of time will usually require that you limit a parent meeting to one or two main items. You should take the initiative to ensure that the discussion moves in a direction that allows you to meet the objectives you have set for the conference. During all phases of the conference you should make a strong effort to act in ways that are essential in any productive helping relationship (i.e., positive regard, empathy, congruence). Here are some additional suggestions for making the meeting a mutually beneficial experience for both you and the parent:

1. Take responsibility for maintaining a pleasant and respectful tone throughout the conference.
2. Accept some irrelevant conversation during the warm-up period, but thereafter gently steer it back to the issue if it's not going in a useful direction.
3. Do not use the conference to talk about yourself or your problems.
4. Emphasize the positive. Be mindful of the personal investment parents have in their children. They will feel that things you say about a son or daughter reflect on them and their abilities as parents.
5. Cite instances of exactly what the student does. Instead of merely saying that "Jamie has a good attitude," elaborate by saying, "Jamie always comes into class with a smile on her face," or spell out "Joe is very helpful," into "Joe loves to give out materials, and always gets the right number of pencils back."
6. Be prepared to take notes on important items parents may mention during the conference, but don't fail to tell parents why you are doing this, or the practice may seem very threatening to them.

7. Avoid any appearance of being hurried or preoccupied during the conference. Nervous glances at your watch or toward the door will give a parent the impression you are too busy to give them your full attention.
8. Make it clear throughout the meeting that you recognize and honor the fact that they want what is in the best interest of their son or daughter, and that that is equally your prime concern.

Concluding and Following Up the Meeting

You will seldom have unlimited time for a parent conference, and it may be helpful if you let the parents know at the outset that (for some tactful and regretted reason such as having to teach, or the need to meet with other parents), you're sure the meeting will be able to get matters settled by *x* P.M. This will both ensure that everyone sticks to the point and it will enable you to bring the discussion to a conclusion in a way that will seem natural and fitting to the parent. It will usually be a good idea for you to provide a brief review of the purpose and the main highlights of the conference, including any conclusions that were reached. Parents should leave the meeting with a clear understanding of what was discussed and any action they and the teacher have agreed to take. If there is a need for further discussion or a follow-up meeting, this is the time to schedule another conference. The closing phase of the conference should allow time for you to end the meeting in a cordial and unhurried fashion.

At the conclusion of a parent conference it is a good idea to make a written record of what transpired. You may want to design a conference form with spaces for various kinds of information that you will want to have on hand for your own record (e.g., date, reason for conference, relevant background information on student, action to be taken). This form could include a bottom line for your signature and that of the parent once the conference was concluded.

Managing Difficult Conferences

From time to time you may find yourself involved in a conference with a parent whose behavior makes it especially difficult for you to engage in productive dialogue. You can anticipate several kinds of parent behaviors that may be tension producing and/or disruptive of your efforts to lead a fruitful meeting, including: (1) shyness and inarticulateness, (2) unusual aggressiveness, (3) debilitating emotion, and (4) self-centered monologue.

Shyness and Inarticulateness

You may encounter parents who have a particularly difficult time articulating ideas or concerns, or even saying anything at all. They may appear accepting of what you have to say, but are essentially unable to offer anything of their own. You will realize very quickly that the conference has turned into a one-person show, and that you need to introduce some simple conversational ploys to get the parents talking.

Try a little light humor as a means of loosening them up. Use low-pressure questions to draw parents into casual conversation on a topic with which they feel comfortable. Showing genuine interest and support in the way you listen may be enough to stimulate conversation. Make some encouraging comment about their child, and ask how the parents managed to help the child be or do whatever it is you mention.

Your key concern must be to resist dominating the meeting or attempting to move the conference to a quick conclusion without the parent taking part. If you don't, this will end up being just another token conference. Avoid showing your understandable discomfort and impatience with this parent's reticence. As the teacher and therefore helping professional, it is part of your job to deal effectively with shyness and withdrawal in your personal interactions.

Unusual Aggressiveness

Dealing with an overly assertive or hypercritical parent can also be difficult. This person may attempt to take the lead and offer a premature perception and resolution of the situation. Generally aggressive people have a need to be heard and to vent what is on their mind. They may begin the conference by being unreasonably critical of your behavior or that of the student. They may also show an inclination to interrupt and disagree with points you are making. If this aggression seems aimed at you, very likely they have entered the meeting with preconceptions of you or the school based on past experiences with teachers or on stories their child has brought home.

In managing encounters with aggressive parents (or students) it is imperative that you avoid overreacting or arguing. The longer you can remain outwardly calm, and in control of your own emotions, the better chance you have of getting them to be reasonable. As in any personal encounter in which other people have pressing concerns they need to get off their chest, your listening skills are paramount. Your ability to employ reflective, empathetic listening techniques (e.g., affirmative nods, confirmatory paraphrases, supportive feedback) can do wonders to turn a confrontational situation into one of mutual sharing and understanding. This will take the personal security and confidence to be able to say, "You may be right," "I understand your feeling," or "I can see how you might get that impression." By rolling with the punches and not arguing, you effectively disarm combative people in their efforts to do battle.

When you provide no immediate resistance to their aggression, their next move is likely to be a show of willingness to temper their strong position. When this happens, you should make an effort to redirect the discussion to talk about factual matters (e.g., the student's failure to complete six out of eight homework assignments). If it is apparent that there is a conflict in values (e.g., the school favors more homework, the parent wants less), point up the conflict, make a case for the school's position, but indicate your ability to understand their point of view. Again, avoid arguing—it is important that you remain reasonable, whether the parent is or not.

Disabling Emotion

A conference in which the parent becomes upset or distraught can create unusual discomfort and indecision for a teacher. Even highly trained counselors sometimes have trouble knowing how to proceed with clients who lapse into weeping and despair. Assuming a nonextreme case, where you can expect the parent to eventually gain emotional control, there are some reasonable steps you can take to deal with the situation and to salvage something worthwhile from the meeting. If you sense ahead of time that this could be a stressful session, it is good to have a box of tissue on hand. Beyond that, it is of course critical not to attempt to push your point. An expression of empathetic understanding and support is also important (unless you have good reason to regard the show of emotion as a ploy to avoid responsibility or to influence you in a particular direction).

Often the most effective way to help these parents regroup and begin functioning in a rational manner is to refocus the conversation on something they are more comfortable discussing. If the disabling emotion resulted from a discussion of their son's failures in school, it could be settling to get them talking about something he excels in outside of school. Above all, in a conference like this it is important for you to be able to maintain your own composure. In a case where you perceive the parent's emotional state is too extreme to justify continuing the conference, the best course may be to suggest postponing the meeting until a later time.

Self-Centered Monologue

It may also be difficult to cope with parents who are self-centered and attempt to dominate the conversation with references to personal status, accomplishments, tastes and distastes, and so forth. The biggest problem with ego-involved parents is their tendency to keep the conversation focused on themselves rather than on the main topic of the meeting. Some self-centered parents will want to use references to their child's school performance as opportunities to talk about their own school experiences and achievements. Like the overly aggressive parent, they have a need to be heard. They are usually looking for occasions to tell someone about themselves.

After demonstrating an initial willingness to listen, you will have to focus the conversation firmly on the reason for the meeting; for example, "I'd like to focus for a moment on something I've observed about Nathan." In conferencing with a parent who shows a disposition toward self-centeredness, it is essential that you maintain the lead in the discussion. It will be up to you to keep the conference centered on the business at hand.

♦♦♦ A P P L I C A T I O N   E X E R C I S E S ♦♦♦

1. Discuss the basic strategies you would consider appropriate to use in conducting each of the following teacher-parent conferences. Give reasons for the approach you would take in each case.

   a. The father of one of your eighth-grade students has made an appointment to talk with you about a failing grade his son has earned in a basic math class. Your preliminary inquiries would indicate this parent is a strong-willed person who is primarily interested in keeping his son eligible for athletics.

   b. You have arranged to meet with the mother of one of your third-grade students to discuss her daughter's continuing aloofness toward you and many of her peers in the class. This girl has been reluctant to join in some class activities (e.g., music, square dancing), claiming her mother objects to her participation in some aspects of the school program. To date, you have not been able to find out what the reasons are, or whether they in fact exist.

   c. You have arranged a conference with the mother of one of your exceptionally talented tenth-grade art students to discuss this girl's interest in pursuing a college scholarship in art. It seems that the mother, a person with limited formal education, has shown little support for the idea, and has left the girl feeling discouraged about her chances of achieving her goal. In the past you have been unsuccessful in getting this parent to come to school to discuss her daughter's situation.

♦♦♦ S U G G E S T E D   A C T I V I T I E S   A N D   Q U E S T I O N S ♦♦♦

1. Define *communication* in your own words. When can it be said that one has communicated? Is communication the process of transferring a message or conveying meaning? Compare your ideas with those of other beginning teachers. What are some main similarities and differences?

2. How effective do you consider yourself to be as an interpersonal (face-to-face) communicator? List some of your communication strengths. Also list any communication weaknesses you think you may possess. List specific steps you can take to overcome these weaknesses.

3. It has been claimed that although most of us are born with the capacity to hear, we must learn how to listen. What do you take to be the difference between the two processes? Discuss some of the main reasons for poor listening in person-to-person interaction. Considering its fundamental importance to human communication, what do you think of the

idea of providing instruction in listening as well as reading and writing in our schools? What kind of instruction would that call for?

4. Consider the following hypothetical criticism of nonjudgmental listening as a communication skill in teacher-student interactions: "If I allow students to use me as a sounding board to vent silly, irresponsible feelings, I'll lose my standing as an authority figure and behavior management will become that much more difficult." Present an argument showing how this attitude could actually lead to more rather than fewer behavioral problems for a teacher.

5. Look for opportunities to interact on a one-to-one basis with students in schools where you are involved (e.g., during tutoring sessions, lunch periods, after school activities). Use these occasions to deliberately practice some of the main interactive skills presented in this chapter. In particular, make it a point to use reflective listening techniques when sharing ideas, experiences, and feelings with these young people. Do you notice differences in the way these students respond to you when you take time to show genuine interest in and support for their personal agendas as well as your own? What are these differences? When interacting with other people, both in a school setting and elsewhere, make a concerted effort to keep the "Yes . . . buts" and "I disagrees" out of your conversational patterns. Do you notice differences in the emotional climate of a discussion when your manner of disagreeing is low-key rather than confrontational?

NOTES

1. Carl R. Rogers, *On Becoming a Person*. Boston: Houghton Mifflin, 1961, see Chap. 3.
2. Robert R. Carkhuff and Bernard G. Berenson, *Beyond Counseling and Therapy*. New York: Holt, Rinehart and Winston, 1967, p. 11.
3. Leslie A. Hart, *Human Brain and Human Learning*. New York: Longman, 1983.
4. Haim G. Ginott, *Teacher and Child*. New York: Macmillan, 1972, p. 69; and Carl R. Rogers, "The Interpersonal Relationship: The Core of Guidance." In Carl R. Rogers and Barry Stevens (Eds.), *Person to Person: The Problem of Being Human*. New York: Pocket Books, 1971, p. 69.
5. Rogers, *On Becoming a Person*, p. 332.
6. Rogers, *On Becoming a Person*, p. 330.
7. George I. Brown, *Human Teaching for Human Learning*. New York: Viking Press, 1961, p. 6. The Caines point to the important role played by "safety" in assisting or standing in the way of communication, and add that "[safety] does not refer only to physical safety. It includes the safety of my ego and who I think I am. Anything that can conceivably diminish me in my eyes or in the eyes of those I value, acts as a threat to my own survival as a person," and as Hart points out, *"cerebral learning and threat conflict directly and completely."* See Renate Nummela Caine and Geoffrey Caine, *Making Connections: Teaching and the Human Brain*. Alexandria, Va.: ASCD, 1991, p. 130. Hart, *Human Brain and Human Learning*, p. 110.

8. Ginott, *Teacher and Child*, p. 64.

9. Joseph Morris, *Psychology and Teaching: A Humanistic View*. New York: Random House, 1978, p. 363.

10. Morris, *Psychology and Teaching*, p. 363.

11. Carl R. Rogers, "The Interpersonal Relationship: The Core of Guidance." In Carl P. Rogers and Barry Stevens (Eds.), *Person to Person: The Problem of Being Human*. New York: Pocket Books, 1971, p. 73.

12. Jesse S. Nirenberg, *Getting Through to People*. Englewood Cliffs, N.J.: Prentice-Hall, 1973, p. 109.

13. Ibid., p. 116.

14. William Glasser, *Reality Therapy*. New York: Harper and Row, 1975, p. 196; and Carkhuff and Berenson, *Beyond Counseling and Therapy*, p. 4.

15. Carkhuff and Berenson, *Beyond Counseling and Therapy*, p. 11.

16. Ginott, *Teacher and Child*, p. 70.

17. Rogers, *On Becoming a Person*, Chap. 3.

18. An exception would be an apparent maintenance-level encounter that uncovers a personal or behavioral problem that needs to be resolved.

19. William Ayers, *To Teach: The Journey of a Teacher*. New York: Teachers College Press, 1993, p. 41.

20. Edward B. Fiske, *Smart Schools, Smart Kids*. New York: Simon and Schuster, 1991, p. 154.

21. Ibid.

22. Seymour B. Sarason, *Parental Involvement and Political Principle: Why The Existing Governance Structure of Schools Should Be Abolished*. San Francisco, Calif.: Jossey-Bass, 1995, p. 23.

23. Realistically, however, a comment of Hart's needs to be borne in mind: "By no means," he writes, "can it be assumed that maximum learning is universally desired. While parents may welcome outstanding performance in certain fields, especially athletics or some form of social approval, it is no secret that many do not jump for joy at having their offspring come home with new and surprising ideas and information, expertise that puts parental abilities to shame. . . . Only a slim minority can be expected to value learning per se." See Hart, *Human Brain and Human Learning*, p. 13.

CHAPTER 12

Managing Your Own Development as a Teacher

Professionals should always be "going to school."

Seymour Sarason

Who dares to teach must never cease to learn.

Charles Dana (Motto of Kean University)

The creative powers of teachers disappear because the teacher tends to lose the learner's attitude.

Willard Waller

Being a Student of Teaching

Teaching affords personal growth opportunities such as few other professions. Your work provides continual opportunities for you to increase your interpersonal skills, your decision-making abilities, your verbal and reasoning powers, your time-management skills, and your self-confidence. These potential benefits often become apparent to perceptive newcomers to the teaching profession:

> Teaching has helped me develop a kind of self-confidence I've never had before. It's especially good for increasing your interpersonal skills since you're constantly interacting with people of different ages and different ability levels.

> I didn't realize teaching was going to require so much of me at a personal level. In many ways this is the most challenging thing I've ever done, but it's also without a doubt the most fulfilling. I've never been involved in anything where my personal skills increased so rapidly.

> The best way to learn something well is to have to teach it to someone else. Another thing you can gain from teaching is the ability to plan and organize activities within certain time limits.

The most fulfilled and successful teachers find ways to take advantage of these opportunities to grow. They insist on being responsible for their own progress as professionals, thereby avoiding the need to rely on external prescriptions and supervisor's evaluations to keep them focused and productive. Yet, because of the complex and fast-paced nature of the work, new teachers often find themselves merely surviving rather than growing (see Chapter 2). This fact of life points up the necessity of developing a viable plan for managing your own professional growth.

This chapter centers on ideas for managing and monitoring your personal development as a teacher. It offers self-governing strategies in three important areas: (1) developing a clear sense of professional direction as you begin teaching; (2) monitoring your own skill development as a beginning teacher; and (3) expanding your horizons as a professional educator.

Firming Up Your Guidelines

As you assume responsibility for your own classroom, the direction you take in developing lessons and managing classes will be largely up to you. At that point it will be important for you to have a reasonably clear notion of the role you wish to play as a teacher and how you will proceed to implement your goals in teaching.

Clarifying Your Concept of Teaching

What Does Research Say About Good Teaching? In formulating a serviceable philosophy of teaching, it is instructive for you to take into consideration the studies that have been done on effective teaching. These have tended to yield results that make it difficult to offer easy prescriptions for sound instruction. For example, studies aimed at determining whether indirect strategies are superior to direct methods of instruction have, as you might imagine, concluded that it depends on the objective. Direct methods are generally more effective when your goal is to teach basic information or skills, whereas an indirect teaching style is more suitable for promoting understanding and higher-level thinking.[1] One frequently cited review of the research on teaching has identified several teaching characteristics that have been consistently associated with gains in student achievement.[2] These characteristics are:

Enthusiasm: Exhibiting vigor, involvement, excitement, and interest during classroom presentations through vocal inflection, gesturing, eye contact, and animation

Clarity: Logical, step-by-step order; clear and audible delivery free of distracting mannerisms

Variety: Variation in instructional materials, questioning, types of feedback, and teaching strategies

Engagement: Businesslike orientation; ability to keep students on task, limiting opportunities for distraction, getting students to work on, think through, and to ask questions about the content

Another attempt to summarize the literature on effective teaching has produced the following list of essential teaching attitudes, knowledge, and strategies[3]:

1. Willingness to be flexible, to be direct or indirect as the situation demands
2. Ability to perceive the world from the student's point of view
3. Ability to personalize one's teaching
4. Willingness to experiment, to try out new things
5. Skill in thinking up and phrasing questions
6. Knowledge of subject matter and related areas
7. Provision of well-established examination procedures
8. Provision of definite study helps
9. Demonstration of appreciative attitudes (evidenced by nods, comments, smiles, etc.)
10. Use of conversational manner in teaching—informal, easy style

Summarizing Your Own Views   The concept of good teaching that guides your professional life will be one that you have chosen on good grounds (not merely on the basis of past experience as a K–12 student), so it is important for you to seek to clarify your present thinking as you make the never-easy transition from student to teacher. You might find the following questions helpful in summarizing your current views on teaching:

1. Now that I have the opportunity to see teaching from the "other side of the desk," has this changed my conception of the teacher's role? In what ways?
2. What are the criteria for *good* teaching? Are certain teaching strategies inherently right or desirable regardless of measurable outcomes (e.g., beginning a lesson with a set), or should good teaching always be defined in terms of the amount and kind of learning it produces?
3. Is teaching primarily a science or an art? What is the difference? What are the implications for learning to teach?
4. What is my conception of the fine teacher? Is it reducible to certain fundamental human qualities, to technical abilities, to intellect, or to a combination of the three?
5. What particular communication skills are fundamental? Are these skills unique to teaching?
6. How much importance will I attach to direct instruction in the subjects I teach? What will be the role of indirect methods in my teaching?
7. As a classroom teacher, where does my ultimate responsibility lie? To the subject matter? To the students? To their parents? To the school system? To the larger society? To the teaching profession? To myself?

Consolidating Your "Game Plan"

You will enhance your ability to be self-governing as a teacher if you will take time *before entering* the classroom to put together a plan of action. This should include a summary of the main procedures you will be setting up. The task will take some careful thought and organization on your part. Considering the variety of theories and methodologies you will have been exposed to during the course of teacher training, it is likely to require considerable effort to sort it all out and to distill from it a concise set of prescriptions for your teaching. That you have consciously settled on the principles that will guide your school behavior will allow you to achieve what Joyce and Showers call *executive control* over your teaching strategies.

Executive control "involves understanding an approach to teaching, why it works, what it is good for, what its major elements are, how to adapt it to varying content and students—the development of a set of principles that enables one to think about the approach and to modulate and transform it in the course of its use."[4]

To help you prepare your initial game plan, the following summary of recommendations and rationales represents a synthesis of some of the central ideas and strategies offered in previous chapters of this handbook.

Becoming Established

1. Make a special effort during the first few days of teaching[5] to get students used to attending to you and accepting your system of expectations. You should place a high priority on having them give you undivided attention when you are talking to the whole class. Refuse to begin class until all students have settled down and are focusing on you. This is one of the first and most important principles of classroom management.

2. Work to make what you say deliberate and penetrating. Nervous anxiety may at first make you tend to hurry through explanations or instructions. Recognize when you are too fast-paced or merely mechanical in your teaching. If students sense you are simply going through the motions of teaching, they will be very inclined to tune you out.

3. Find occasions to "walk" your students (as a group) through some short tasks or exercises so they can get into the habit of responding to your voice and following your instructions. Take this opportunity to make sure they've got the message. Respond quickly and good-naturedly when you notice students who lag behind or become inattentive, and make a mental note to find out why. Be patient, but deliberate and insistent, when it comes to keeping individuals on task and in tune with you and the rest of the group. The precedents you set here during these early stages of teaching will be crucial to your success with a particular group.

4. Do not expect everything to fall perfectly into place during your first days of teaching (or at any other stage in your career). Classroom teaching is often hectic and unpredictable. Things will not always work out as logically and precisely as you had planned. A sense of humor,

careful thought about what went on and some planning to deal with the problem—and then a good night's sleep—will usually do wonders after "one of those days."

Relationships with Students and Supervisors

1. Strive to develop natural authority, the regard students give you because they respect you as a person rather than as someone just doing a job, filling a role. This requires that you be authentic in your interactions with students, even if that sometimes means showing something of your real feelings. It is important to avoid coming across as too stiff, subject-centered, and impersonal at the one extreme or too wishy-washy and ingratiating at the other. Attempt to be honest and unpretentious in all your relations with students, and be ready to take personal responsibility for anything you ask them to do.

2. Do not allow a desire for natural authority to lead to peer-level relationships with your students. Students usually prefer teachers who are friendly and approachable, but they seldom expect teachers to behave toward them like peers. Avoid behaving in ways that might signal an inclination on your part to be just one of the gang. Most young people have more friends than they do stable adult models in their lives. Addressing groups of students as "you guys" or allowing them to call you by your first name is not recommended.

3. Recognize that you are the moral leader in your own classroom. You will generally create the mood for the day. Try always to be positive, but not falsely so, in your approach to classroom business. Use positive rather than negative phrasing when stating expectations or when reprimanding (e.g., "I'd like everyone's attention up here at the front of the room," rather than "You people are going to have to stop talking back there"). When you feel you are doing your part to promote a positive and constructive classroom environment, you have a right to expect students to reciprocate. Recognize and comment on students when they do so. Bear in mind the fact that teacher praise, especially when it is seen as gushing, can be counterproductive, and students who get it are perceived as the teacher's pet, or as some sort of nerd.

4. Maintain an interest in and respect for individual personalities, in spite of the tendency for personalities to be obscured within the crowd atmosphere of the school. Your ability to be patient, understanding, appreciative, and perhaps most of all concerned and able to help individual students will go a long way toward earning the trust and cooperation of the young people with whom you work.

5. Find ways to clear the necessary space in your life to enable you to devote your best energies to teaching, and do everything you can to manage personal problems and outside concerns in ways that prevent them encroaching excessively on the time and attention you need to give to

the business of being a teacher. In your relationships with other adults in the school, do all you can to have yourself seen as a resourceful adult who is able to handle problems and setbacks.

Getting Students Involved in Learning Activities

1. Personalize your teaching as much as possible. Appeal whenever you can to students' imagination, curiosity, personal experience, moral sensitivity, problem-solving ability, and desire for competence when introducing new learning. The more abstract and impersonal your teaching, the more difficult it will be for students to learn, and the more frustration and boredom[6] will lead to fidgeting, daydreaming, and disruptive behavior.

2. Make sure that you don't teach in ways that lead students to conclude that what happens in your classroom is just a part of a game played to satisfy the needs of an impersonal system. When you begin a class by saying, "O.K, carry on with exercise number 23," or "Don't forget we have a test on Chapter 5 on Friday," or "All right, we have to start our demonstration speeches today," you're giving students the message that class is just a matter of going through routines rather than of doing some worthwhile learning. You are (at least until now unwittingly) contributing to the dullness, impersonality, and artificiality that many students have come to associate with classroom learning. You're more likely to get some genuine learning when you appeal to the internal motivation of students rather than when you rely on anxiety about grades, satisfying parents, getting into college, or other forms of external leverage. As a general rule it is better to start a class by asking, for example, "Could anybody suggest a connection between the lab experiment we did yesterday and what you ate for breakfast?" or "Did any of you notice the headline on the front page of yesterday's local paper?" or "What would you do if you were faced with this sort of situation?" than by telling them to take out their homework or by plunging into a lecture.

3. Plan your lessons so your instruction converges on main points or "big ideas" (or definable skills). Be able at any stage in a lesson to say, "This is the point I'm trying to make here," "This is what we're leading up to," or "This is what I'd like everyone to be able to do when we're finished." Using an advance organizer will help you do this. Always try to achieve clarity and simplicity in your instructions and in your explanations. Be as conversational as possible without resorting to slang or inappropriate colloquialisms.

4. Give some attention to the pacing of your teaching. A deliberate, unhurried approach is the thing to strive for. The abundant use of questions, pauses, and opportunities for thought and laughter help create an environment in which students are comfortable and genuinely involved with learning tasks.

5. Do not hesitate to put a good deal of yourself into your teaching. Your personality should not be left out of the teaching-learning process. Students will be more interested and attentive when they see you as a whole person. You can share personal thoughts, experiences, and humor with your students and still retain dignity and an orderly classroom provided you do not come across as self-centered, corny, eccentric, or easily sidetracked.

◆◆◆ **A P P L I C A T I O N   E X E R C I S E S** ◆◆◆

1. Using the questions on page 271 as a basis for your ideas, develop a one-page summary of your view of teaching. Spell out some of the ways your beliefs about teaching will affect what you do in the classroom.
2. Carefully review the summarized prescriptions presented on pages 272–275 to determine how well this suggested game plan represents an extension of your present philosophy of teaching. Highlight those rules of procedure that you feel prepared to implement in your own teaching. Modify or reconstruct this set of recommendations to make it best represent your own plan of action.

Monitoring Your Own Skill Development

Making the Necessary Investments

Competent teaching calls for complex skills that do not come easily and naturally for most new teachers. As a prime example, the ability to interact effectively with groups of students while also performing a control function involves doing several things at once, something that requires most people to give a lot of thought, maybe for the first time, to how to maintain students' attention and how to communicate with people individually in a crowd, that is, in a classroom. For most beginning teachers it entails considerable *unlearning* of old patterns before new skills can be properly mastered. In the process of acquiring complex teaching behaviors, there will normally be a point at which you can expect to get worse before you get better! As in the learning of athletic maneuvers, a degree of skill can just be picked up but competence or excellence require high levels of coordination (e.g., a fully effective golf swing), so what doesn't work must first be eliminated. This may mean a retreat to square one, to starting all over, so that one can gradually advance to higher levels of competence.

During this period of unlearning, it is normal for learners of complex skills to feel awkward and off-balance. As teachers-in-training often testify, this can lead to feelings of vulnerability and defensiveness:

> I grew up in a family where the adults were the authorities. When I'm working with younger people, I tend to be better at delivering information than I am at sharing ideas. Learning these new communication skills is not going to be easy for me. At times I feel like I'm being moved away from what I do best.

> I tend to be a practical-minded person, so I'm feeling a need to get on with the action. Taking time to examine the reasons for what we do in the classroom hasn't exactly been my cup of tea. I know I'm feeling threatened by the fact that others in the group seem to be better with theory than I am.

When the new behavior does not come easily and quickly, the temptation is to revert to the old and more comfortable pattern, such as frequent lecturing. This accounts for the fact that many people fail to advance beyond a relatively low level of performance in learning various complex skills (e.g., driving, tennis, reflective listening). It helps to explain why some teachers remain fixated at the level of information giving and assignment checking as the sum and substance of their teaching repertoires.

If you understand and accept the fact that complex skill development is an arduous task, you will be more psychologically prepared to master the requirements of competent teaching. According to psychologist Joseph Russo, the route to "creative behavior change," such as that required to learn new teaching skills, includes the following[7]:

1. *Awareness* of the need for new ways of acting, coming from the recognition of the inadequacy of existing ones.
2. Willingness to accept your present level of skill as the place from which you must start. Such *affirmation* is important to maintaining a positive self-concept, a vital ally during difficult periods in complex skill development.
3. *Acceptance* of the simple fact of *present lack of knowledge or skill,* and a resisting of the temptation to blame others or the environment (e.g., *your* teachers, your college program, your teaching schedule, the makeup of a class of students, parents, television) for those inadequacies. You are not responsible for their presence, only for their removal.
4. *Identification* of the new capacities you wish to acquire and formulation of a plan for achieving your goal.
5. *Frustration* in some degree (and perhaps demoralization) when you discover that the previous four steps have not automatically produced change.
6. Strengthening of resolve or commitment to *focus on the new goals* until the new behavior begins to be automatic. This is the step at which goals are translated into intentions.
7. *Acting* on one's intentions over and over again. This is the step at which intentions are translated into actions.
8. *Accepting the need to work your way through the vulnerable stage*—with its attendant awkwardness and frustration—that follows on your letting go of an old, familiar behavior, until you begin to feel secure with the new behavior.

Using Available Mirrors

There are several good ways of obtaining self-initiated feedback on your classroom performance in order to check on your progress and to identify what you still need to work on. One is to get tape-recorded samples of your teaching. Another is to solicit information from your students. A third means of gaining insight into the quality of your teaching is to invite observations by fellow teachers.

Audio and Video Recordings One of the quickest and easiest means of finding out how you are coming across in your classes is to get an audiotaped sample of yourself interacting with a group of students. It is normally a simple matter to obtain audio-recorded teaching segments whenever you want to know how you sound to groups of students. In listening to a simple audio recording of your teaching you are able to screen out other classroom events and to concentrate on one main indicator of the quality of your performance, namely, what you are saying to students and the way you are saying it. It is generally a good idea to take samples of your teaching voice at some early point in the school year. By listening to an audiotaped segment of your teaching, you can determine:

> *The quality of your teaching voice*—Do you speak clearly, intelligibly? Is your delivery well-paced and unhurried? Does it include a full range of expression? Are you speaking loudly enough to be heard throughout the classroom?
>
> *The adequacy of the directions and explanations you are giving*—Are you being deliberate and emphatic in stressing important points? Are you giving students a chance to ask questions? Are you meeting the criteria for good explanations? Are you reinforcing them visually?
>
> *The nature of your questioning patterns*—Are you asking only one, easily understood question at a time? Do you pause long enough (three to five seconds) at the end of a question to allow students to think? Are you using different types and levels of questions during a lesson? Are you calling on a wide selection of the students?
>
> *The overall mood you generate*—Do you sound confident? Are you positive and encouraging? Is there ever any laughter in the class?

It is a fairly simple matter to obtain these audiotaped samples. Put the recorder in some inconspicuous spot at the front or side of the room and explain why you are using it. Let the students know that you are using it to critique yourself, not them. They may be quite willing to assist you in the process. In the event there is another teacher in the room with you, you might ask that person to do the taping. You should be sure to use a good-quality tape as well as tape recorder. The process won't serve much useful purpose if you have to strain to hear your voice while analyzing the tape.

A videotaped segment of your teaching will, of course, allow you to do a more complete analysis after you have taught a lesson. Many schools presently have video equipment for this purpose. You can usually arrange to have a fellow teacher (or a mature student) videotape one of your lessons during a free period. One possible drawback to videotaping as a way of analyzing what you do is the potential for this equipment to be a distracting influence for you and your students, resulting in a nonrepresentative teaching sample. However, once you and the students are accustomed to having a video camera in the room, and if they are engaged in interesting work, they tend to lose interest in the camera.

Studies on the use of videotapes and audiotapes for reconstructing teaching performances have shown that, if used appropriately, these tapes can be a great assistance in helping teachers analyze and improve their teaching. However, because the behavior on the tape is rapid and complex, it is necessary at first to have help in critiquing your performance. "If teachers do not know what to look for, they will not see very much. . . . When teachers view tapes with a colleague or supervisor who can provide specific feedback or with materials describing what to look for, positive change occurs. . . . Such materials are effective only if specific teaching behaviors are highlighted and discussed."[8]

Obtaining Feedback from Students Another easily available method of getting useful feedback on your teaching is to draw on student perceptions of your class and its activities. Students can provide helpful data on the extent to which your teaching is succeeding. They can tell you whether they are understanding your explanations, whether they are having enough time to complete your assignments, whether they are comfortable with your interpersonal style, and so on. From this kind of information you can make inferences about the effectiveness of a particular teaching approach. It can help you decide whether specific methods are producing the results you had hoped to achieve.

The easiest way of all to find out what students think of your teaching is to take note of their reactions to your classes. If students appear apathetic, bored, restless, or ill-tempered, you can take it that something is wrong. Although other factors may also be playing a part, this kind of behavior should alert you to the possibility that a particular approach is just not working. Boredom, as one classroom investigator sees it, "is a kind of pain born of unused powers, the pain of wasted talents and possibilities,"[9] and people naturally try to escape it anyway they can, passively or actively. Interested, attentive, and actively participating classes, on the other hand, are sure indications that whatever you are doing is working well. Another way of obtaining feedback during the course of a lesson is periodically to ask your students, "Are you hearing me in the back of the room?"; "Does everyone understand the point I'm making?"; "Does what I'm asking you to do seem fair and reasonable?"; "Will you now be able to complete the rest of this assignment on your own?" If, as often happens, there is no response, you may need to ask one or more students directly. Although it may take some experience to know just how to interpret the feedback (or lack thereof) that you get in these situations, once you have developed a productive relationship with a group of students, such inquiries will usually result in sincere efforts on the students' part to provide accurate feedback. This is, of course, only true when they know that their criticism will not change your attitude toward them.

Besides methods that involve keeping your fingers on the pulse of the class during instruction, you can also get useful information on your teaching by asking students to respond from time to time to questionnaires or rating sheets that you have prepared for this purpose. If the responses are to be candid, you should take measures to assure students that their ratings will remain anonymous. With this in mind, forms that call for check marks are sometimes more appropriate than those that ask for handwritten comments.

It will be important to ask the right questions in soliciting student feedback on your teaching. Students have no training in pedagogy, so they can only tell you how they are being affected by your teaching. They cannot tell you how to teach. It would probably not be appropriate, for example, to ask most students whether a particular concept would be best taught through direct or indirect instruction. However, it would be useful to know which of the two approaches students are finding more interesting and understandable. These are some of the kinds of questions that you might use with students beyond the primary level to obtain useful feedback on your teaching:

Are students in the class treated fairly?
Does the teacher seem interested in the students?
Is the class orderly?
Are the assignments and explanations clear?
Are you having enough time to finish assignments?
Is the teaching interesting and stimulating?
Do you feel free to participate in the class?
Does the teacher do anything too often? too rarely?
Would you like more . . . ? less . . . ?
Can you suggest any way the teacher could help you learn better?

Utilizing a Neutral Observer A fellow teacher or supervisor of your own choosing can also be a source of helpful feedback on your teaching. You should attempt to find someone to give a critique of your class with whom you feel comfortable and gather data on the particular area of your teaching that concerns you at the moment. It will entail finding a time when this other person is available, then settling on a focus and a format for the observation. Considering the number of concurrent happenings in a typical classroom, it is important that you pinpoint ahead of time what you want the visitor to observe or to comment on. There are several kinds of focuses that a neutral observer might adopt. For one thing, you could ask this person to collect information on the degree of attention being paid by students during the class period. From a strategic spot in the back of the room, an experienced observer might, for instance, notice particular points in the lesson when a sizable number of students begin to lose interest, starting to fidget or gazing out the window, and other times in the lesson when they refocus on what the teacher is doing.

For another focus, you might ask an observer to concentrate on dominant tendencies that you exhibit in your teaching, patterns of which you may be oblivious. For example, it would be useful to be made aware of an inclination to teach primarily to one side of the room, or of a disposition to favor certain students in a discussion and to ignore others. It could also be important for you to get descriptive feedback on irritating and unhelpful verbal or vocal mannerisms such as a habit of overusing "O.K.'s," "you know's" or "Right's" in your speech, or a tendency to slur your words at the end of sentences.

Interaction Analysis This is a more formal approach to the examination of teaching patterns. Here the observer might record who talks during the class and how often, the types of questions being raised, or other kinds of data relating to the nature and frequency of both teacher and student input during the lesson. Some interaction analysis techniques are relatively easy to use, making it possible for you in certain instances to do the analysis yourself with taped samples of your teaching. One simple method allows you to determine the ratio of teacher talk to student talk in your classes by recording a "T" for every instance of teacher talk and an "S" for every time a student talks. If one of your overriding objectives is to have students actively involved in your classes, this kind of feedback can be an indication of whether or not you are meeting that objective.

A more sophisticated interaction analysis technique is a well-known scheme developed by Flanders (*Flanders' interaction analysis*) that attempts to categorize all verbal interactions that occur between teacher and students in a classroom setting.[10] Using this system to analyze a segment of teaching, an observer would make a tally every three seconds to indicate what the teacher is doing. For example, the teacher might be giving directions, praising a student, criticizing, or asking a question. The Flanders system contains a number of categories, some of which reflect *direct* teacher influence during instruction (lecturing), others representing *indirect* teaching behaviors (accepting or using ideas of students). This technique is a systematic way of gaining a comprehensive picture of what is happening in a class. It is especially worthwhile for determining the extent to which you are allowing indirect as well as direct influence to be a part of your teaching strategy. An outstanding source of in-depth information on techniques for classroom observation is *Looking in Classrooms* by Thomas Good and Jere Brophy.[11]

A Summary of Criteria for Assessing Teaching Ability

As you proceed to develop techniques and skills for assessing live teaching, whether your own or someone else's, it will help for you to have a comprehensive set of criteria for evaluating teaching ability. These criteria can then become the basis for an evaluation form or rating scale that represents your concept of good teaching. This gives you a solid basis for self-evaluation, and a frame of reference for discussing your teaching with other interested parties (such as administrators and parents).

The following groups of criteria should assist you assess how well you are doing as a teacher:

Classroom Presence

The teacher:

Demonstrates a personal presence strong enough to gain the attention and cooperation of the class

Is able to develop relationships with students based on natural authority rather than on power or position

Is calm, confident, and unhurried in dealing with the demands and pressures of the classroom

Is able to maintain a focus and a sense of direction in the face of interruptions, unexpected happenings, and other potential distractions

Is able to handle discipline problems in a confident, low-key manner and to avoid creating unnecessary anxieties and distractions for the class

Is genuinely interested, enthusiastic, and good-humored

Keeps his or her finger on the pulse of the class and recognizes when to adjust strategy accordingly

Clarity of Communications

The teacher:

Gives the class a clear idea of the point of the lesson

Provides a sufficient tie-in for new learning by using advance organizers or connections to previous learning

Has lessons that center on main ideas or skills

Uses terms that are unambiguous and within the students' experience

Clarifies and explain terms that are potentially confusing

Provides sufficient examples, illustrations, and analogies in explanations

Takes time at the end of class periods to achieve effective closure

Interactive Skills

The teacher's:

Lessons begin with lead-ins or "grabbers" that appeal to students' curiosity, imagination, previous experience, or problem-solving interests

Dealings with students convey respect, support, and concern for them as individuals

Teaching approach is thoughtful and well-paced, and his or her questions, pauses, and challenges encourage students to think and to question

The teacher:

Engages students in learning by appealing to internal needs and interests rather than authority, grade anxiety, or extrinsic rewards

Encourages students to become engaged in learning by asking them questions that appeal to them on the personal level (e.g., "Can *you* imagine . . . ?" "Have any of *you* ever seen . . . ?" "What do *you* think about . . . ?" "What would *you* do if . . . ?").

◆◆◆   A P P L I C A T I O N   E X E R C I S E S   ◆◆◆

1. Record of one of your lessons. Do a self-analysis of it based on a set of criteria you have devised for assessing the verbal aspects of your teaching.
2. Using the teaching prescriptions on pages 272–275 as your frame of reference, construct a comprehensive rating scale you could use to assess your own teaching, based on videotaped samples and/or feedback received from a classroom observer.
3. Find opportunities to observe two or three other teachers in discussion activities with students. (You might use videotapes for this purpose.) Focusing exclusively on the teacher's behavior, make a tally each time the teacher (1) asks a question, (2) gives an instruction or an explanation, (3) praises or acknowledges a student idea, or (4) criticizes or arbitrarily corrects a student. At the end of the class period, total the number of tallies in each category. What kind of balance do you find between direct and indirect teacher influence based on these interaction samples?
4. Devise a practical scheme for doing an interaction analysis (see page 280) of your own teaching based on data that you would be able to obtain from audiotapes or videotapes in which you determine the focus of the analysis.

Developing Your Understanding of Teaching and Maintaining Your Professional Commitment

As you enter teaching, you are in the initial stages of your development as a professional. You will need to continue to expand your knowledge and capabilities in order to realize your full potential. The strength of your commitment to teaching will be reflected in, and fostered by, the kinds of professional activities you continue to undertake on your own initiative. There are several kinds of ongoing pursuits that will help keep you vital and up-to-date as a teaching professional. These include (1) substantive professional reading, (2) membership in professional organizations, and (3) continuing education and inservice work.

Professional Reading

Change in the educational field is rapid, and the flow of new ideas—not all of them by any means good ones—is constantly expanding. If you are to maintain, and increase, your effectiveness as a teacher, you must, in common with professionals in other fields, such as medicine, engineering, or the law, stay in touch with the literature in your own field. This will both keep you apprised of developments and help you to decide which ones you might most usefully adopt. You will be in effect joining in a conversation with people who are confronted by and attempting to deal with some of the same questions and problems as you are experiencing. In addition to its potential practical value, stimulating professional reading can prevent you from feeling isolated and powerless within the confines of your own classroom and school.

There are several kinds of educational literature that have relevance to you as a classroom teacher.

In Your Field of Concentration/Grade Level One or more journals or periodicals cater to teachers in every subject area or field of interest, such as, for example, *Social Studies* and *The Arithmetic Teacher*. A number of publications cater to the needs of elementary school teachers, among them *Teaching pre-K–8*, *Young Children*, *Learning*, and *Instructor*. If you have not already done so, you should make a practice of regularly reading one or more of those that apply within your field, or even better, take out a subscription to at least one of them.

In Curriculum and General Classroom Practice A number of publications will help to keep you up-to-date in relation to instructional techniques, curriculum development, and new ideas in classroom management. The two outstandingly useful journals are *Educational Leadership* and *Phi Delta Kappan*, both readily available in any college library, and often found in faculty rooms in schools.

In the General Field of Education A proportion of the articles in the preceding category regularly deal with schoolwide issues and developments, of which it is important for you to be aware, but the best single source of current information on the national scene is undoubtedly *Education Week*. Needless to say, any teacher should keep an eye on the local newspaper and a national newspaper such as *The New York Times* or *Washington Post*.

This reading is, of course, a supplement to, rather than a substitute for, the more extensive treatment of whatever major interests you have in your subject area or grade level. Major studies of schools, such as John Goodlad's *A Place Called School*,[12] theoretical and practical works such as Howard Gardner's *Frames of Mind: A Theory of Multiple Intelligences*,[13] or scholarly works dealing with current controversies, such as Berliner and Biddle's *The Manufactured Crisis*,[14] should be on any teacher's reading list, to be gotten to when time allows.

Participating in Professional Organizations

Membership in professional organizations is another way to keep abreast of new ideas and developments related to your teaching. Every subject matter has its own national organization as, for instance, the National Council of Teachers of English, and the National Council of Teachers of Mathematics. The Association for Supervision and Curriculum Development (ASCD) covers the entire field of instruction, curriculum, and supervision. Other organizations, such as the the National Association for the Education of Young Children and the National Middle School Association, are oriented toward a particular level of schooling. The activities of professional organizations usually include regular meetings (involving discussions or speakers), conferences, conventions, and various service projects. These meetings, which often include the opportunity to discuss experiences with other teachers who have similar problems and concerns, can be energizing and inspiring. In many cases such memberships entitle you to receive the professional journal of that particular organization. Information about many of these organizations, and details of their meetings and conferences can most easily be obtained by checking their Web sites, addresses of which appear at the end of the Notes in Chapter 5.

Membership in another type of professional organization, a teachers' *network*, is another possibility. The *1997 ASCD Year Book* describes these networks as

> engag[ing] school-based educators in directing their own learning . . . encouraging them to collaborate with a broad variety of people. . . . Participants have opportunities to grow in a professional community that focuses on their development. . . .

Such networks are to be found regionally scattered around the nation—such as *Bread Loaf Rural Teachers' Network* in Vermont—or as nationwide groups such as the *National Network for Educational Renewal* based in Seattle.[15]

When you take a teaching position, you will normally be expected to belong to the local teachers' association and its state and national parent organization. The two large professional organizations are the National Education Association (NEA) and the American Federation of Teachers (AFT). Both organizations are politically active in promoting working conditions and higher salaries for teachers through collective bargaining, and both play a role in promoting the professional development of teachers and the improvement of educational practices. In some school districts you may have a choice between joining one or another of these organizations. Before making a decision on which to join, you should look carefully at their goals and programs to determine which is more closely in line with your professional philosophy.

Continuing Your Formal Learning

A third means of maintaining your enthusiasm and commitment, and keeping up-to-date in your teaching is to continue to be involved in education classes and workshops that will help you to increase your professional knowledge. If your school is within commuting distance of a local university, and as soon as you feel reasonably secure in the classroom, you should seriously consider taking graduate courses in professional education. These courses should be chosen with specific goals or applications in mind, and, carefully selected, they can help you to increase your teaching skills in areas of perceived weakness. They are a good way of meeting fellow professionals and exchanging ideas, and they will alert you to new methods and materials, and provide you with new insights into the students with whom you work.

Some states already require a certain amount of graduate work as a condition for the periodic renewal of teaching certificates; other states, New Jersey for example, are considering moving in this direction. It is important for you to be aware of any such requirements when you take a teaching position. Also, most school districts allow teachers graduated salary increases for completion of a specified amount of graduate work, with larger increases for advanced degrees.

In addition to university graduate courses, you will have opportunities to be involved with inservice programs sponsored by your school system. Most school districts budget a certain amount of money each year for the inservice development of teachers. They frequently provide on-site classes or workshops aimed at helping teachers increase their competence in some aspect of instruction (e.g., classroom management, questioning techniques). Teachers are often allowed some choice in selecting programs related to their needs.

The quality and usefulness of such inservice programs vary greatly from one school to another. With the participation of highly motivated teachers, some districts put a great deal of effort into offering practical and relevant inservice workshops. Other districts do relatively little to encourage the inservice development of their teachers. It will be worth your while to inquire about district-sponsored inservice opportunities whenever you interview for a new teaching position. The seriousness with which school districts approach the inservice education of their teachers can be an important indicator of the vitality of that school system.

It is important to remember that the ultimate responsibility for keeping yourself in touch with what is happening in the educational world is yours. We live in times of particularly rapid change, and in times when the public in general is vitally interested in, and often well-informed about, a wide range of developments, either because they may affect their children's future, the future of their nation or, most immediately, their taxes! New and often controversial ideas such as charter schools, school choice, vouchers, inclusion, national standards, and the extended school year are part of the national debate on education, an activity that in all its forms accounts for well over $100 billion a year. As functioning professionals, we owe it to ourselves, to our students, to the parents of our students, and to the nation at large to know what is going on. We have to go on adjusting our practice in the light of increasing understanding of how young people learn best, what young people need to know and be able to do in order to live fulfilling lives in a free society, and to contribute to the improvement of that society for all its citizens.

The wise words of a long-time student of schools and teaching may provide the best conclusion. As a teacher, writes Seymour Sarason in his little book, *You Are Thinking of Teaching?*

> your obligation to yourself and your profession is to know what is going on; that is, what others are experiencing, studying, and writing. Teaching need not be, must not be, a lonely profession. Reading is one of the better prescriptions for diluting the sense of intellectual professional isolation as well as the sense that you stopped developing. No profession more than education provides as exciting an opportunity to understand the society in which we live; how it has changed, will change, should change. Will there be problems, frustrations, ups and downs, even despair? Of course. Is personal, intellectual, professional "growing up" easy. Of course not. End of sermon![16]

◆◆◆ SUGGESTED ACTIVITIES AND QUESTIONS ◆◆◆

1. Mention aspects of classroom teaching that you find most challenging. What are some things you can do to prepare yourself to meet these challenges?

2. Consider the best teachers you have had during your years in school. Attempt to list shared qualities and actions that made these teachers exceptional? Compare your list of characteristics with the teaching behavior that research has found to be most indicative of effective teaching (refer to pages 270–271).

3. Is it ever appropriate to say a teacher has taught when the students have not learned? Can you think of arguments for both sides of this question? Does it make any practical difference how we answer the question? Elaborate.

4. Why is it that teachers have a difficult time being aware of everything that occurs in the classroom? Mention specific strategies you intend to

use to enhance your awareness of classroom behavior, and particularly your own teaching behavior.

5. What are some things you can do to ensure that your efforts at self-evaluation do not disrupt the natural flow of classroom events, and thereby invalidate the self-assessment?

6. What are some of the pros and cons of using students' evaluations to judge teaching performance? Mention several guidelines for obtaining and making best use of student evaluations.

7. Think of several kinds of information about your teaching that a discerning classroom observer might be in a more advantageous position to provide.

8. Investigate one or more professional journals in subject areas that you teach. Also find opportunities to examine the content of several of the educational journals mentioned in the chapter. What kinds of articles within these journals do you find most interesting?

Notes

1. Ned A. Flanders, *Analyzing Teaching Behavior*. Reading, Mass.: Addison-Wesley, 1970, pp. 401–2.

2. Barak Rosenshine and N. F. Furst, "The Use of Direct Observation to Study Teaching." In R. M. Travers (Ed.), *Second Handbook of Research on Teaching*. Chicago: Rand McNally, 1973, p. 167.

3. Don Hamachek, "Characteristics of Good Teachers and Implications for Teacher Education." In J. Michael Palardy, *Teaching Today: Tasks and Challenges*. New York: Macmillan, 1975, p. 36.

4. Bruce Joyce and Beverly Showers, "The Coaching of Teaching." *Educational Leadership* 40, no. 1 (October 1982): 4–10.

5. For detailed guidance on the first few days of school, see "Getting Off to a Good Start," in E. T. Emmer, C. M. Evertson, B. S. Clements, and M. E. Worsham, *Classroom Management for Secondary Teachers*, 4th ed. Boston: Allyn and Bacon, 1997. There is a parallel chapter for elementary teachers in *Classroom Management for Elementary Teachers*, 4th ed., Chap. 6. Boston: Allyn and Bacon, 1997.

6. On boredom in the classroom, see Seán D. Healy, *Boredom, Self, and Culture*. Cranford, N.J.: Fairleigh Dickinson University Press, 1984.

7. Adapted by permission from the teaching files of Joseph Russo, Department of Psychology, California State University, Chico.

8. Thomas L. Good and Jere E. Brophy, *Looking in Classrooms*, 7th ed. New York: Harper and Row, 1997, p. 37.

9. Susan J. Rosenholtz, *Teachers' Workplace: The Social Organization of Schools*. New York: Longman, 1989, p. 150.

10. Flanders, *Analyzing Teacher Behavior*, p. 34.

11. Good and Brophy, *Looking in Classrooms*, see Chap. 2.

12. John I. Goodlad, *A Place Called School*. New York: McGraw-Hill, 1984.

13. Gardner, op. cit.

14. David C. Berliner and Bruce J. Biddle, *The Manufactured Crisis: Myths, Fraud, and the Attack on America's Public Schools.* New York: Longman, 1997.

15. Andy Hargreaves (Ed.), *1997 ASCD Year Book: Rethinking Educational Change with Heart and Mind.* Alexandria, Va.: ASCD, 1997. Two other sites that offer professional discussion are *Teacher-2-Teacher Web Forum, http://www.teach-net.com/t2t.html,* and *Teachers' Meeting Place, http://www.planet.net/ptmpheal.*

16. Seymour B. Sarason, *You Are Thinking of Teaching?* San Francisco: Jossey-Bass, 1993, p. 138. For an introduction to the Internet for teachers, see http://www.capecod.net/schrockguide/index.htm. Lesson plans involving the Internet, designed by teachers, can be found at http://www.trms.ga.net, while TeachNet (http://www.teachnet.org) has descriptions of over 500 classroom projects designed by teachers. Further suggestions, plus a mass of information about teachers and technology are provided in the November 10, 1997 issue of *Education Week,* "Technology Counts: Schools and Reform in the Information Age."

INDEX

The *n* following page numbers represents items found in the notes.